31 ESSENTIAL PRINCIPLES OF LEADERSHIP

This book will inspire, challenge and equip you to be the best leader you can be. It can be used as a textbook by individuals, in groups, in homes, in politics, in churches, in mission agencies, in schools, colleges and universities. May God help you as you read and apply this book to improve your leadership effectiveness!

Also by Charles Balenga

Africa, It's Time!

What others say about the author and his books *Africa, It's Time!* and *31 Essential Principles of Leadership*

"*In* 31 Essential Principles of Leadership, *Charles has compiled an extensive list of all the attributes that will make a leader as effective as possible. Each attribute is clearly explained with examples of how you can apply them to both your everyday life and your leadership. Charles' passion for leaders, both young and old, to be as effective as possible is inspiring and contagious; he truly desires to see Africa, and the world as a whole, become a stronger place for all. He uses his own considerable leadership experience through being a teacher, a missionary, executive director, board president and a pastor to compile this list. Listen and learn from his wisdom, and become a better person and a better leader for it!*"

McKenzie Spies,
editor of *31 Essential Principles of Leadership* –Freelance
Editor at Gold Raven Editing – Alberta, Canada

"*Depending on the angle from which one stands and looks at Africa, the conclusion that one would draw concerning leadership would be entirely different from that of another analyst. For instance, when I look at Africa today, I see a set of heads of African States who are mostly individuals with an acute deficiency when it concerns leadership, solely because they were almost all born from a womb of slavery and into a terrain of slavery, only to be oriented into what would have been "leadership" by the heirs of the masters of their forefathers. The scope of orientation was never genuine and/or aimed at liberating Africa, but on extending and converting colonization into academic democracy. Africa needs leaders who can be heads of states, not heads of states who should be leaders. Discourses such as the ones which are being released by my dear brother, Charles Balenga, are beginning to sprinkle resilient seeds despite the ground upon which they would fall, as long as it is an African ground: some* uncommon and non-compromising leadership plants would pop up and grow to the salvation of Africa."

Dr. Convy Baloyi,
Independent Specialist in Education, Governance, Leadership & Strategy Development – Republic of South Africa

"Charles' passion to see Africa achieve its potential, both in biblical spirituality and economically, shines through in his writing. Charles invites all friends of Africa to join in the development effort. It is especially refreshing to see Charles' approach of challenging his fellow African nationals to work hard to develop industry and trade opportunities, rather than asking for aid. Then, he follows this up by reaching out to his fellow African Diaspora, who are now living in developed countries around the world, asking them to participate by joining forces in a true partnership with Africans to mentor and to participate with their brothers and sisters in this building process. You will be encouraged as you read his book; it will give you a better understanding of Africa's potential."

Ron Plett, CPA, CMA,
Independent Business Consultant; Board Member of several organizations, including FCE Canada (a mission to Africa and beyond) – Alberta, Canada

"We first met Charles at my parents' dining room table, Christmas 1996. Charles was new to Canada, a quiet, humble, very perceptive, and intelligent young man, whose confidence came from knowing his God. My father, a former medical missionary in Zaire (DRC), 'adopted' Charles with the same love that he had faithfully served his adopted country. After Christmas, my father and husband moved Charles to Regina, where he studied and finished his Masters. His phone calls and visits were always welcome to my folks. My father and Charles would discuss complex issues facing many African nations, as well as life's problems, at length. Later, Charles would speak at my father's funeral. Charles asks hard questions of others which he has asked himself, questions which do not have easy answers. The gospel of Jesus Christ that he preaches is a call to action.

His book Africa, It's Time! explores African traditional values as well as its leadership roles, which have been threatened by modernization and war. He examines leadership models and proposes new values, which will truly serve the nation's people. His frank discussion of poverty and its culture, manipulation by the rich to maintain poverty, the emergent extreme rich, as well as the exploitation of women and children, can be uncomfortable. These are hard truths that challenge Western practise of giving to the poor, which can actually perpetuate poverty. Becoming part of the solution requires a new paradigm of partnership and problem solving in our global consciousness. The challenge to the African Diaspora to serve their country of origin with skills and education they have gained from abroad is particularly nouveau. The paradigm he suggests is that of Africans of the Diaspora being agents of change. His insights from his personal experience living as a family and serving as Canadian missionaries in Africa make his propositions very practical and insightful. Each chapter is constructed in a way that is conducive to classroom or group discussion. They are more than ideas, but carefully thought out plans for individuals/groups partnering with nationals in such a way that transformation of a nation can take place. We recommend his books to anyone who cares about building a better world!"

Joanne Lepp,
Former missionary kid in DRC –Regina, Canada

"Pastor Charles is a good person, loving, kind, and respectful. From the time he was teaching us at Gitega International Academy, I found him to be a courageous person, because he never got tired of encouraging us. He used practical examples that we find in our community. I like how in his book, Africa, It's Time!, he talked about the need for African leaders to leave power peacefully. I agree with him on the need for the African Diaspora to come to Africa to contribute with their skills and knowledge. In his Leadership and Christian Education lectures, I learned the value of 'we' not 'me', because working alone you cannot achieve much but when you work together, you can. The Bible says that where two or three are gathered, God is with them. God can bless Africa if we work together."

Divine Habiyambere,
former student at GIA, Burundi

"You have been more than a friend for me. You have been a mentor. Pastor Charles, it was a blessing to know you. You helped me know Christ better, and for me, that is a big gift you can give to somebody."

Andy Karl Irambona,
former student at GIA, Burundi

"I met Brother Charles Balenga at the Theological College of Central Africa (TCCA), now Evangelical University (EU), where we were both theological students in 1994. He was a young foreign student. Being an interdenominational evangelical college, you would expect exciting theological debates. Sometimes there was so much heat among us that it affected relationships. I observed that even in the heat of raw emotions, Brother Charles was always calm and thoughtful. Always with a smile, he treated everyone with respect and consideration. It was very difficult for anyone on campus to stay away from Brother Charles, and he never stayed away from anyone. We all found ourselves pulled to him and ended up in unity. He is a natural leader, now made better by sound biblical truth. He speaks from his heart under the guidance of the Holy Spirit. You will benefit a lot from his experience."

Reverend Godrey Mambwe,
Executive Director of Zambia Baptist Association - Zambia

"The success of true leadership is determined by the legacy of passing on the leadership mantle. True leadership is about inspiring and influencing others to follow you. It is this process that builds one's reputation to be a mentor for someone. In his books Africa, It's Time! and 31 Essential Principles of Leadership, Charles exhibits his passion for leadership and the need to transform leadership of those who lead. A leader is the voice of the voiceless. As a leader, you are expected to stand in the gap, lobby and advocate for those whose freedoms, rights, and privileges are trampled upon. Effective leadership trains other leaders, as 2 Timothy 2:2 says, "And the things you have heard me say in the presence of many witnesses entrust to reliable people who will also be qualified to teach others." You will be remembered as a true leader by the number of faithful people that carry on your leadership dynamics and attributes to signify the continuity of your leadership, even when you are no more. I therefore recommend that these books be used as resources that will promote effective and competent leadership in the home, church, schools, universities and business in the whole world."

Revd. Fr. Dennis Milanzi,
Executive Director of Theological Education by
Extension in Zambia (TEEZ) - Kitwe-Zambia

"I knew Pastor Charles for about two years. I found him to be a great leader. He made a sacrificial decision to come serve in Burundi with Burundi Youth for Christ as chaplain at Gitega International Academy. Him and his family were the first big family serving as volunteers at BYFC. It was a blessing to have them. I am so grateful to know Pastor Charles Balenga as a good model who exemplifies servanthood leadership by serving others and ministering to the African community. I read his first book Africa, It's Time! and I would encourage everyone to read it. In it, he demonstrates how Africa can become the best place to live. His book challenged me to see Africa in a different angle and to remember the life I lived in England. I thank God for the impact I am seeing with my own service in Burundi which is beyond what I could have achieved if I had remained in the UK. Thank you so much Pastor Charles for your ministry in Burundi by serving especially in Gitega. We wish you *could come back. We thank God for your contribution in raising-up a generation of leaders in Burundi."*

Jean Paul Ntakarutimana,
Burundi Youth for Christ regional coordinator based in Gitega, Burundi.

"After meeting Charles at a book event and after reading his book, it became evident that he has a strong passion for Africa and a God given vision for Africa. I believe that Charles' destiny is greatly tied into Africa's future. Chosen much like King David was, a man after God's own heart, Charles has the courage to stand with Africa. Africa is his passion and destiny."

Jenny Rumancik,
Author of *I met Jesus at the gym* – Canada

31 ESSENTIAL PRINCIPLES OF LEADERSHIP

One Principle Every Day for a Month

CHARLES B.M. BALENGA

31 ESSENTIAL PRINCIPLES OF LEADERSHIP
One Principle for Every Day for a Month

Copyright © 2018, Charles B.M. Balenga.

Edited by McKenzie Spies.

Published by Charles B.M. Balenga, Edmonton, Canada

ISBN:
 paperback: 978-1-77354-060-3
 electronic: 978-1-77354-068-9

Publication assistance and digital printing in Canada by

PAGEMASTER
PUBLISHING
PageMaster.ca

Contents

ACKNOWLEDGEMENTS:

We are who we are because God chose to create us in His own image, to save us through His Son Jesus Christ, and to make us intelligent human beings. Right from the beginning, in the Garden of Eden, God established us as leaders. In Genesis, God gave power to Adam and Eve to rule over all other creatures.

> *Then God said, 'Let us make mankind in our image, in our like-ness, so that they may rule over the fish in the sea and the birds in the sky, over the livestock and all the wild animals, and over all the creatures that move along the ground'. God blessed them and said to them, 'Be fruitful and increase in number; fill the earth and subdue it. Rule over the fish in the sea and the birds in the sky and over every living creature that moves on the ground'.* Genesis 1:26, 28.

The Bible tells us that in Him we live and move and have our being: With God we have everything, and without Him we have nothing. We owe everything to Him! Therefore, the first and most important acknowledgement goes to our God who deserves all the glory, all honour, all the credit, all praise, and all gratitude.

God has blessed me with people who have been so good to me and to whom I owe gratitude. Many people have contributed to making me who I am, and to each and every one of you, I say thank you from the bottom of my heart. Since God calls us to be grateful, I just want to take this opportunity to say thank you. I would like to personally thank some people with special mention of their names. To anyone I will forget to mention specifically, please know that you matter and I thank you.

I would like to thank my wife and our children for being so understanding when I spent so much time writing this book. Thank you for being so accommodating. Your support is very much appreciated! Thank you to my wife, Darla Balenga, for proofreading the draft manuscript.

I want to thank my late mother, whose love for me went beyond expectation! Your love and care for me made me understand clearly why God compares his love to the love of a mother. What a special privilege to have been raised by you. You taught me many things. You taught me the value of work. I remember you gave me my first job of cleaning over and above the regular house cleaning. I remember the particular assignment you gave me of cleaning the large table that was in your room and you paid me a wage every month for that; how I am indebted to you for that! Receive in your rest all my gratitude! I miss you every day. I wish you were here to celebrate the success of your son's two books now. I remember how it made your day when anyone spoke well of me! I thank you for being my mother!

I want to thank my father for educating me. I want to thank him for one special day I have always remembered. I had scored first in my class and dad was so proud of me that he took me to Bukavu, where he asked me to choose new clothes and shoes and took me to a special restaurant where he also asked me to order anything I wanted to eat. Thank you dad for that special time! I thank you too for showing me the value of generosity in how you paid for the high school education of four young people and helped them through university degrees.

I want to thank my father- and mother-in-law, Albert and Linda Liebelt, especially for their help with all our children. Thanks to a number of people who took me in like their own son, and others as their own brother, in Canada and in Zambia: Former Deputy Chief Justice George and Sylvia Baynton, Dr. and Mrs. Ernest and Leona Schmidt, Bishop John Osmers, Mr. and Mrs. Sandford and Marion Mulundika, Mr. and Mrs. John and

Cynthia Goodbrand, Dr. Alan and Barbara Barr, and Elder and Mrs. Edson Lumbila.

There are many people I met during my African tour with my first book, *Africa, It's Time!* These people were helpful to me and I want to thank them: Bishop Peter A. Mphande, Bishop and Mrs. Kajolo, Pastor Isaiah, Bishop Mwinga, Bishop Kampeshi, Apostle Kunda, Joseph Mphande, Karori, Apostle Dr. Convy Baloyi, Dr. Juniel Matavire, Father Dennis Milanzi, Reverend Godfrey Mambwe, Dr. Manana, Dr. Joe Kapolyo, Dr. Lazarus Phiri, Pastor Isaac Makashinyi, Pastor Martin Kapenda, Bishop Enocent Silwamba, Pastor Victor Chaungwe, Leonard Mutono, Jonathan Longa, Pastor Elbo Museremu, Pastor Rame Kasaro, Pastor Maipambo, Sammy Matwali, Fazili Mwemera and his wife Refilwe, Musa Mwemera, Marcel Bigi, Florence Naki, Kaposho Kape and Espoir Mahinanda.

Thanks to PageMaster for the assistance with publishing. Thanks to McKenzie Spies for editing my book. Thanks to Rich and Joanne Lepp, Eric Carrillo, Justin Watkins, Shuni David Masikini, Jenny Rumancik and Ron Plett. Thanks to Holly Andony. Thanks to Patrick Mwemera and Sarah Mwemera for their donations which enabled the printing of 60 books.

To all my friends and family all over the world, to all of you who care for a better world in which Christ reigns supreme, thank you, and may God bless you abundantly!

Leadership is an everyday need.

Life is such that every day we face leadership decisions we need to make and actions we must implement. Leadership is a universal need. Everywhere you go, in any community or any country, leaders are needed. Effective leadership must be contextualized but it is a necessity everywhere.

Now, because leadership is so crucial for any community to thrive, we must make sure leaders know who they are, what are their roles in society, and how equipped they must be to effectively lead. This book has been written to train and equip leaders to lead successfully. We have all heard that a community or a country would go as far or as high as the leader goes. The leader is the driver and members of his community are like passengers. He can choose to drive them into a ditch or take them to the Promised Land.

I have provided in this book *31 principles for effective leadership*. This is not an exhaustive number. Some other authors have written 11 principles, others 21, and others different numbers. In the number 31, I have done my best to provide what I consider to be the main essential principles of leadership.

If you read, understand, and apply these 31 principles, I can assure you that your leadership's effectiveness will rise to a greater height. Although it is meant to be read as a daily devotion for each day for a month, you can read two, three, or more principles a day, depending on your reading speed and understanding. The important thing is your comprehension and application of these principles.

In this book, I will discuss leadership at a global level, but I will have some discussions on African leadership specifically. The principles addressed in this book are applicable anywhere in the world and can be used in any community, country, or kingdom. These principles are meant to help every leader, wherever he or she may be, to lead well.

When you look at world history, you find that almost every country or kingdom has had great leaders. Some leaders are well known at a global level and others at a national or community level.

Basketball has people like Michael Jordan. Hockey has Wayne Gretzky. Soccer has Pele. In the world of humanitarians, we have people like Mother Teresa. In the world of business and innovation, we have people like Bill Gates, Warren Buffet, Mark Zuckerberg, Steve Jobs, Africa's richest person Aliko Dangote, and others. In the world of science, we have Albert Einstein. In the world of influential talk shows and media, we have Oprah Winfrey. In the world of faith and evangelism, we have Billy Graham.

In African politics, there are great leaders who have been elevated to heroic status. Leaders such as the first Congo Prime Minister Emery Patrice Lumumba, President Kwame Nkrumah of Ghana, President Julius Nyerere of Tanzania, Burkina Faso President Thomas Sankara, and President Nelson Mandela, and many others.

In Canada, there is the former Premier of Saskatchewan, Tommy Douglas, who is credited for the establishment of Medicare. Prime Minister Pierre Trudeau is credited for official bilingualism and the Charter of Rights and Freedoms, among other things.

In the United States of America, there is President Abraham Lincoln, who is credited for the abolishment of slavery. Dr. Martin Luther King has attained heroic status for his civil rights movement. Before Dr. King, we have great pioneers for equality such as Sojourner Truth. Consider what she accomplished in the 1800s:

> *Sojourner Truth was an African-American abolitionist and women's rights activist. Truth was born into slavery in Swartekill, Ulster County, New York, but escaped with her infant daughter to freedom in 1826. After going to court to recover her son, in 1828 she became the first black woman to win such a case against a white man.* (1)

You also have overcomers such as Catherine Coleman Goble Johnson, an African American woman who excelled in the world of physics and mathematics. She broke the barriers of race and gender to become a key contributor to the genesis of NASA.

Throughout history, the world has been filled with many great leaders. Whenever there has been a need for leadership in any area of life, God has raised a leader. When the Israelites had been living in slavery for 400 years, God raised Moses to lead His people out of Egypt. You can go back as far as creation. After creating all other creatures, God created Adam and Eve and established their leadership over everything else that He had created.

Today, when you look at Africans in Africa and Africans in the Diaspora, you cannot help but see that there is a need for leadership. When you look at the conflicts and wars, the problem of poverty, the unfair treatment of the poor by the rich, the gender inequalities, the injustice, the ever-increasing inequalities between rich and poor, it is clear that Africa is in dire need for leadership. It is extremely sad that the most

Christianised continent is the one in which evil seems to have established its dwelling.

Evil has continued to devastate Africa: the rape and violence against women and children, child labor and abuse, tribalism, discrimination, the refugee crisis, the exploitation of Africa by the West, and the exploitation of Africans by Africans, corruption, and bribery. When you think about all these problems Africa faces, you realize that the problem of Africa today is not families having seven or eight children, as President Macron thinks, but rather it is a problem of leadership.

We are living in extremely difficult times; everywhere you turn, there is bad news. Globally, you have terrorism that is proving hard to control; kidnapping of innocent people, such as the girls kidnapped by Boko Haram; wars in Iraq, Afghanistan, and Ukraine; racism and discrimination; frequent killings in the United States, and so on. There are also increasing natural calamities such as earthquakes, tsunamis, and mudslides. You can turn on your television and you can hardly hear any good news.

Economically, we are now experiencing back-to-back recessions. Global inequalities are so wide that there is no logic to explain them. The gap between rich and poor is widening every day, so that the poor are becoming poorer and the rich are getting richer in both the under-developed and the developed countries.

In fact, in the developed countries, the rate at which the world is making instant millionaires and instant poor is alarming. Today, if you are an elite basketball player in the National Basketball Association, you can be paid per year what 1,000 regular employees make per year in the same country. Without mentioning names, there are sports players earning 40 million US dollars per year, while an average American makes less than 40 thousand dollars per year. This is the same for soccer/football players in the European league.

There are games today, such as *Who Wants to Be a Millionaire*, where you can make a million dollars if you answer all the questions correctly. Imagine making in one day what most working employees do not make in their entire working life. There are reality shows where a single season can help you win a contract and a million dollars. Think of the gap when you realize that in Africa, the poor working person is still making less than 360 US dollars per year.

Yes, we will always have the poor among us; that is the reality of life. Even in the socialist system, there were those who were poor and very few others who were rich. The goal is not to equalize the income of everyone; that is as impossible as chasing the wind.

Jesus said very clearly that we will always have the poor among us. But He also expects those in positions of power to bring good news to the poor, to deliver those in various forms of imprisonment, and to give freedom to the oppressed. It is the leaders' responsibility to be aware that there will always be impoverished people and that they must always be defended. Leaders must be a blessing to the poor by finding ways to advocate for them and improve their lives.

> *"The poor you will always have with you, but you will not always have Me."* John 12:8

> *"The Spirit of the Lord is on Me, because He has anointed Me to preach good news to the poor. He has sent Me to proclaim deliverance to the captives and recovery of sight to the blind, to release the oppressed."* Luke 4:18

We are living in exceptionally difficult times and we need exceptional leaders that God will use to take us to the Promised Land. Let me take this opportunity to praise African countries and their leaders who are showing exceptional leadership and are combatting these evils head on. It is encouraging when we see some African leaders work hard to fight corruption and injustice. I am thankful for leaders who are championing the cause of the poor, fighting waste and inequalities and improving the economy. If this kind of leadership can be seen in more African countries, the African continent can soon start to feed its own children and hopefully one day grow to lead the world.

But I know that some people who have already been crippled by corruption, bribery, and selfishness are unfortunately engaging themselves in fighting the leadership of those who want to bring the continent out of its current mess to a respectable status. Some have developed fault-finding, an agenda just to make great leaders look bad. We need to understand that even great leaders make mistakes; they are human.

Fault finding, a strategy to make someone appear guilty, is bad for Africa just as it is everywhere. We saw this strategy used in Canada when Stockwell Day was leader of the Canadian Alliance and leader of the opposition. Just because he was unashamed to say that he was a Christian, the media did all that they could to find fault in him. He was heavily attacked for his faith in Christ, and of course, they found a way to make him look bad. They tried to make even his very innocent actions look bad, just because they were determined to make it look like one cannot be a strong Christian and be a country's political leader.

Fault finding is a cruel technique that has been used for centuries. In the book of Daniel, when his opponents could not find fault in him, they made false accusations just to make him appear guilty. The Swahili people have an expression for this: *Kisiki ni kwale nipate sababu.* It means that when someone wants to find the wrong in you, they will make sure they get it. They can come, bump into you, fall down, and accuse you for their falling.

As Africans, we need urgently to graduate from this disastrous fault-finding practice. Let us encourage those who are trying hard to lead exceptionally well. The Moses and Aaron type of leaders are very rare, and when God sends us leaders, let us encourage and support them. It does not mean we cannot correct them when they make mistakes, but we must also support them when they make right choices.

African leaders should imitate the good in each other and gracefully correct each other's errors. I call on fellow Africans to be supportive of each other. I am not saying that we must not address the wrong and correct it, but rather, that we should also energetically support the good in each other. African countries must be each other's primary trading partners. One day, I heard President Uhuru Kenyatta respond well to criticism about importing sugar from Uganda. He said he would rather import sugar from Uganda than import it from Brazil. This was not about taking a shot at Brazil, but rather an emphasis on Africans trading primarily with Africans.

African countries must trade with each other. African countries must partner in trade, in keeping the African culture, in innovation, in education, in agriculture, in governance, in the establishment of the rule of law, in combatting poverty and discrimination, and in many other ways. African leaders must champion the African way of doing things. The development of Africa must be African.

Recently, I was encouraged by the East African Community's decision to promote the establishment of local clothing factories and the production of cotton, therefore ending the importation of second hand clothing.

> East African countries could ban imports of used clothes and second-hand cars in the next three years, putting an end to a lucrative trade in the region...Burundi, Kenya, Rwanda, Tanzania, and Uganda could all ban second-hand clothes and leather...The EAC directed member countries to buy their textiles and shoes from within the region with a view to phasing out imports by 2019...The idea is to give a boost to local manufacturing, and help the economy. (2)

My advice to the East African community leaders is that they should not stop there. Making our own clothes is one thing, but wearing them is another thing. I am appealing to all African leaders to start wearing African clothes, made in Africa by Africans, to truly promote the African clothing industry and African culture.

Leaders must lead by example. When almost all African leaders wear western suits at the African Union meetings, what statement do they make by that? When you are a leader, people follow you. If you cannot wear the clothes you are promoting, then you are contradicting yourself, and your people can see that.

When then President Mobutu brought in authenticity and started wearing short sleeve jackets, the *abacost*, and long sleeve jackets with buttons all the way to the top, everyone followed suit. It is crucial that African people see their leaders wearing African clothes to truly authenticate their devotion to promoting African culture and industry.

It is important that as Africans, we be authentic, true to who we are. It is important that we are proud of who God made us to be. Yes, we do not have to erase everything we have borrowed from the west, such as the foreign names we have taken, but we can start choosing what is truly African.

It is important to be comfortable in our identity and to promote it. We have been followers for too long. Now is the time to truly relate to all other people groups as equals. It is time for us to start leading the world in our areas of expertise. We must now have a development authentically African.

Africa must be a strong player in Africa and on the world stage. But while the development of Africa must be typically African, Africa can no longer live in isolation. Africa is, and must be, part of the global village. This means that Africans will do all they can to keep their heritage and cultures, while also being able to compete internationally.

Leaders trained in Africa must be able to lead in Africa, as well as anywhere in the world. Clothes made in Africa should find markets in Africa and throughout the world. The African Diaspora should participate in the promotion of African clothes by personally investing in them and wearing them.

African celebrations, throughout the Diaspora, should also promote African clothing. This is not a call to reject non-African clothes, but rather an appeal to show and demonstrate African pride. For example, African clothes are suitable for Western summers; why not enjoy your summer in refreshing African clothes.

The time for African leaders to rise up is now. As the title of my first book puts it: Africa, it's time. This is our time. Every other continent has had their time. This is now our time. Fellow Africans in Africa and fellow Africans in the Diaspora, let us join forces to lead Africa to join other continents in development and even becoming the world leader. Everything is at our disposal to make it happen.

We have qualified human resources both inside and outside Africa. We have fertile land and most countries have enough rain to produce good crops. Africa has the best climate in which one can farm throughout the year. We have minerals and oil. We are now a multicultural and multiracial society. We have amazing forests and parks.

God has blessed the continent of Africa in an amazing way. What remains is our own resolve to work hard and utilize well all that God has given us. Let us take away fear and doubt. Both have power to cripple us. Let us chase away pessimism and negativity. Let us restore the African *Ubuntu*.

It is important we each know that the greatness of any human being, the ultimate success of any leader, is in the 'we', not in the 'me', doing well. Greatness is in my ability and your ability to rejoice in the others' success. The more I rejoice in the blessings of someone else, the closer to coming my blessing is.

This means then, that jealousy, rivalry, and negative competition with others are all chasing after the wind. A leader blesses others. He empowers others. He throws a party to celebrate the success and achievements of others. He works with others to ensure community success. Wanting to be the only successful person in the community is not being a leader.

As I said in my first book, the best success is shared success, because it has the power to benefit many. Let us work together for our common good and we will get there. Trust me, we will get there.

This book is intended to make leadership an everyday part of our lives. Leadership must be lived and exercised from the first day of the month to the last day of the month. This means, in other words, that leadership must be practiced every day.

In this book, I am going to address 31 principles of leadership, one principle for each day of the month. You will realize that some months only have 28, 29, or 30 days. But each year has seven months with 31 days in each month. If you read each principle seven times a year, you will be in good shape in terms of your leadership development and responsibility.

It is important for me to clarify something here. You will notice that some days, instead of one quality, I have added a subtitle to include principles that are similar to the subject I am talking about. I have underlined each of those additional principles to make it easier for the reader to identify. Those added principles complement or help explain the subject of that day.

So, instead of giving each one of them its own day, I have chosen to include them as subtitles and a complement to the main subject. An example of that will be 'caring' and 'compassionate'. People who are caring are usually also compassionate.

My hope for you, the reader, is that you will learn some things here that will empower and equip you in your leadership so that you can lead better. You may already be a great leader, but there is always room to improve.

Read this book, and you will become an even better leader. Knowledge, even if it is not new because you have heard it before, is still valuable when it comes as a reminder. This book can be used by everyone: those who are new in the world of leadership and those who have served as leaders for a long time. So stay turned and be inspired!

KNOWLEDGEABLE

True knowledge begins with knowing God. Knowledge must go hand in hand with wisdom!

The first and primary knowledge any human being must have is that of knowing God. Other knowledge such as science, history, mathematics, physics, philosophy, and many other subjects come after knowing God.

Any true leadership begins with knowing God and having an established relationship with Jesus Christ, the Saviour. Any human being is very limited and is unable to lead others on his or her own ability alone. Dependency on God and wisdom from God will constitute the biggest assets or qualifying criteria for good leadership.

It is important to note that the knowledge of God I am referring to is knowledge that is based on relationship with God. It is not the mere knowledge that God exists, but rather it is the kind of knowledge that trusts in God. It is knowledge that believes in God, Jesus Christ as one's Saviour. It is the kind of knowledge that has God as our Master and King. It is the kind of knowledge of God that recognizes our sinful nature and that seeks God's forgiveness and surrenders oneself to God. This is the knowledge that Jesus Christ himself described as the true knowledge, because it is the knowledge that has eternal consequence:

"Now this is eternal life: that they may know you, the only true God, and Jesus Christ, Whom you have sent." John 17:3

Knowing God is a mutual relationship. It means that we know God and God knows us. In fact, it should be that we know God, because He first knew us and first loved us. We know God because we belong to Him. He is our Father. We are His children, and so we belong to His family. Jesus explained that this relationship is based on mutual knowledge, in that we know God because He first knows us.

"I am the good shepherd; I know my sheep and my sheep know me. Just as the Father knows Me and I know the Father- and I lay down my life for the sheep. I have other sheep that are not of this sheep pen. I must bring them also. They too will listen to my voice, and there shall be one flock and one Shepherd." John 10:14-16

Knowing God must not be kept as a secret. We must share this knowledge with other people so that they too would know God personally. We all know that what makes good news good is the fact that it is good to many. Because knowledge changes and transforms us, we must invite others to know Him so that more people are changed and transformed. The more people truly know God, the more communities are changed and transformed.

We saw what happened in Zambia when then President Frederick Chiluba declared Zambia as a Christian nation. Evangelism and Christian mission work exploded. More people came to know God. Churches were packed every Sunday. In fact, we can trace the beginning of the true church expansion in Zambia from that declaration. Workers started lunch hour fellowships so that they would go to church during their lunch hours. There were prayers at State House. That seed of declaration of Zambia as a Christian nation continues to produce good fruits even today.

Zambia today is more advanced than most African countries. Democracy has worked there consistently. I am not saying that everything became perfect, but Zambia performed much better with the expansion of the knowledge of God. The country did better living under the Lordship of Christ. It is my prayer that the people of Zambia will continue to live under the Lordship of Christ. My prayer is that they will continue to build on the legacy of Zambia as a Christian nation.

Knowing God is rewarding. Consider what this knowledge has done to countries such as the United States of America. The United States of America's motto is "In God we trust". Their knowledge and trust in God has elevated the country to superpower status. Many other countries have been blessed through the United States of America because its very foundation is based on knowing God and paying allegiance to Him.

Today, America is struggling in its relationship with God by approving evil practices; no wonder we are starting to see a decline in the American economy and power. A country cannot keep falling down morally and ethically, and expect to keep being blessed by God. You cannot racially discriminate your own people and think that there will be no consequences for your actions. American leadership needs to start re-giving value to the Christian faith and practice. It is my prayer and hope that America goes back to knowing and loving God like they once did.

Canada was founded on Christian values and principles. Canada as a country has prospered because of its relationship with the Living God. But since Canada has begun rejecting the principles of God and has become so secular that it has started embracing immoral practices, rejecting prayer in schools, and restricting Christian practice, the country is slowly declining. Unless we can stop the bleeding before it is too late, we may soon find ourselves in a country with more problems than we can solve.

Africa in general and African countries specifically must find a way to acknowledge God in all they do. We have to resist the evil immoral Western influence that is taking us away from our knowledge of God. We see what Europe has become. We see how empty churches are in Europe today. We see how far extreme secularism has taken Europe. Even the notion of right and wrong has disappeared in the continent that brought the gospel to Africa. They have made truth to be relative. Truth has ceased to be universal. They claim that what is right for one is not necessarily right for the other.

Family structures have changed. The definition of marriage has changed. There, common law unions are becoming the norm of the day. Divorces are more common than lasting marriages. Europe is now totally bankrupt morally and spiritually. Africa must guard jealously its heritage that has come as a result of knowing God and having a relationship with Him.

A leader must have knowledge. We cannot teach what we do not know. A leader must make sure he makes learning his lifelong pursuit. To lead well, a leader must continually be a few steps ahead of those he is leading. In today's world, knowledge is accessible through different means, so there is no excuse to remaining ignorant. For any organization or any country to succeed, it must have a knowledgeable leader.

It is important, however, to note that real knowledge must be accompanied with wisdom. It is not enough just having knowledge; wisdom is needed for the best application of knowledge. Knowledge alone, or what is often referred to as head knowledge, is not of any value if it is not useful or applied. Just having a medical degree is not helpful if it is not used to treat patients. Knowledge must be put into practise for it to have value.

Knowledge and wisdom go hand in hand. When a leader is both knowledgeable and wise, he will greatly lead his people. Knowledge without wisdom is like being a talented player with an injury. When you are seriously injured, you cannot perform to the level of your skill. Sometimes you cannot even be allowed to play. Trying to lead a community based on knowledge without wisdom will be just a matter of time before total failure is inevitable. Leaders need wisdom to best apply their knowledge.

A knowledgeable and wise leader doesn't have to be the most intelligent person in his group or community. He just needs to make good use of the minds surrounding him.

Poor leaders tend to push away anyone who seems to know more than them, but that is a big mistake. Great minds are to be valued and appreciated for their contributions. Great minds are part of the team. Great minds are the leaders' assets. A wise leader creates a conducive atmosphere of work in order for the great minds around him or her to continue expanding.

When Joseph explained the dream of King Pharaoh, a dream which all the king's wise men could not explain, Pharaoh quickly saw in him a great asset at his disposal. When Joseph advised him to appoint a manager of the resources who would plan well and avoid famine in Egypt, Pharaoh could not appoint anyone else but Joseph. He made him Premier Minister of Egypt. Joseph used his God-given wisdom and knowledge to manage the resources and applied a great saving system that helped Egypt go through seven years of drought unharmed. The lesson is clear; when you as a leader discover a great mind, use it to everyone's benefit.

Africa is suffering today because we think that there is only one person with all knowledge and wisdom to lead the country. Often leaders surround themselves, not necessarily with great minds, but with those who tell them what they want to hear. But a great leader realizes that being human means we know some things and we do not know other things. So for those things we do not know, we ask help from others. It is when we pretend to know everything and when our inner circle tells us that we do indeed know everything that we become fools and damage our communities in unbelievable ways. Only a fool thinks he knows everything. In fact, to pretend to know everything is to make oneself a god, and that is nothing less than blasphemy. If you are truly a leader, beware of those who want to make you divine. Haile Selassie knew the danger of being made supernatural and he refused it. He recognized that only God must be worshiped:

> "Do not worship me, I am not God. I'm only a man. I worship Jesus Christ." (3)

Great minds make the leader look great. The leader may already be knowledgeable and wise. But when a leader adds to his knowledge and wisdom the knowledge and wisdom of others, great things happen. We saw this when Canada had Paul Martin as Minister of Finance. His expertise in Finance combined with Prime Minister Jean Chretien's good leadership produced wonders for Canada. We saw the same with Prime Minister Stephen Harper and the late Finance Minister Jim Flaherty. These two Ministers of Finance made the already great Prime Ministers more successful.

A leader is like a coach who is not necessarily the best at playing the game, but understands the game and his players and how to make the best use of the team. The coach's job is to teach, guide, and lead every player to give his maximum and to play as a member of the team. The leader's job is to empower others to give their contributions and to motivate everyone to buy into the team concept and to do everything for the team.

So, to be effective as a leader, seek knowledge and wisdom. Start with knowing God, because that is the most important knowledge that has eternal reward. And because no human being knows everything, use the knowledge and wisdom from others, making them part of your team.

Lord, help me know you more and make you known to others who do not know you yet! Lord, give me knowledge and wisdom to know how to share that knowledge wisely!

Application of Day 1

1. Why is it important for a leader to seek knowledge?
2. Why is it that knowing God is the primary and most important knowledge?
3. Does the leader have to be the most knowledgeable of the team? Explain why you opt for yes or no.
4. How do great minds make the leader look good?
5. Why it is that knowledge without wisdom is ineffective?

VISIONARY

A visionary leader is ambitious, has a dream, and is driven!

A leader must have a vision. Vision allows a leader to see where he or she is going, and where he or she is taking the people. He is a guide. He knows the place where he is taking people and he knows how to get there. He also knows what needs to be done there. He has a clear picture of the entire adventure.

Sometimes during our missionary service in Burundi, we would go visit their important sites, such as the Zoo in Bujumbura, and the Karera Falls, which are both great sites to visit. What made these sites more enjoyable were the tour guide personnel. These tour guides know the site very well and what is in it. They know what is safe and what could be dangerous. They know the history of the site, and it is that history and the site itself explained that makes the tour more interesting.

A visionary leader is like a tour guide. He knows the place well, including the history of it. This is why he can be trusted to lead to the destination. Also, his knowledge of where he is taking himself and the people makes the journey more interesting. Just like deciding to see a new movie requires one to see the preview, a visionary leader gives you a preview that informs your choice of buying into the vision or not.

Without vision, people will be lost. Without vision, they will beat around the bush. It is like embarking on a journey without a destination. Vision is so important because it sets the agenda. It gives direction. A vision is much clearer than a GPS. When it is well-thought through, it allows a leader to have a plan from beginning to end.

This is why for any country to succeed, it must have a visionary leader. A leader must be able to see far away. A leader must see what is good for his people. A leader must be able to have a big vision for his community. Too often, we have self-proclaimed leaders with visions so small that cannot improve even the lives of one family. Such so-called leaders are so crippled by their small-minded visions that they get busy chasing after rats instead of antelopes. A leader must have an enlarged vision. When the whole community or country is depending on you, you must have a vision big enough to carry your community or nation into greatness.

Vision is a quality that is given to one person, who in turn uses it for the benefit of his community. Martin Luther King was a visionary leader. Even when the realities of his time saw racism and discrimination everywhere, he envisioned a society that will one day allow for people of all races to enjoy a relative freedom and equality, and be able to succeed based on effort and not on race.

While it is difficult to eradicate racism and discrimination, we can all agree that King's vision has been realized in the United States of America to some degree. It is reasonable to think that Barack Obama's presidency in America is a product of King's vision. It is very sad to see that the racial tensions have risen again and are sharply dividing Americans. Black Americans experience more brutality and killings as if they were still not equal to other Americans. So, while progress has been made in racial relations in the many years following King's death, much more has to be done to bring about equality of all races. It is at least encouraging to see some American leaders speak forcefully against racism in America. One of those leaders is former president George W. Bush. He said:

> Our identity as a nation, unlike other nations, is not de-termined by geography or ethnicity, by soil or blood. This means that people from every race, religion, ethnicity can be full and equally American. It means that bigotry and white supremacy, in any form, is blasphemy against the American creed. We've seen our discourse degraded by cas-ual cruelty. Too often, we judge other groups by their worst examples while judging ourselves by our best intentions, forgetting the image of God we should see in each other. We need to recall and recover our own identity. (4)

Jesus, our greatest leader, was also our greatest vision-ary. He envisioned a world where his twelve disciples would be used to spread the Good News of the Gospel that would eventu-ally turn the whole world upside down. To make that happen, he took time to teach and empower his disciples to take the baton after him. Today, we are the partakers of the fulfillment of that leadership transfer. The gospel has now reached almost every part of this world, and its impact cannot be stopped, even under the severe persecutions and rapid moral decline of our present age.

The problem we have today is that we have people who want to be given a position of power and leadership when they do not even have a vision. If you do not have a vision, how are you going to lead people? As a leader, you have to know the way so you are equipped to take people with you. You can-not take them anywhere good if you yourself do not even have an idea where to go and how to get there. We all know that if a blind person leads another blind person, they will both fall. Jesus said it well:

"Can a blind man lead a blind man? Will they not both fall into a pit? A student is not above his teacher; but everyone who is truly trained will be like his teacher." Luke 6:39-40

Africa and the world need visionary leaders who know a better place to take their people. Africa will become what our leaders make her to be. Time has come for African leaders to lead their people with great vision and help Africa join other continents in development and soon become the world leader among other continents.

This visionary leadership should not be limited to political leaders. The church, in fact, should take the lead. Africa is currently the most Christianized continent on Earth. Imagine how many people fill up churches throughout Africa every Sunday! What if all those people were led by visionary leaders who inspire and challenge them to live out their faith in Christ in action? The time has come for Christian African leaders to start having God-given visions big enough to change and transform not only their congregational members, but also their entire communities.

Give credit to the pioneer Western missionaries; I know sometimes we just focus on finding all that they did wrong, forgetting to give them credit for the many wonderful things they did. One of the great things visionary missionaries did was to be used by God to change and transform not only the lives of those who believed in Christ, but entire communities where they served.

We had in our Bafuliiru kingdom specifically, and in Kivu in general, the Swedish missionaries. They came and preached the gospel that was holistic. It was the kind of gospel in words and in deeds. They did not stop at just the proclamation. They built the community structures, hospitals, schools, workshop centres, bookstores, and more. They did not just give people fish; they taught them how to fish. Many of the leaders today were former students in the missionary schools. Many doctors today work in the former mission hospitals. Their visions impacted entire communities.

But today, we have our own Christian African leaders whose visions are only limited to proclamation and not extended to practical action on the ground. Their visions are so small that they cannot even create a small bookstore, or chicken farm, or brick-laying projects, or anything practical that is worth taking people out of the beggar mentality to become responsible Christian adults. They have crippled themselves and their members with the never-ceasing need for Western aid, as if that should be their permanent solution.

Thank God that in the midst of the visionless leadership, we still have exceptions to the rule. One of those exceptions I have come across is an organization called Foundation for Cross-cultural Education (FCE) that started in South Africa and has now gone into many countries in Africa. I love their vision. I like many things about them, starting with their vision or mission statement:

"Jesus Christ, making disciples through us world-wide, by building a highway of holiness, through education and training." (5)

They let themselves be used by God to make disciples whose lives are changed in body, mind, and spirit. Their transformational vision is training people to be Christians who are doing well in faith and in life. It is not about 'claiming and naming it' and it miraculously happens, but about faith and work that builds our relationship with Christ our Lord and makes us providers for our families. God is using this ministry greatly, and changing and transforming lives that are in turn contributing greatly to building the kind of Africa that will soon change from being the receiver of aid to the giver of aid to others.

Here is my vision that I will suggest to fellow African ministers of the gospel. Can we reduce the two weekly prayer meetings to one and use the other meeting to build a community farm, where, as a church, we can have our own farm from which we can harvest food that we can use to feed the needy and our guests and we can use for our functions such as church fellowships? Can we create our own companies, such as brick-laying companies, so that we can start employing our own people and develop self-sustaining churches?

We must balance prayer and work, as both are important and complimentary. That is leadership. Leaders must be able to think outside the box and be visionary enough to create practical solutions to the world's problems.

A leader must be ambitious enough to want to create the best possible life for his people. I know that the word ambition has a connotation of selfishness. But it must be understood in terms of a leader being so driven to do great things for his people. His expectations must be high so that he can push himself to achieve much.

I have met a few extremely ambitious and driven people. One of those people is my good friend, Dr. Daniel Zopoula. He is the founder and CEO of Bridges of Hope and the Archbishop for Misericordia Fellowship. Daniel always seems to achieve whatever he puts his mind to. He is so successfully driven and ambitious that he lives and does things as if the word fear or failure no longer exists in the dictionary.

The good thing about him is that he is ambitious for the right cause. He is always advocating for the betterment of others. He has established orphanages, clinics, and many other humanitarian projects and programs to help alleviate poverty and empower people. So, being ambitious, driven, or a dreamer, for him, has worked out to produce wonders for the many suffering poor. We need more of that kind of unselfish, ambitious dreamer in Africa, leaders who will do all they can to make a lasting difference in the lives of their people.

Lord, make me a visionary leader so that I may lead the people in the right direction!

Application of Day 2

1. What does it mean to be a visionary leader?
2. How it is that a visionary leader is like a tour guide?
3. We know that visionary leading is not limited to political leadership. What other areas need visionary leaders?
4. What does vision do for a leader and his community?
5. Think of two or three biblical visionary leaders. How did their God-given vision help them lead well?
6. Think of two visionary leaders that you know. How did their visionary leadership help them to help their people?
7. Think of yourself. Do you have a vision? What is it? How is your vision making a positive difference in your life and in the lives of those who are in your sphere of influence?

PURPOSEFUL

A purposeful life is a life that leaves positive legacy!

There is a reason why we are on Earth. There is a purpose to our existence. God did not place us on Earth to merely exist; He placed us on Earth to live a purposeful life. There is probably nothing more wasteful than living a meaningless life, a life without purpose. A leader makes sure his life counts for something meaningful. A leader makes sure he leaves a positive legacy.

I was in Pretoria, South Africa, and I went to take a picture at the monument of Nelson Mandela. I observed one thing there, a crowd of people, group after group coming to take their picture with Mandela's monument. He has been dead for a few years now, but his legacy continues. He lived a purposeful life.

Jesus Christ, our Lord and Master, lived a purposeful life. In just 33 years on Earth, he secured salvation for humanity, for anyone who repents of his sinful nature and trusts in Christ for salvation. Even extreme suffering could not deviate him from his purpose. He endured everything, including death on the cross for us. His life and death inspires us to purposeful living.

Purposeful living starts with knowing God because without him there is really no purpose. God is the reason why we even exist. He gave us life by creating us. We find purpose, meaning, and significance in Him. Rick Warren, the author of *Purpose Driven Life*, says it well:

> "*Without God, life has no purpose, and without purpose, life has no meaning. Without meaning, life has no significance or hope.*" (6)

Living with a purpose gives us a reason for a meaningful life. It says to us that we are on Earth to make a difference, a positive one. It says that we have a contribution to make to the betterment of ourselves and our society. It is living in gratitude to the God who gave us life in the first place, and saying to Him that we will fulfill the mission He assigned us.

Myles Munroe says that every human being must answer five important questions of life. I would like to quote these questions because they are very fundamental to understanding our purpose on Earth:

1. **Who am I** - *This question deals with identity. The average human being has never answered the question, who am I? This is not what you do or did. Most people don't know who they are, so they die as someone else.*

2. **Where am I from** - *this is not an ethnic question. It is not about whether you come from Africa, China, Kenya, Coast, Nyanza, Kiambu or Teso. No, it is where you are from in regards to your creation. If you can find out where you came from, you can also find out your ability, your strength and your potential.*

3. **Why am I here** - *This is a question of progress, why do you exist, what did you come to earth to do. Did you just come to go to work and pay bills and die, as many people think? It has to be more than that. There has to be a purpose for your existence.*

4. **What can I do** – *what is my true ability? They say the average human only uses 10% of their brain. No one knows your ability, except the manufacturer. So never let anyone judge you based on their measurements or their tastes.*

5. **Where am I going** – *This is a question of destiny. No one was just born to die; we were born to fulfill an assignment. What you are looking for is right where you are all the time. You don't have to go to US or UK to be great; you can be great where you are. (7)*

God, the great Creator, designed every one of us with a purpose, a mission to fulfill. We all must answer the question, why am I on Earth? We all must discover our uniqueness, our gifts and talents, our skills, and use all that God gave us to leave wherever we are a better place than we found it. What a waste when all we ever did was spend time existing on Earth!

A true leader must ask himself some important questions: What is my role? What can I do? What cause can I champion and fight for? Who can I help over and above my family? What is my purpose in life? Who can I motivate? Who can I inspire? Who can I encourage? Who can I empower? Who are the oppressed that I must defend and advocate for? Why am I here on Earth? To live a purposeful life, a leader must put his brain to action and find what cause needs his involvement.

Purposeful living requires sacrifice. It usually requires the crucifying of self in order to make the lives of many better. Selfish living is really the opposite of purposeful living. Selfish living is all wrapped up in the 'I' and 'me' while purposeful living is all about 'we' and 'us'. Purposeful living is about making decisions and choices that will impact our community positively. It is a sacrifice for many to benefit from it. Purposeful living is about investing in helping and inspiring others to succeed. It is about not being satisfied in succeeding alone. There are many people who will do well if only we took time to inspire them.

I remember one day in 2006, I was preaching in the Jerusalem City church where my good friend, Pastor Noah is the Senior Pastor. Pastor Noah is from Africa, and the church was predominantly African. In my application of the message, I urged my fellow Africans who were already Canadians to start enjoying their full Canadian citizenship. I told them that we were not visitors in Canada but full citizen and we needed to start participating fully in building a better Canada for ourselves and for all Canadians. Many Africans were living in Canada as if their Canadian citizenship was not equal to that of other Canadians of European decent. I told them that a Canadian citizenship gives us full rights just as it does for all other Canadians and that we needed to start enjoying Canada as our country.

One example of living in Canada as a Canadian was to work hard and one day buy a home in Canada. I said that while we all start with renting, once we have worked hard and saved some money, we should buy a home for our families. I did not know how much that message inspired the congregation until about two years later when one of the members of the congregation who heard that message came to see me and to thank me.

He said, "Pastor Charles, I have come to thank you for inspiring us to buy a home." He reminded me of the sermon I had preached in their church and how I encouraged them to live in Canada as full Canadian citizen and to buy themselves a house. He told me that they bought a house a year after that message as they started saving money toward the house the first month after I had given that message. Many others bought houses and became more and more involved in contributing to building our wonderful country, Canada. Purposeful living is about inspiring others to maximize their potential. The world will be a better place if we all live purposefully and making a positive difference in the lives of many other people.

Purposeful living often finds joy in personal sacrifice for the benefit of many. Think of the sacrifice of Charles Mully, a successful businessman, a millionaire who gave up everything, all his wealth, to establish homes for the desperate poor children in Kenya. It is said that by now, more than 10,000 children have been supported through his foundation. Some of them are the leaders in Kenya in different fields. Imagine the difference that 10,000 educated people are making in their communities! But it took Charles Mully's sacrifice and dedication to live a purposeful life to have 10,000 lives changes and transformed, and the impact is still growing.

Consider also Oprah Winfrey, who invested $40 million to establish the Oprah Winfrey Leadership Academy for girls in South Africa. Imagine the kind of leadership training these girls get there! Imagine the empowerment they are getting and the kind of opportunities it creates for them in the future! Imagine the sacrifice Oprah had to make, to spend all that money educating thousands of future leaders. I know Oprah is one of the most blessed people on Earth, but spending $40 million on others is a huge sacrifice for anyone. She could have chosen to buy a huge mansion anywhere in the world with that money, or a bigger airplane, or a hotel, or anything else. But instead, she thought of others' needs before her own; that is what it is to live a purposeful, sacrificial life.

I know some people have criticized her for spending that much money on one school. They claim that she could have built many schools with that. But I agree with Mandela, who saw in Oprah's sacrificial giving something worth so much praise.

The Oprah Winfrey Leadership Academy for Girls—located near Johannesburg and educating girls in Grades 7 through 12—is therefore a wonderfully appropriate gift to the people of South Africa, one that will endure over many lifetimes. When I went to the opening of her school, I looked at the shining faces of these young women and thought every one of them has the potential to be an Oprah Winfrey. The school is important because it will change the trajectory of these girls' lives and it will brighten the future of all women in South Africa. Oprah understands that in Africa, women and girls have often been doubly disadvantaged. They have had the curse of low expectations and unequal opportunities. (8)

Some people specialize in criticism without doing anything better. As humans, we have the tendency of the disciples and the Pharisees who do not want a good expensive perfume to be poured on Jesus, claiming the money from the sale of it could be used to help the poor. It is as if they only think of the poor when someone else does something good that they could not do themselves. We need to specialize in appreciation. Oprah gives a reason for why such an elite school in South Africa:

I think the reason not just Africa but the world is in the state that it is is because of a lack of leadership on all levels of government ... and particularly in regard to schools and schooling for poor children. ... The best way to effect change long term is to ... give children exposure and opportunity and nurture them to understand their own power and possibility. (9)

That school is and will continue to be instrumental in generating great African women leaders, and provide a balance in the continent that has seen many worthy and intelligent women and girls marginalized.

Purposeful living is about picking up the cross and carrying it as Jesus commands us. It is giving all, like the poor widow in the Bible gave. The good news is, contrary to what we think humanly, sacrifice produces fruits in abundance.

Today, the tragic fate of the raped women and girls in Eastern Congo is known worldwide because of the sacrifices of Doctor Denis Mukwege, who has risked his life and profession to repair the damages on the beloved women of his country. He has advocated for them both verbally as a great Christian and humanitarian, and practically as a gynecologist. Even after escaping death, he went back to continue his devoted work for the women he dearly cares for.

Jesus said that he who wants to save his life will lose it, but he who loses his life for Jesus will save it. Living a purposeful life is losing one's life just to save it in abundance. Best success, best accomplishment is found in one's giving up on his own selfishness to be of service to those in need; that is indeed purposeful living. Father Damien's story illustrates very well what purposeful living is all about:

Father Damien or Saint Damien of Molokai was a Roman Catholic priest from Belgium and member of the Congregation of the Sacred Hearts of Jesus and Mary, a missionary religious institute. He won recognition for his ministry from 1873 to 1889 in the Kingdom of Hawai'i to people with leprosy, who were required to live under a government-sanctioned medical quarantine on the island of Moloka'i on the Kalaupapa Peninsula. During this time, he taught the Catholic faith to the people of Hawaii. Father Damien also cared for the patients himself and established leadership within the community to build houses, schools, roads, hospitals, and churches. He dressed residents' ulcers, built a reservoir, made coffins, dug graves, shared pipes, and ate poi from his hands with them, providing both medical and emotional support. After sixteen years caring for the physical, spiritual, and emotional needs of those in the leper colony, Father Damien realized he had also contracted leprosy when he was scalded by hot water and felt no pain. He continued with his work despite the infection but finally succumbed to the disease on 15 April 1889. Father Damien has been described as a "martyr of charity". He was the tenth person in what is now the United States to be recognized as a saint by the Catholic Church. (10)

While we must recognize that not everyone is called to such extreme sacrificial and purposeful living as Father Damien, we all must find our purpose on Earth and live to fulfill it. Unfortunately, the church of today that is supposed to live out this selfless and purposeful life is busy joining the world in the very pursuit of self-gratification and selfish success.

Christian living must be a purposeful living; it must be meaningful. Jesus told us that while we are to expect the full realization of the Kingdom of God in heaven, kingdom joyful living begins right here on Earth.

Every human being has been sent here on Earth to live purposefully and to leave a positive legacy. Every day we live must be lived in a meaningful way. We all know that time or days of our lives are rare assets, that once you lose time, you cannot get it back. John Bevere says in his book *Driven by Eternity*:

> *"Many things lost in life can be restored; however, time misused can never be recovered. Once the sun goes down, the day is forever gone."* (11)

This is why the apostle Paul tells us to be wise in how we live our lives. He advises us to maximize our usage of every opportunity, so that it counts. He urges us to understand God's will for us, to understand God's purpose for creating us. Paul says it so much better than I:

> *"Be very careful, then, how you live—not as unwise but as wise, making the most of every opportunity, because the days are evil. Therefore do not be foolish, but understand what the Lord's will is."* Ephesians 5:15-17

The apostle Paul is saying that our life matters so much that we cannot afford to waste it. Right from creation, God placed value in us human beings. We are the only creation to whom God used dust, formed us, breathed life into us, and created us in His own image. We are the only creation to whom God gave authority to rule over other creatures. Jeremiah tells us that God Himself has great plans for us:

"For I know the plans I have for you, 'declares the Lord,' plans to prosper you and not to harm you, plans to give you hope and a future." Jeremiah 29:11

When you consider the value, the meaning, and the purpose God has placed on a human life, then you realize how offensive we are to God when we live as if life itself is meaningless. I am sure God looks down from Heaven and says to Himself, 'If only you knew your value; if only you knew how much you are worth; if only you knew how much work I put into your life.' You would make great use of your life so much that you will live to build a lasting positive legacy that will count even after you exit planet Earth.

The time has come, and it is now that we must rediscover our value on Earth and especially our value in Christ. There is a purpose for our being on Earth and every second of our life matters. We must eradicate from our minds the whole concept of 'wasting time'. We have to live in such a way that what we do counts for eternity. The time to live for self is over; it should never have been there.

Purposeful living has eternal consequences. One day each one of us will give an account of our life on Earth. I wonder what will be our answers when God asks us: 'What did you live for while on earth?' I can see someone saying, 'I lived to make lots of money.' Someone else will say, 'I lived to care for my family.' Another person will say, 'I lived to enjoy pleasure.' But someone will say, 'I lived to evangelize so as to give an opportunity to as many people as possible.'

And although none of those answers are evil in themselves, still God will be pleased with the evangelist, because he lived to extend himself for the eternal benefit of many. A leader lives to make a difference in the lives of many.

We must always remember that we are on Earth for a short while and we have eternity ahead of us. Purposeful living then is about seeking the kingdom of God and its righteousness. This kingdom includes extending ourselves for the benefit of others. It is to that kind of meaningful living that in the end Jesus will welcome us as His faithful servants into His eternal Kingdom. The Bible tells us that He would say to us:

> *"For I was hungry and you gave me something to eat, I was thirsty and you gave me something to drink, I was a stranger and you invited me in, I needed clothes and you clothed me, I was sick and you looked after me, I was in prison and you came to visit me."* Matthew 25:35-36

Lord, help me live a purposeful and meaningful life that makes a difference for eternity!

Application of Day 3

1. What is your purpose in life? Why are you here on Earth?

2. What is the value of having a purpose?

3. How does purposeful living make life meaningful?

4. How does purposeful living often require sacrifice?

5. From a biblical perspective, explain how purposeful living has eternal consequences?

6. Are you truly living a purposeful life? Ask God to show you the purpose of your life. Can you choose and decide to fulfil God's purpose for your life?

PERSON OF INTEGRITY

Honesty and good reputation are qualities that go hand in hand with integrity!

Integrity is one of the top marks of a true leader. A leader must be a person of integrity. The apostle Paul gives us the qualities of a leader, an overseer, in 1 Timothy 3:1-7. He also continues to talk about leadership qualities regarding deacons. Let us consider the first instructions to overseers:

Here is a trustworthy saying: Whoever aspires to be an overseer desires a noble task. Now the overseer is to be above reproach, faithful to his wife, temperate, self-controlled, respectable, hospitable, able to teach, not given to drunkenness, not violent but gentle, not quarrelsome, not a lover of money. He must manage his own family well and see that his children obey him, and he must do so in a manner worthy of full respect. (If anyone does not know how to manage his own family, how can he take care of God's church?) He must not be a recent convert, or he may become conceited and fall under the same judgment as the devil. He must also have a good reputation with outsiders, so that he will not fall into disgrace and into the devil's trap.

Integrity helps a leader have a good reputation. You cannot buy a good reputation, but you earn it. People know that you are who you claim to be. Integrity is about being the same person in private and in public. A leader must guard his integrity and good reputation jealously, because they set you apart as a good leader. King Solomon tells us in his book of Proverbs that a good reputation or a good name is of great value:

A good name is more desirable than great riches; to be esteemed is better than silver or gold. Proverbs 22:1

A good name or a good reputation is the most valuable asset of a leader. People want to work with someone of good reputation. A good name makes the sale for you; it advertises you. A good name speaks for you even in your absence. You can afford to lose many things because you can get them back with hard work. But you cannot afford to lose a good reputation, because it is very difficult and, in fact, close to impossible to get it back.

Integrity goes hand in hand with honesty. A person of integrity refuses to get anything in a dishonest way. What do you do when you are tempted to gain something in a dishonest way? In 2017, we sent a container to Africa. When it arrived in Tanzania, the person we contracted to help us declare the container at customs suggested to my cousin, who was in Tanzania at that time, to lie about the size of the container. We had sent a 40–feet-long container, but he suggested that we say it was only 20 feet in order to save money. My cousin called me and told me the situation. So we decided to tell him that no matter how expensive 40 feet would be, we would never lie to save money. So we required him to declare 40 feet.

It is very unfortunate that Africa keeps going backwards in some areas because more and more people are not being honest. It is as if integrity does not matter. But they forget that if we all cheat the government, there will be no money to build roads, schools, hospitals, and also improve the wages of workers.

It is very alarming to see the level of dishonesty that is prevailing now on our beloved African continent. When even Christian leaders, not all, have their consciences sealed so that clear dishonesty does not bother them anymore, they deliberately lie to make dishonest gains; something has gone terribly wrong. It used to be that when a Christian sins he would not be at peace until he humbly repents of his sin. But now sin, dishonesty, or lack of integrity is accepted, and sometimes embraced, because we have reduced the meaning of life to 'the end justifies the means.'

Sin has ceased to bother people as it used to do in the past. And it is not because it has ceased being what it is, but it is because we have done away with God's warning on the 'love of money'. People are ready to throw away their integrity as long as dishonesty can benefit them financially. They would even sell you, like Joseph's brothers did to him, if they get an opportunity to do so. It is very sad how far we have fallen.

Sin must bother a Christian. Integrity is important in any circumstance. We must never overlook or justify sin. Satan often whispers to us that some sins are too little that we should not bother about them. It is like bribe, some people have become so used to bribing that it no longer bothers them. I have seen in my various travels in Africa where taxi drivers would constantly bribe the police officers just so that they can keep driving their commercial vehicles without proper documentations. Sin is so blinding and does not even make economic sense. These taxi drivers do not even realize that it is cheaper to have proper documentations than it is to keep paying a bribe every day to avoid the cost of an annual fee for the proper documentation.

The problem of bribe is not only an African one. It is a universal problem. It has its variances and degrees of severity depending on the culture it is operating in but it is a problem everywhere. No matter where we are, we have to guard against it. In most cases, it is a constant battle that we need to ask God's grace to fight it. For example, with the conveniences of technology; how many of us still resist the temptation of just copying a CD or DVD instead of purchasing that CD or DVD and paying the right dues to the producer of it? Someone worked so hard to produce that CD, DVD, song or book and you just want to copy it without properly paying for it; how is that not a sin of stealing?

I have seen situations where a cashier forgets to charge for something and people think they were just lucky. It should not matter that the cashier, the bus driver or anyone else forgot to charge us for their service; we must pay for the services that we receive that require a charge. God and our conscience see what humans could not see. We owe to God to let our God-given good conscience guide us into doing the right thing. Yes, Satan will never quit tempting us while we are still in our healthy sinful nature but we must resist him. The book of James gives the best formula to resisting the devil; it starts with being submitted to God.

"Submit yourselves, then, to God. Resist the devil, and he will flee from you." James 4:7

One day I went to do grocery shopping at the Lloydminster Superstore and because I had a number of items, I put the container of vinegar on the bottom shelve. But when I went to pay for the items, I did not remember that the lone container of vinegar was on the bottom. The cashier also did not see it, so he did not charge me for it. When I went to unload the items into the car, I saw that vinegar container and immediately I realized that I did not pay for it. I checked the receipt and for sure I noticed that the vinegar was not itemized there. The devil quickly whispered in my ears that I should run the items that I paid for home so that my wife can get started on the supper for which we were already late in making. But I did not want to open the possibility of me forgetting to pay for the item. I thought that it is better to eat supper late than to delay making things right. Integrity, honesty is more urgent than supper. So, I quickly run back to the store and went to tell the customer service that I was not charged for the vinegar so I had come to pay for it. She looked at me with a great smile on her face and said, "Thank you for your honesty!"

I hope you do not think that I am trying to think of myself as a sinless person; far from it. We all need to constantly ask God to supply us with more of his grace to overcome sin. The lack of integrity is very damaging. It destroys leadership. It destroys families. It destroys lives. We all know powerful leaders who have fallen badly because of it. Such leaders once thought they were being smarter or clever by avoiding paying taxes, cheating systems, getting away with fraud and many other evils.

Unfortunately, the world is now saturated with so-called leaders. Such people pursue worldly gain at any cost. They live and act as if their consciences have stopped working. They reject anyone who tries to bring them to the right path, because they think others are being jealous of their success. They have chosen to ignore Jesus' challenging question of eternal consequences, truly a question of life and death:

"What good is it for someone to gain the whole world, yet forfeit their soul?" Mark 8:37

These often self-proclaimed leaders are the ones who seem to attract large audiences. They are making everyone look bad. But thank God, we still have many leaders who have continued to live a life of integrity. I met a few of them while on my African book tour. It is my prayer that they will be discovered and given more leadership responsibilities so that they can help turn the African continent in the right direction. As African leaders, especially Christian leaders, we must stop and see how far we have fallen and repent. For our African land to be healed, true repentance from our lack of integrity and honesty and from other sins must happen. It is only then that we can expect to lead our people and Africa to where we should be.

"If my people, who are called by my name, will humble themselves and pray and seek my face and turn from their wicked ways, then I will hear from heaven, and I will forgive their sin and will heal their land." 2 Chronicles 7:14

Lack of integrity has very damaging consequences. Everyone who thinks they are getting away with cheating does not realize that in the end, we all pay the consequences. Why is it that in the West, most people easily pay taxes that are required? I do not mean that the West is free of tax avoiders and cheaters. But, in general, most people are law-abiding citizens, and they pay to Caesar what belongs to Caesar.

A missionary once told me his own story of being confronted with dishonesty to save money. He had brought in a car for his personal use while he was a missionary in Congo. He was told that if he declared his vehicle as for missionary use he would be tax–exempted, and he would give the agents a bribe for the favor of letting him know. But if he declared it for personal use he would have to pay a heavy tax. He chose to pay full tax on it because he was convinced that even though he would also use it for missionary purposes, most of its use was personal. The Congolese agents could not believe such a choice. But that is what integrity means.

One day I had packed my car in Gitega, Burundi, in a place that was considered not for parking, so I was told. After I came back from the store where I quickly went to buy something, I found two police officers waiting for me. They told me I had packed in a non-parking spot. I told them I was sorry, as I did not notice it was a non-parking spot. They told me I had to pay the fine. They showed me in a booklet that the fine was 50,000 francs. So I said that I would pay the fine since I am in the wrong. Then one of the two officers said, "But you can talk." So I said again, just in case they did not hear me correctly, that I would pay the fine. Then the officer asked me where I lived and if we could go talk at my home. Our cook whispered to me, "Boss, just give them 5,000 or 10,000 francs and it will be ok." I told him I could not do that. To make the long story short, I asked them to write me a ticket, which they did. I went to the bank to pay the ticket. Now, 50,000 francs, equivalent to $30 USD, was a lot of money to me at that time, considering we were on a tight missionary budget. But keeping my integrity was more valuable than saving 50,000 francs, and it serves as a lesson and a testimony to the officers that bribery is wrong, and that integrity is of value.

How is Africa doing when it comes to integrity? It is so refreshing when you hear stories such as that of the President of Tanzania, Dr. John Magufuli. It is said that though he had held prominent cabinet ministries prior to his presidency, he did not get rich. He always puts his integrity above money. He lives well but refuses to gain more through dishonest means. Other presidents are wealthy, and Magufuli just has enough to live decently. How I wish that his personal integrity would be imitated by all other leaders. Integrity is a personal choice, but it benefits many, and as Africans, we have to start making integrity a part of who we are.

When people trust you, they are often willing to follow you at any cost.

Integrity is very rewarding for a leader. When people know that you are the same in public as you are in private, then they want you to be their leader. A person of integrity can be entrusted with anything.

When someone becomes a leader, he must be willing to be like an open book. Privacy goes out of the window with leadership. That is why Bill Cosby's allegations of affairs could not go untold. It is the same with Tiger Woods. It is also the same with Jimmy Swaggart and President Bill Clinton. These celebrities' scandals were made public because they were leaders in their fields who were expected to be people of integrity.

In the movie *Courageous*, a test for integrity is given to different people who are seeking a leadership position. A person seeking the leadership position is asked by management to lie on the report and give a false number so that the company can make more profit. This test is given to Martinez Javier, a Mexican worker who has struggled with finding work. The boss requires him to lie on the report so they can make more profit.

Martinez is a man of integrity and chooses to obey God even though it could cost his job. He goes to consult his wife. The wife is ok with him accepting to lie so he could keep his job. She does not want them to go back to Mexico. He finally convinces his wife that he would rather be fired than lie just to keep his job.

When his boss asks him for his thought-through answer, he replied:

"Mister Tyson, I am very grateful to have a job here. I cannot do as you have asked...because it is wrong. It will be dishonoring to my God and to my family to lie on that report." (12)

To keep his integrity, even when faced with losing his job, Martinez refused to lie. He would rather have lost his job than lost his integrity. Honoring God meant everything to Him. As a result, the boss ends up rewarding him for his integrity and gives him the job. The boss was encouraged to see that people of integrity, though extremely rare, are still living in this world.

What is the lesson we can learn from this man's story? Integrity pays, and it is pleasing to God. Yes, it can make us lose our job because some people cannot handle having people of integrity in their companies; they would rather hire people who will do anything wrong as long as it brings them profit. Integrity can sometimes put us in a lonely position, but it is worth it. Integrity often requires our sacrifice. As Christian leaders, and as any leader for that matter, we must be willing to go to the grave as people of integrity. The world needs more trustworthy people, people of integrity.

Lord, make me a person of integrity so that I can be your true ambassador on earth!

Application of Day 4

1. Why is integrity so valuable for a leader to have?

2. Think of Martinez's exhibition of integrity. In your own assessment of leaders today, how many would act like Martinez, knowing that they would lose their jobs and face deportation?

3. What are some of the areas in which most people struggle with to keep their integrity and why?

4. Do you consider yourself a person of integrity?

5. How can leaders help establish a culture of integrity?

6. When we see the wicked and the dishonest prosper, how tempting is it to throw away our own integrity? How can we resist prosperity that comes as a result of lack of integrity?

7. Integrity often demands sacrifice. What can we do to live a life of integrity, even when it will cost us?

CARING

Caring goes hand in hand with being compassionate, loving, and gracious!

A **leader must care for others.** A leader must be compassionate, loving, and gracious to others. Caring must start with the leader's own family, but it should continue to care for everyone else in need, as well. My mentor, Mr. John Goodbrand, reminded me earlier on in my ministry in Youngstown of Theodore Roosevelt's powerful statement, that:

"People don't care how much you know until they know how much you care." (13)

The inability to care makes the message and the messenger irrelevant, and therefore ineffective. The leader's ability to care usually lands his message on a fertile ground and makes it productive.

Jesus, our greatest role model, cared about people. When they were hungry, he fed them. When they were sick, he healed them. He made the blind see. He advocated for the poor. He honoured children and challenged the adults to be like children. Throughout the New Testament, we read about Jesus having compassion toward people in need. For Martha and Mary, he raised their brother Lazarus. Jesus cared even for the rejected in society, such as the prostitutes and the lepers. He also cared for the evil doers such as the tax collectors like Zacchaeus.

A true leader must care for people of all kinds. A leader cares for those who support him or those who oppose him. President Obama said, after winning the election for the presidency of the United States of America, that by being elected president, he would be the president for those who elected him and those who did not elect him. A leader must care for all people.

How are we caring as African leaders? How are we compassionate as African people and leaders toward those in need? How practical are we in our compassion? It is one thing to feel compassionate toward someone, and it is another thing to show that compassion in a practical way. Abraham Lincoln felt compassion for the suffering Black American slaves and made sure to act on that feeling; once in power, he abolished slavery.

When we look at the extreme suffering of the African poor today, we cannot help but pray for true compassionate African leaders to arise. African leaders must now tangibly work to combat poverty. They must now provide solutions that will reduce drastically the gap between rich and poor and provide standards of remunerations for all employees, so that even the lowest paid can provide for his family.

Consider the millions of orphaned African children. Why is it that these desperate children have to get sponsors only from the West? Are Africans unable to take care of their own children, or at least be among the sponsors, so that the load is not carried by Westerners alone? Why have we become so dependent on others to do what we should be doing? The role of the foreign helper or partner is to subsidize the efforts already made by the local helper. But now we are asking our friends to do everything for us. How tragic and irresponsible on our part!

Sometimes you wonder what has happened to our African hearts! It is terrible when the extreme suffering of others no longer moves us into action. Why have we become indifferent to poverty, children's abuse, exploitation of fellow Africans, and so many other evils? Why have we become so selfish that we are losing any ability to care for and even to feel the pain of the suffering Africans? We have to go back to *Ubuntu* and refuse to be satisfied with selfish gain. It is time we regain our God-given compassion toward others, the kind of compassion that seeks and works at making everyone's situation better. We can do it when we allow our God-given compassion to freely and fully operate within us.

Love makes all the difference. If you love what you do, chances are that you will do it well. If you love your family, chances are, you will care for them. If you love the people under your leadership, chances are you will treat them well.

For a leader to truly love his people or to love others, he must first love himself. I know that some people may not agree with me on that statement, but it is actually biblical. The Bible says that we are to love others as we love ourselves, assuming that it is natural that we love ourselves. If we did not love ourselves, loving others would be practically impossible. But God, who created us with the inner, natural ability to love ourselves, is the one who asks us to go a step further in loving others. It is not enough to stop at simply loving ourselves. Each one of us should do more, extending himself to loving someone else.

"And the second is like it: 'Love your neighbor as yourself.'"
Matthew 22:39

Love gives birth to so many good things. Love made God send His only Son to die on the cross for sinners. Abraham loved God so much that he was willing to offer his own son Isaak as a sacrificial offering to God. Jesus loved us so much that He willingly died for us. He sacrificed everything for us. Sometimes I wonder, when we claim to have love for others, if we truly know what we are talking about. Take Africa, for instance. When a rich, Christian employer pays his worker or servant less than a dollar a day, does he really love his worker or servant? There must be a certain level of sacrifice in our love for others. We cannot just keep making mere statements about our love for others, when in practice there is not even a hint of that love. Sacrificial love is practical love, because it does not stop at the verbal expression of love but goes further into tangible actions.

I once heard a story of a mother who loved her son so much that she was willing to sacrifice herself for him. One day, fire broke into the house where her son was sleeping. When the mother saw the blazing fire burning the whole house, she quickly remembered that her son was sleeping inside the house. She ran like a crazy person and dunked a blanket under water and covered her son with it. Then she quickly stormed out of the house, protecting her son. But because the fire was so intense, it burned her so badly that her face was disfigured. The once beautiful mother was no longer good-looking, to say the least.

Her son, who had many friends, started visiting them in their homes. He quickly noticed that all his friends' mothers were more beautiful than his mother. He was deeply troubled by that, as the difference in beauty between his mother and other mothers was so big that it was like a night and day difference. He decided to one day ask his mother why she was not beautiful like his friends' mothers. For a long time, he could not gather the courage to ask his mother, as he was afraid of the consequences such an inquiry could bring. But as he became so troubled about it, he gathered the courage and asked.

He said, "Mother, please don't be upset, I just have a question I would like to ask you." The mother said, "Please go ahead, son." The son said, "Why are you not as beautiful as my friends' mothers?" The mother then asked her son to sit down and hear the story about it. She then explained how one day the blazing fire broke into the house and was burning everything and quickly. That she remembered that he was sleeping in the house. She ran like crazy into the house and wrapped him in a wet blanket and rushed out to save him. She told him that in the process, the severe fire burned her to the point that she is even lucky to be alive, but it disfigured her face. She told him how she used to be very beautiful, but she was willing to sacrifice her own life to save his.

By then, the son was already in tears, crying like a baby as he heard how much sacrifice his mother paid for him to be alive and healthy. Then the son uttered, "Mother, you are the most beautiful of all mothers." That is what love can do.

How are we Christians doing in terms of loving one another? Africa is the most Christianized continent today. If love is the central way of life for a Christian, and Africa is the most Christianized continent on Earth, Africans must therefore be the most loving people on Earth, starting with loving God and continuing on to loving one another. Unfortunately, we are observing that the more Africa becomes the most Christianized continent, the more unloving toward each other Africans are becoming. It is sad to witness a flagrant contradiction between faith and practice within Africa when it comes to love.

Let me be clear here, the decline in love toward God and one another is not just an African phenomenon, it is a problem worldwide. We see that in the West, too. Some people have become so unloving that they cannot offer even a mere smile. And if they cannot even give a smile, there is no hope for them giving love to others. As humans, we need to go back to the basics, and looking at someone with a smile is one of those basics. Mother Teresa said it well:

"Let us always meet each other with smile, for the smile is the beginning of love." (14)

What has gone so wrong that almost everyone is practicing self-love and completely refusing to extend love to the neighbour, as the Bible commands us? Jesus said that the world will know we are His disciples by looking at how we love one another.

Unfortunately, most of us have reversed that command by focusing on selfish love. We are concerned by loving ourselves and we fail to love others. Today, if you want to see love, you look at the pagans, the philanthropists, the humanitarians, and the like. This is truly a challenge to the church today. We must wake up from our deep sleep and start to go back to obeying Christ's command.

We have become so selfish that we are not ashamed to seek power that we will use only for personal gain. A true mark of a leader is his love for the people. The lack of it is what has drowned Africa into unbelievable poverty. When a leader owns huge farms, farms that he will never be able to put into community-use benefit, he is depriving people of land. Some people now own land for prestige's sake, while many poor who would like to farm and support their families are left without any portion of land to utilize. You find people with fifty hectares of fertile land, but they only utilize one hectare for the most and refuse to let those who are without any land of their own use a portion of it. Such unloving actions have contributed to drowning people into poverty. When we live as if loving others does not matter, and when we pose deliberate actions that only benefit us and not others, we have chosen hate over love.

Grace and love go together. A loving person is usually a gracious one. In sending His only Son to die on the cross for the sinners that we are, God loved us so much that He offered salvation to us by grace. Grace is unmerited favor. Sometimes, when we run out of time to do an assignment, the professor can choose to offer a grace period by extending the due date so that we have time to finish the assignment. Even though, in that case, we deserved a zero, grace says you have another chance to do better. Sometimes world leaders offer grace or pardon to offenders in prison and offer them a gracious release before their due date.

Grace is a wonderful thing when you are on the receiving end of it. I remember getting a ride from my nephew Kape from Denmark to Amsterdam, Holland, to catch my flight to go back to Canada. I arrived late due to road construction in Germany and Holland. If I had checked my suitcases, I could have travelled on that flight because there was still half an hour before departure. But time had run out for checking in luggage. So I was asked to go change the flight. I was already feeling bad, as normally it costs about $500 to change a flight. Then the flight agent asked me why I was late catching the flight. I told her that we experienced many delays due to road repairs.

Then she told me that, not only she would not charge me any extra fees, but she would also give me a direct flight and avoid me two lay-overs, one in Paris and another in Toronto, as per my previous itinerary. She was so gracious. God surprised me with his grace, as He always does only what God can do. I arrived six hours earlier even though I left four hours later.

A leader must be gracious. I do not mean that he should not apply the law, because it is important that the law be applied. It is important that people know that in the end, there are consequences for our actions. But as a general rule, let us be gracious toward one another. We must shower each other with undeserved grace. The people we lead must receive our grace.

Grace refuses to be revengeful. It does not pay back evil for evil; it pays back grace or good for evil. This is how David responded to his enemy, King Saul. Saul had attempted to kill David. In fact, he was consumed with the desire to kill David. But he could not. Later, David gets an opportunity for revenge and to kill Saul. But instead of paying back evil for evil, David paid back good for evil. It is a wonderful demonstration of undeserved grace:

"He said to Saul, 'Why do you listen when men say, 'David is bent on harming you'? This day you have seen with your own eyes how the Lord delivered you into my hands in the

cave. Some urged me to kill you, but I spared you; I said, 'I will not lay my hand on my lord, because he is the Lord's anointed.' See, my father, look at this piece of your robe in my hand! I cut off the corner of your robe but did not kill you. See that there is nothing in my hand to indicate that I am guilty of wrongdoing or rebellion. I have not wronged you, but you are hunting me down to take my life. May the Lord judge between you and me. And may the Lord avenge the wrongs you have done to me, but my hand will not touch you." 1Samuel 24:9-12

It is also important that, in our application of grace, we do it fairly. God loves humanity so much that He offered his grace to all who believe in His Son. A leader must show grace to all his people and not just to a select few. Grace makes people feel loved and cared for. Grace makes people feel that they matter.

Grace is what differentiates Christianity from other faiths or religions. Many religions put too much emphasis on humans' good works, as if good works, in themselves, can save someone. But we know that, as much as there are many good deeds we see done by practitioners of various religions, Christian faith tells us that we are only good when we are under God's grace. No goodness on our part can save us. Grace says that we are good because we have been made good. We are good because of what God has done for us. Our goodness comes from the grace of God. Grace makes all the difference. C.S. Lewis says it best:

> *During a British conference on comparative religions, experts from around the world debated what, if any, belief was unique to the Christian faith. They began eliminating possibilities. Incarnation? Other religions had different versions of gods' appearing in human form. Resurrection? Again, other religions had accounts of return from death. The debate went on for some time until C. S. Lewis wan-*

dered into the room. "What's the rumpus about?" he asked, and heard in reply that his colleagues were discussing Christianity's unique contribution among world religions. Lewis responded, "Oh, that's easy. It's grace." (15)

A story is told of two brothers. One brother was a biological son and the other was an adopted son. The biological son told his brother, "You just thank God because my parents adopted you. You were not part of our family." The adopted son replied to his brother and said, "You just thank God because our parents did not have a choice, they just happened to give birth to you. But for me, they loved me enough that they went all the way to adopt me. At least for me they made the choice to make me one of them."

Grace makes a choice to lavish favour on the unmerited. It is through the grace of God that we have been adopted as sons and daughters of God. Like the adopted son, God went all the way to choose us. We too must show grace to others.

Lord, help me to be caring, compassionate, loving, and gracious to others, as you are to me!

Application of Day 5

1. Why is it important to care for others?

2. We have received grace, unmerited favor from God. How then can we be gracious toward others?

3. Do you agree with the statement that people do not care how much you know until they are convinced how much you care? Explain why you agree or disagree.

4. King Saul was determined to kill David, and David knew and ran for his life. David later got the opportunity to kill Saul, but instead he spared his life. What lesson about grace does David's act teach us?

5. Love requires sacrifice. God sacrificed His Son for us. How sacrificially loving are we to be as Christians toward others?

6. Can you think of ways we can love others as we love ourselves?

7. Why is compassion valuable, especially for a leader?

8. Our Lord Jesus is our true example of a compassionate leader. When people were hungry, He fed them. When they mourned for their loved ones, He cried with them, and that authenticated his ministry even more. How can we imitate His compassion?

GOOD LISTENER

A good listener is one who listens with undivided attention.

The ability to listen well can never be underestimated for a leader. Whenever a leader listens well, people under his leadership feel validated and are willing to share their concerns. A leader is a good listener to all, not just to those who agree with him; he listens to even those who disagree with him or oppose him.

The problem with not listening well or not listening at all is that the outcome is already faulty. One cannot expect to lead well if he cannot listen well. To listen well includes listening to your opponents. There is a tendency for leaders to listen mostly, or even solely, to those who tell them what they want to hear. The problem with that approach is that very often, such friends can easily mislead the leader. These false friends sometimes only tell the leader what is good for the leader to hear while it is for their own personal benefit.

A leader must listen also to his opponents and his fierce critics. Even though the opponents tend to exaggerate in their critique of a leader, often they have a point. A leader must listen to all criticisms and then discern what is right and what is wrong. It is fact that some of the best advices come from one's critics.

Listening is really a must-have asset for a leader. When you talk with someone who is a good listener, it is so refreshing. Over the years, I have talked to many people, some who are good listeners and others who can hardly let you finish your sentence before they start theirs.

When you listen well, people feel that you value them. You can solve many problems by simply listening, paying attention, and showing the person you are talking to that he or she is the most important person at that very time. People are willing to share their hearts when they know that you are listening to them with undivided attention.

A leader must develop the listening skill. There is no such thing as 'I am not a listener, I am just a talker'. That may be your natural predisposition, but anyone can develop a listening skill and tame the talking impulse. Being more a talker than a listener can often put a leader in trouble. People who speak more than they listen often speak before they think, and by the time they realize this, they have already committed a blunder. The Bible commends us to practice listening more than talking.

> *"My dear brothers and sisters, take note of this: Everyone should be quick to listen, slow to speak and slow to become angry."* James 1:19

A leader must listen to the general population. The unfortunate state of leadership in Africa is the fact that many leaders want to stay in power, even when the whole population is demanding their departure. One must know that a leader leads people who want him or her to lead them. Once those very people want the leader out, it is in the best interest of the leader and his or her people for the leader to go peacefully. I know there are some complicated situations that must be taken as exceptions, but the general rule must be, 'if your people don't want you any more, leave before they force you out.'

Unfortunately, in Africa especially, leaders think that they can maintain their power by force. But the truth is, even the weakest people, once they stand up against you, your days in power are very short. So do yourself a favour, listen to your people, and follow their will. Don't listen to only your close friends who often find pleasure in lying to you to protect their selfish interests.

One of the biggest enemies of any leader is the selfish selective listening. Some leaders have specialized themselves in only listening to what sounds good to their ears. They choose to listen to the lies as long as it feeds their ego and makes them feel that they are in control. You look at some countries in Africa where everything is going wrong, but the leader still listens and believes those who are telling him that he is doing a great job.

I understand that sometimes the opposition is so negative that they can make even the obvious good look bad, just so they can topple the government. I also know that just because a group of people demonstrate on the street, it does not necessarily mean the leaders are bad.

I am aware that politics is so complex that some people want to remove others when they themselves have no better programs. I was once quite involved in politics, and I understand quite a bit about them. I know that goodness is often too good to survive in it. But given all those facts, the truth still remains; sometimes a leader must evaluate himself or herself, and then seek proper counsel from people who do not depend on their leadership for survival, and then clearly listen to the counsel and act appropriately.

Late Dr. Ernest Schmidt is a great example of an excellent listener. Dr. Schmidt was a highly respected gynecologist at a hospital in Saskatoon, Saskatchewan, in Canada. I must also mention that he and his young family served as missionaries in

Belgian Congo before independence and had to come back when his wife, Mrs. Leona Schmidt, was diagnosed with cancer.

To say that his work in Congo was very sacrificial is an understatement. He was the only doctor, not only at the main hospital where he served, but in the whole district. He and his family lived in a very simple house. His wife Leona gave up her own nursing profession to support him in the mission and to help raise their children. Here is a man who could be making lots of money in Canada, but chose to go live in a rural area under very difficult conditions, especially during the pre-independence era.

When Dr. Schmidt reached about 70 years old, he approached a fellow doctor, his partner and colleague gynecologist, Dr. Yeboah, and asked him a very important and serious question. He asked him to look at his work from years ago and then the present and tell him honestly if he thought he was still doing an effective job as a doctor. Dr. Yeboah could not believe the humility he witnessed in Dr. Schmidt's request. After all, Dr. Schmidt was his senior in the profession and contributed much to building his career. He was like a father to him in the field. But Dr. Yeboah was being entrusted with the advice that could dictate Dr. Schmidt's decision to keep working as a doctor or to retire. When Dr. Yeboah told Dr. Schmidt that his efficiency was on the decline, Dr. Schmidt immediately retired. That is called great listening, and it takes a truly humble leader to act on great and honest advice.

African leaders need to imitate attitude such as Dr. Schmidt's and start listening to wise counsel. Some leaders need to listen to those who are telling them the truth. When some of them keep listening to those who are telling them that people still want them after 35 years in power, are they not able to question if what they are hearing is the truth or the lie from their inner circle? Why can they not ask counsel from neutral people who can tell them the truth?

True leaders prepare others to take over. This is my advice to leaders who have overstayed: Start preparing someone else to take over. Listen carefully to your people. They appreciate all that you have done for your country, but they want you to leave while they still love you. Do not wait until they are demanding that you go. Do not wait until they start going into the streets to demand your departure. Leave on time, like Mwalimu Nyerere, so that they can forever hold you in high esteem.

Overstaying will tarnish your accomplishment. Overstaying will write off your legacy. Listen well and leave before everyone is praying for you to go. The worst thing you can do for yourself is maintaining your power by force. Listen and leave while you still matter. Let someone else continue building on your foundation. Let someone else bring something new and keep taking the country to higher and better levels.

Leaders listen to those who are telling you the truth. The truth is that there is life after the presidency. Learn from other leaders, such as President Kikwete. President Kikwete is happily retired and now he can enjoy his farming passion and working on his foundation that is making a great contribution to humanity. Consider what Kikwete says about leaving the presidency:

"I'm so happy, I played my part, now I have to move on, let a new team come and take the nation further." (16)

He said that he is now enjoying his time with his family, his cattle, and his farm. Now he can play a peaceful role on the international stage and just enjoy his retirement. Is it not the best way to end your active working years of life? Why do other leaders have to wait to be hunted and forced out? We saw what happened to Yahya Jammeh, former president of Gambia. The man ruled Gambia for 22 years. Then he organized the election and lost. At first, he acted as a hero by accepting the election results and called his challenger to congratulate him for his victory. Then, I do not know who he listened to, but he chose to change his mind, rejected the election results, and tried to maintain himself in power by force. His people and neighboring fellow leaders tried to talk to him about leaving power peacefully, but he refused to listen. He ended up leaving anyway, as a thief, not a leader; how tragic! African leaders must renew their listening skills and start listening well. The truth is that to lead well, a leader must listen well.

Lord, make me a good listener so that I can use my ears more than my mouth!

Application of Day 6

1. In your own words, what is effective listening?

2. Why is listening a must-have asset for a leader?

3. Who do you listen to, as a leader: those who tell you what you want to hear, or those who tell you the truth even when it is not what you want to hear?

4. Can a person develop listening skills? If yes, how?

5. What are some hindrances to effective listening?

6. How do you ensure that you are giving the person/people you are talking with undivided attention?

7. Improving our listening abilities is an on-going process. Think of your own listening abilities. Make a detailed list of how you can improve your listening skills.

HUMBLE

Humble is similar to approachable.

Humility is one quality that is losing its power in the Western world. Humility is seen as lack of confidence and even lack of ability to do what is required. I remember my first job interview in Regina, Saskatchewan, Canada. After the interview, my interviewer said to me, "Charles, you seem like a real good person. But you didn't sell yourself. You seem so humble, but I needed you to be tough. So for your next interview, don't portray a humble attitude; show toughness and high confidence." I followed his advice and for sure I got the next job right away. But I had to become a different person to get the job, as humility could not pay for me in that situation.

Humility is one quality that we need to re-value again. We know what the opposite of it, pride or arrogance, can do to our society. We must resist pride and arrogance. Dictatorship style simply oppresses people, and they work for you not because they like you, but only because they have to. When people work for you out of fear and obey you just so they can keep their jobs, at that very moment your title is 'boss', not 'leader'. The problem with the title 'boss' is that it turns people away; everyone working for a mean person, a 'boss', always views his employment as temporary and is always on the lookout for a better opportunity. So, the turn-over is often very high in any organization where you have a boss on top, even if the job pays well.

I often wonder why someone would enjoy overpowering others, mistreating those who work under them, bossing others, overloading those who are already weak, taking advantage of the oppressed. Do they ever ask themselves this question: if the voiceless could miraculously be empowered to speak, what would they say? If the weak could become the stronger ones, what would they do?

One day I heard a story about a man who used to beat his wife almost daily. He beat his wife so much that it became almost a hobby for him. His own wife had become to him an object to do whatever he wanted with. He enjoyed his power over his wife; he abused her in every way possible. But then something happened. His wife got fed up with it. She decided enough was enough. She vowed to herself never to get any more beatings from her husband. She gathered all the power within herself and prepared to reverse the equation. She resolved in her mind that if he tried one more time to beat her, he would be the one to get the beating. Her husband didn't know anything about his wife's plan. So, as usual, he came to do what he always did, he came to beat his wife. But that day, he was not prepared for what he was about to experience. When he tried to throw his punch at her, she blocked the punch and instead she quickly punched him. She was so strong that this time she beat him so much that the husband started pleading for her mercy. Then she told him that he had a choice to never again abuse her, or he would be the one enduring the beating. The beating in their marriage stopped right there. You see, the problem with pride is that it blinds a person so much that one doesn't see the suffering of others.

Humility is about considering others equal to us, not inferior or superior to us. God created all human beings equal. We are all made in God's image. It is when we realize that any human being is made by God's own hands, just like us, that we find every reason to be considerate toward any human being. When you put down anyone, you are making a statement, and it is a very negative one.

Humility pays in a long run. I know that it is tempting to give up on humility when you look around and see that it is the arrogant, the proud, the boss, the dictator who seem to prosper. But we are never to feel less of ourselves because we seem to have failed and the arrogant and mean boss has prospered. Pride can seem attractive from the outside, but if not addressed, it more often than not single-handedly leads to a tragic fall. Pride is one of the character traits that God opposes. But God rewards humility.

"God opposes the proud but gives grace to the humble." James 4:6

Humility is an underrated quality and yet so essential to leadership. The opposite of humility is pride. When you read the Bible, you will not find many things which God said to resist. But pride makes the list. On the contrary, God is in the business of lifting up those who humble themselves. Unfortunately, humans are so deeply depraved that, even though they know that pride always lands us in trouble, they still choose it over humility. But I hope we can all choose humility over pride.

"Humble yourselves before the Lord, and he will lift you up." James 4:10

Humility, however, does not mean self-pity or weakness. A person can be humble and yet confident. Jesus was humble and meek, and yet, He was confident. Being humble does not mean letting other people push you around or bully you. Being humble is having a proper consideration for self and others. The apostle Paul, knowing that being young could make people look down on Timothy, urged Timothy to be confident so as not to let other people look down on him.

Humility is about being authentic. Being humble is living simply without the need to prove anything to anyone. People today spend so much time trying to prove they are superior, or better, than others. They are not satisfied doing their best without comparing themselves to others; they only see themselves as successful when they think they are doing better than everyone else around them. Humility is being satisfied with who God made us to be, while appreciating others the way God made them to be. What makes people approachable is the ability to value themselves as much as they value others.

Humility gives a leader a proper perspective and respect for those under his leadership. When your employees or servants see you as a humble and approachable leader, they serve the organization better. They work with self-esteem, and not under fear or compulsion. Yes, some would try to walk over you, because in their minds, a leader must dictate, order, and impose on his workers. I know all about that. Our first cook in Burundi could not handle the freedom and the value we gave him as an equal human being, so he walked all over us and ended up doing half of his job. But it is the leader's responsibility to help those under his leadership to see the benefit of being treated as equal and valuable, regardless of the positions they occupy in the organization. The bad thing is that most leaders enjoy the fact that they are feared by their employees, so that they see no need to fight; in fact, they embrace it wholeheartedly. People have been oppressed for so long that they have come to accept that they are inferior and that you, their employer or boss, are superior to them, but you do not have to treat them as inferior. It is the responsibility of a leader to bring others up, those who are feeling inferior, to a place where they realize they have equal human value with anyone else.

This is really a needed topic for discussion. Let me address one area where this leadership responsibility is needed. It is the area of Whites working in Africa. In most places in Africa, Whites are considered superior to Blacks. In Gitega, where we served and lived for more than a year, I became known because of my White wife. A number of people knew me as the White lady's husband.

I remember when we had an accident with our van; a Good Samaritan came to help us through the ordeal. We went first to drop my wife and our children at home. Then we went to report the accident to the police. My Good Samaritan tried to introduce me to the police officer who was going to investigate the accident and make a report. But the police officer quickly stopped him and said, "Who doesn't know him? Isn't he who is married to the White lady?"

Another time another police officer, a lady, mistook me for my wife's driver when she said, "Hey you, can you ask the *Muzungu* to give me some money so that I can buy airtime on my phone?" She was surprised when I said to her that the *Muzungu* she was asking for money was my wife. She had just assumed that a Black man could not possibly be the husband of a White lady.

One day, when we didn't have our vehicle yet, we hired two motorbikes to give us a ride home. No motorbike driver wanted to take me; the two drivers were fighting to carry my wife, as it was prestigious to carry a *Muzungu*, rather than a Black person like myself.

A similar story is that of a White missionary friend of mine, who had to go use the Internet at one of the hotels in Gitega. Normally, to use the free Internet there, you have to buy food, or you have to be a client who has booked a room in the hotel. It happened that my host would go regularly to use the Internet at the hotel. So, I asked him how he could afford to eat at the hotel regularly, as that was the condition to use the Internet there. He told me that he eats there once in a while. But he also told me that the hotel manager likes to have the White missionaries use the Internet there, as it serves as publicity, that the hotel must be a good one to attract White people. I was not surprised, because that is what other managers would do, and it is indeed true that it creates good publicity for the hotel.

When we took our children to school for the first time in Burundi, all the children came to surround them, touching their skin and shouting *Muzungu*. Teachers struggled for a long time to stop them from touching our children's skin and calling them *Muzungu*. We also helped. My wife helped change the whole *Muzungu* name with the children, and asked them to call her 'Mama Savana', as they would call any other mother.

At Gitega International Academy, where we served as missionaries, the principal was a White American, and several teachers were White missionaries. The school quickly gained a reputation as an elite school because it had a strong White missionary presence. Sometimes, we would get stopped by the police and they would ask us what we were doing in Burundi, and we would tell them that we were missionaries working with Gitega International Academy. Then they would say, "Oh, that international school that is led by White people."

But what is the point I am trying to make here? The point is this: when you are being honoured to a point where the one honouring you does so out of fear and a feeling of inferiority, you owe it to yourself and to the one honouring you to correct that inequality. It is ok to be respected, but it is not ok to be feared by another fellow human being. Just because many Black Africans view White people as superior, you don't have to view yourself as superior to them. It is your responsibility to treat them as equals.

It is easy to justify oneself in the sense that no one asked to be viewed as superior to someone else, and therefore it is the other person's problem if he chooses to view Whites as superior; but it is important to realize that, to expect the one who considers himself inferior to correct that false view of himself is almost as impossible as expecting a cow to fly. The person responsible to change that false conception is the one who is considered superior.

I know that, as Africans, we have to do our part educating our people on self-respect and a proper appreciation and consideration of the other. I am of the view that our friends, the Whites or any other non-African peoples, must be appreciated for coming to serve in Africa. Many of these friends sacrifice much to come help make a positive difference in Africa, and they deserve our appreciation and thanks. Fearing them or considering them superior to us is, in fact, not appreciating them. Proper appreciation says thank you for the good deeds in a mutual respectful relationship.

Leadership is about setting the example of proper humility. It is about living modestly, within reason. It is not a call to suffering but rather to decency and simple living. Leadership is about sharing the country or the community resources with all the people, not with just a selective few. It is unfortunate when leaders are at peace with amassing so much wealth when their country's men and women keep their children home because they cannot afford to buy books and pens for school. Humility is one of the true marks of a leader. Humility is about putting others first and making sure they too can afford the basic necessities of life. The advantage of being a leader is that you get to have choices. You can choose to invest in personal and selfish gain, or you can choose to sacrifice for the sake of lifting everyone else up. When you are the leader, it is up to you to choose to be humble or to be proud, to oppress people or to treat them fairly, to be greedy and exploit people or to be generous and simple. It is always encouraging to see leaders who are humble enough that they choose to sacrifice themselves in order to invest in the good of others.

One leader who exemplified humility is the former president of Uruguay, José Mujica. Unlike other presidents, who have pocketed thousands of dollars every month, President Mujica gave 90 percent of his salary to charity, remaining with about $1,200 per month. His choice of simplicity is a proof that true leadership is unselfish and full of humility. All the world leaders can learn true humility from President Mujica. Consider what is said of him:

> *"He has been described as 'the world's "humblest" president' due to his austere lifestyle and his donation of around 90 percent of his $12,000 monthly salary to charities that benefit poor people and small entrepreneurs."* (17)

A leader is one who views himself as equal to those under his leadership, not superior or inferior to him. It is this kind of attitude that helps a leader work with people, as one of them and not as the master among his slaves or servants. All leaders must resist the temptation of feeling superior to their servants or employees, or people under their leadership.

Western partners must start collaborating and working with Africans in Africa on equal basis. They should stop going to serve in Africa with the attitude of the masters, even though that is the way many Africans, unfortunately, still see them. We all have the choice to choose how we respond. Westerners can chose to feel superior to others because that is the view colonialism, slavery, apartheid, and neo-colonialism have conditioned Africans to think of them, or they can choose to reject that view of themselves and treat Africans as equals. This is really a matter of the heart.

My friend Gary told me his experience of serving as a volunteer in Africa, building a new school. Gary is a White Canadian. He went to serve with other missionaries from a different country that I will not mention for the sake of not stereotyping people. One time, Gary was carrying bricks at the construction site. He was working enthusiastically and enjoying serving with both local and international workers.

When his international co-worker saw him carrying bricks, he screamed, "Gary, put those bricks down. That is not your job. That's why we have all these local people here." Gary could not believe that in the 21st century, some people are still stuck at the slave to master consideration. They are far from even a minimal understanding of what humility is.

A humble leader evaluates the practices in his culture and decides in his heart which practices are fair and worth keeping and which ones are unfair and must be rejected. In many of our African cultures, women are overworked and undervalued. They hold full-time jobs outside their homes, just like their husbands, and when they come back home from work, they are the ones to do all the housework while their husbands watch TV or visit with their friends. If you ask the husband why it is only his wife doing all the work, he will tell you that his wife does not mind. But even if it true that she does not mind, can you not see that it is unfair? If Africa is to be great, men have to humble themselves and start sharing the home workload with their wives. All leaders can use a measure of humility.

It is different if the couple decides for one parent to stay home and look after the children while the other parent works outside the home to support the family. But in any case, the Bible is very clear on how we can live a life of humility:

> "Do nothing out of selfish ambition or vain conceit, but in humility consider others better than yourselves. Each one of you should look not only to your own interests, but also to the interests of others." Philippians 2:3-4

Humility is needed in African leadership. It is sad when you see leaders, especially in Africa, behave as if they were super-human and that those under their leadership or management are lesser humans.

A true leader wants his employees to be respectful but not afraid of him. He makes himself approachable. He lets his workers enjoy an open-door policy so that they can reach him or talk to him anytime, especially when they have a problem that requires the leader's involvement to resolve it.

A leader must overcome the false assumption that humility will make him weak and make those under him walk over him. There is usually confusion between being assertive and being humble. Some people think that you cannot be assertive and humble at the same time. They would argue that you have to choose one or the other.

This confusion is a result of the society that has become fascinated with self. From a young age, children are being bombarded with the pressure to be assertive, to have strong self-esteem. The emphasis on belief in self and being assertive has diminished the value of humility in our society today.

But the truth is that you can be humble while being assertive at the same time. You can be humble toward others while not allowing them to walk over you. Being humble has nothing to do with low self-esteem. Humility is about being respectful and considerate toward others.

Humility can be tricky. It is possible to be falsely humble. Putting yourself down, beating yourself up, is not humility. False humility is often consumed with always presenting self as humble. I remember a friend in college who always proclaimed himself as being very humble, when in actual fact, he was the least humble of all. True humility is proper consideration of self and others. Humility is not easy. We need to constantly ask God to help us be humble because the moment we think we have mastered humility, then we have officially signed in for arrogance and vain pride.

Lord, make me humble and approachable so that I can avoid the sin of pride!

Application of Day 7

1. What is the value of humility in a leader's life?
2. Explain how humility is different from weakness?

3. James 4:10 commands us to humble ourselves before the Lord, and as a result, God will lift us up. Can you think of situations in your life or in someone's life where humility has been rewarded by God?

4. There is such a thing as false humility. How do you see false humility manifested? Give some examples.

5. There is also authentic humility. How does true humility manifest? Give examples of true humility.

6. Does being the leader make you superior to your servants or workers, or is the leader equal to his servants or employees? Explain your answer.

JOYFUL

Another word for joyful is passionate!

J oy and passion are true keys to successful living and working. They are must-have assets for any person, especially any leader, who wants to make a positive impact on their life and that of other people in their sphere of influence. Sometimes we underestimate the power of joy and passion. Who wants to learn from a grumpy, unhappy person? Who wants to work with an unhappy co-worker or for an unpassionate boss?

I once worked with an extremely unhappy, unmotivated, unpassionate co-worker. He would start work already unhappy and would finish work unhappy. He was unhappy to see other co-workers happy. Nothing seemed to cheer him up. If it rained, it was too bad because he did not like rain. If the sun shone then he hated the heat. He did not like the snow, but he also did not like summer. He was just unhappy no matter the situation. Other co-workers would always wish he was not on shift while they were working. He would try to create problems for others just so everyone could be as unhappy as him. Working an eight-hour shift with him felt like a year. One time, he tried to create problems with me. Then I talked to the supervisor about it, and he told me just to let it go, as the administration had done everything to help him but could not do anything more. I wonder how much harder it would have been if he was the boss!

Joy and passion create wonders. Joy attracts people to a leader. Joy is contagious and creates a happy atmosphere, which in turn creates a positive atmosphere for learning and working. Passion enables a leader to achieve great things. Without joy or passion, whatever one does becomes too heavy a burden and so discouraging that the temptation to quit is high and the performance is often mediocre as a result. When you do what you are passionate about, you are likely going to be successful in it, and people under your leadership find pleasure in learning from you.

I remember in grades 10 and 11, I had a very passionate French and Literature teacher; it was so fun to be in his class. He was very knowledgeable on the subject he was teaching, but more than that, he was very enthusiastic in the way he taught his class. I remember that even when I was sick, the moment I saw on the schedule that he was teaching literature that day, somehow I would feel like I was well enough to go to school because I did not want to miss his class. He would teach about the heroes of the Négritude movement, such as Léopold Cédar Senghor, Aimé Césaire, Léon Damas, and others, as if he was one of them. In every one of his lectures, our eyes would be glued to him. I can see that even my passion for writing on Africa came in part from having had him for two years.

Wikipedia says

"Individuals who enjoy their work will have higher levels of performance for several reasons. These include creativity, trust in their colleagues, and reducing levels of stress." (18)

Also, John Maxwell adds that a leader needs passion and not position to achieve his vision:

"A great leader's courage to fulfill his vision comes from passion, not position." (19)

David Lucatch, founder and CEO of Yappn Corp., speaks on the value of passion. He says:

"The people I have seen achieve the greatest success in their professional and personal lives are passionate people that lead, support, and mentor others with that 'zeal and zest' for the work and people. A person with passion typically exudes confidence, and confidence creates value for themselves and others by leading the way, not showing the way. Professionals who are excited create enthusiasm in their teams and with others, and are viewed as great supporters." (20)

Joy gives energy. Passion is a great motivator that renews strengths so that you are energized to keep working and to keep going. Because of the presence of joy in what you do, those around you are contaminated, and they too become more productive. When you do something that you enjoy doing, you and those under your leadership are empowered to work harder. The apostle Paul knew the value of joy and the act of rejoicing that he had to repeat it twice in Philippians 4:4:

"Rejoice in the Lord always. I will say it again; rejoice."

True joy is found in living in and for Christ. Christ gives us joy. When Christ is our Lord and personal Saviour, we have every reason to rejoice. In Christ there is abundant and overflowing joy. Joy in Christ is never ending. We can rejoice in Him always. It is joy, not in small portion, but in abundance.

Our God is the greatest joy-giver. Sometimes, as Christians, we let the cares of this world rob us from the realization of eternal life that God has prepared for all those who have believed in His Son Jesus Christ. Eternal life is one in which joy is enjoyed to the fullest, and it will never end. Imagine living joyfully, non-stop, pain-free for eternity! That is the life God has promised us in His Word:

> *"And I heard a loud voice from the throne saying, Look! God's dwelling place is now among the people, and he will dwell with them. They will be his people, and God himself will be with them and be their God. He will wipe every tear from their eyes. There will be no more death' or mourning or crying or pain, for the old order of things has passed away."* Revelation 21:3-4

Being joyful is a matter of choice. Sometimes we make a mistake, thinking that you need to have material stuff in order to be joyful. Yes, it is necessary to have a decent living standard, and material things make life much more bearable and can influence our feelings about life, and overall, our joy, but joyful living can be attained apart from material things.

It is very sad when the church becomes so legalistic and a joy-killer that Christians, especially the youth, feel like they are in prison and not in the house of the Lord. In God's house, there must be joy. Our God is the Lord of abundant life. Why is the church competing with funeral homes for which of the two is the number one place of mourning? We want people to be saved, but how can they be when our churches have no joy? Should not the hope of eternal life be enough to keep us joyful? God's kingdom should be a place of celebration. I agree with Tony Campolo that 'The Kingdom of God is a Party.' If we cannot party in God's Kingdom, where else should we? Our God is the joy-giver.

I know that we have to avoid the extreme that says that a Christian cannot be poor, cannot be sad, cannot be sick, and cannot experience suffering. That is not true. It is unbiblical, because suffering can also be part of our experience in Christian living. But even in the midst of suffering, we can still be joyful. In fact, it is when we are able to be joyful regardless of our difficult circumstances that we positively affect non-believers. Joy, therefore, must be an on-going experience.

We also have to be reminded that the presence of joy does not exclude order. Some church services have become chaotic, but claim to do it in the name of freedom in Christ. The Spirit of God is the Spirit of order. It is important not to confuse the two. We must fully rejoice in the Lord, but we do it without losing order or proper conduct.

Unfortunately, there is a tendency to lose the balance and emphasize one way or another. The legalistic ones are so serious that it seems that joy was forced to go away because it could not be allowed to operate. The other extreme emphasizes freedom, and some of them go as far as making the worship indistinguishable from wild, secular parties. I think there must be full joy in the house of the Lord, but that joy must be in reverence to God; hence the need for order and not chaos. Order is not an enemy of joy; in fact, order is joy's partner. It keeps joy under a positive control and balance. It is not about quenching the joy or limiting joy, but about expressing joy properly.

What kind of a leader are you? Are you joyful? Are you passionate? Do your co-workers or your employees enjoy being around you? Do people work for you just because they need to get a pay cheque, or because they love working for you? Is your passion contagious? Does your joy or passion motivate others to work more and to put in all their effort? If you are a leader, you are responsible to a large degree on how well your company succeeds.

A leader's passion, or lack of it, can determine the success or failure of an organization. When people complain that their employees are lazy, grumpy, and unproductive; they must wonder what they have contributed to make their work environment unhappy and unproductive.

I think that joy or passion is not necessarily an inborn trait or quality, but rather something we develop over time and continue to enhance. I agree with John Maxwell that a person needs to have two ingredients to successful living: a job that pays the bills, and a job that a person enjoys or is passionate about. We need both, because one is not good enough.

If you enjoy a job that does not pay, soon you will be in trouble financially. But if you do what you hate to do, chances are that your performance will be so poor, you will not be productive, and you will lose the job because no employer would want to have you on his team. This is another reason why joy and passion are both keys to successful living and successful working. So, let us cultivate a joyful spirit.

Lord, fill me with joy and passion so that I can always be excited to do your work and also be joyful and passionate to serve others!

Application of Day 8

1. How does being joyful and passionate help a leader?

2. Why does the Apostle Paul repeat the same word, 'rejoice', twice in one verse, Philippians 4:4?

3. Can you list some advantages of joy and passion in someone's life? If you do this exercise in a group, let each person make their own list and then share everyone's lists with the group.

4. Some people are joy and passion killers. How can you protect your joy and passion from them?

5. It is important to keep joy and passion in order to keep leading well. What must you do to keep joyful and passionate?

THINKER

Another word for thinker is creative!

A leader puts his mind to work. He is a thinker. He creates something. He innovates. He doesn't just copy what everyone else has done. There is nothing wrong with being influenced by others' creativity, but a leader uses his own thinking creatively to make something. A leader makes or brings something new. He also thinks to improve what exists already.

One of the best gifts God gave us is the thinking and creative mind. We can choose to use it to create something beautiful, or we can choose to be lazy and subdue it. One of the greatest gifts that separates humans from other creations is our God-given ability to think. So, we must value our minds and use them. In giving us the mind, God gave us the best gift. The mind has the power to think, to create, to innovate, and to achieve success. Napoleon Hill was right when he said:

"Whatever the mind can conceive and believe; it can achieve." (21)

I like the use of the verb can, because it makes it a possibility and not a guarantee. It is important to note that it is possible that, just because the mind conceives and believes, it does not mean it will certainly achieve. Yes, there is a strong possibility that it will achieve, but we have to guard from putting too much confidence in human ability. For example, just because the mind conceives and believes that it can create a living human being as we are, we know it cannot. Anything human remains human, and therefore limited in power.

So, we need to guard ourselves from equating ourselves with God, as only He can do whatever He wants and conceives. Still we need to understand that Napoleon Hill is simply demonstrating to us how powerful our God-given mind is. I think the point Hill is really making is that a human being with such a powerful mind must realize that he has the power to think and to create a better living situation, not only for himself, but also for others that he is able to influence.

It is amazing to see what thinking and creative minds can do and achieve. You think of leading innovators and what they have been able to achieve; often, it is mind boggling. You take people like Steve Jobs and his innovation of the iPhones and iPads, and how these tools have made communication easier and more effective. You think of Google and how it can answer so many of our questions. You think of what Mark Zuckerberg has done with Facebook, and how it has revolutionized the world of communication. Now you can post something on Facebook, and it will be seen all over the world. Now you can talk to someone thousands of kilometres away on Facebook video call. Every time I fly to go overseas, I often wonder how a human mind could conceive and create an airplane. Such a huge vehicle that can take hundreds of people, plus luggage, in the air and be sustained for many hours; it is simply unreal. Last time I boarded on a huge plane that had a capacity of close to 500 people. Looking at the number of people on the plane, it was like a sea of people. It is simply amazing to think of what the mind can do!

It is amazing to think of what minds have conceived, believed, and achieved, even in just the last four decades. Four decades ago, I still remember when we introduced my late grandmother to a tape recorder; it was in the late 1970s. We showed grandma the tape recorder and told her that it could record her voice and she would hear herself talking in it. Grandma could not believe it. She exclaimed, "How?"

As we were talking, we were recording her. Later, we played the tape and she heard herself talking. She could not believe it; she was shocked. She still asked in amazement, "Who is that talking?" We said, "It is you, Grandma." She asked how we had put a big person like her into a small machine. It was simply hilarious to see how surprised she was at what is considered obsolete technology today. Our world is changing so much and so fast that we can expect that what we consider fascinating technology in 2017 will also be obsolete before a decade is over because the mind keeps creating and innovating.

The gift of thinking and creativity is truly a wonderful gift God bestowed upon human beings. We need to keep using it wisely - thinking and creating wisely and positively. It is important to realize that not everything our minds have created has worked out for our good. Some innovations, though wonderful, have brought to us as much harm as they have brought good. You think of the use of technology. One of the problems technology has created is the taking away, or at least the reducing, of human's active thinking. Today, if we want to add, multiply, divide or subtract, we ask the calculator to solve the problem for us. When we want to know something, we quickly ask Google and deprive ourselves of using our minds to find answers. This full dependency on technology is slowly rendering us as thinking handicap or inept.

Africa, and the whole world for that matter, needs to go back to using our God-given thinking and creative minds, without taking shortcuts such as calculators for even simple calculations. When leaders refuse to think and instead choose to let technology or other people do the thinking for them, they cease to be leaders, even when they still think they are. If a leader can't think, he has chosen to be like anyone else, a follower, and should therefore stop leading to avoid leading people astray.

Africans must think for themselves and for Africa. African leaders must not let foreign leaders think for them and dictate their decisions to them. This is not a call to stop learning from others, including our friends from the West, but rather an urge to African leaders to think for themselves, to think African in order to lead Africa with African thinking and African creativity.

Africa is a continent of more than a billion people. Think of how much can be done when a billion people begin to think creatively; the sky is the limit! But instead, we are always quoting non-Africans when it comes to innovation and creative thinking. African leaders must pioneer a movement of African thinking and creativity so we can start talking about African innovations.

We need to stop limiting ourselves with the 'victim' mindset that always finds excuses. We have to elevate our own African pride and start refusing to lead Africa with Western thinking and creativity. We must have our own; we must think and do it creatively and innovatively. And trust me, if we have not yet done so, it is not because we do not have creative thinkers, but because we have not created an environment for them to think and to create.

African leaders must lead Africans into thinking culturally. Africans, we are the only people on Earth who continue to pride ourselves on being able to think as Westerners. We are people who have continued to pride ourselves in thinking and acting like our colonial masters, as if more than 50 years of independence are still not sufficient for us to have our own minds. What an insult to our Freedom Fighters, who gave up everything to secure our political independence! Ghana got independence in 1957. As I write this book in 2017, Ghana has celebrated 60 years of independence. Many other African countries will soon celebrate 60 years of independence. How long should Africans wait before they have to also celebrate their independent thinking? When will Africans be finally proud to think and to promote thinking culturally?

I like Zack Mwekassa's analysis of Africans in terms of supporting one another. He said and I will paraphrase what he says because I am also translating what he said in French into English. He said that 'When a White person (here he is referring to a non-African White person or a Westerner) writes a book, everyone buys. Again here he means every African buys a book written by a Westerner or non-African. But when an African writes a book, his fellow Africans want to find mistakes. They want to know where he studied. They question his academic credentials. But they do not ask those questions when it is about a White, non-African person.

What is wrong with thinking African? As Africans, we owe it to our good God, who wonderfully created us the way He did, with our unique culture and unique thinking patterns and abilities, to use our minds and think creatively as Africans proud of our culture. We can learn some things from other people without throwing away who we are. When we think creatively, within our own culture, we will create an innovative African development that is full of African pride and dignity.

We must resource and fund creative thinking. Research that results in innovation does not just happen; it is enabled to happen. As long as African leaders will continue to spend more on meaningless overseas government mission trips, expensive government functions, and allocating almost nothing to fund innovation and research, we will still be going backward instead of forward as a continent.

It is important for me to clarify what it means to think African and even be an African. Contrary to popular opinion on Africa, Africa is not a continent exclusively for Blacks. Africa has a large population of Arab Africans, East Indian Africans, White Africans, and Black Africans.

One day, I was invited to a mission presentation by White South Africans. They were as much Africans as I am and their mission in Africa is contributing greatly to building a better Africa. I was proud of their work just as I am proud of any work that contributes to bettering our world. My family doctor in Canada is a White African. He and I connect as Africans. So, when I am calling on us Africans to start thinking creatively as Africans, I am including every African regardless of their colour or race. If there is one thing Black Africans must never do is discriminate against non-Black Africans.

We must think creatively together, all Africans without distinction, in order to build together the best Africa for us all and our generations to come. We must also welcome all non-Africans who care for Africa to join forces with us in the building of a better Africa. Inclusion, not exclusion, is the key to proper development. We must also include the newly naturalized Africans. Anyone who has chosen to become African must be welcomed and given full rights of participation into this creative thinking that will help build the best Africa.

The world has become a global village, and color or race no longer determines a person's citizenship. Yes, there is still faulty thinking that must be corrected everywhere. For example, in the West, the fact of being Black makes people assume you are a foreigner. When I was serving as a Canadian missionary in Africa, visiting White missionaries assumed I am local. Many of them were surprised when they found out that I am Canadian citizen. It is the same response I got from fellow Africans who also assumed you cannot be Black and be Canadian. But we have to face the reality of the 21st century, in which our world is so much a village that you can now find people from all over the world in any country. I visited Vancouver and saw more Asians than Whites.

For Africa to be great, we must sharpen our creative thinking minds. We must include Africans in Africa, the Diaspora, and friends of Africa who love Africa and are passionate about the development of Africa. When we put all these minds together and truly work together as unselfish teammates working to secure a win for Africa, we can be assured that we will succeed.

Lord, I thank you for the brain you gave me. Help me use it to think well and to be creative!

Application of Day 9

1. Why is it so important that a leader must be a thinker?

2. Why it is important for a leader to build a team that includes creative thinkers?

3. Africa today counts many creative thinkers, both inside the continent and in the Diaspora. How come Africa is still lagging far behind other continents in innovation?

4. What must Africa do to be creative and innovative?

TEAM PLAYER

A similar word to team player is partner!

Team work begins with God. We see team work in the creation when God uses the pronoun 'Us' and 'Our'. We have the God who operates as Three-in-One. He is the Triune God; that is where we deduce the word Trinity. He is the 'We' God, in God the Father, God the Son, and God the Holy Spirit. He said in Genesis 1:26:

> "Let us *make man in* our *own image, in* our *likeness, and let them rule over the fish of the sea and the birds of the air, over the livestock, over all the earth, and over all the creatures that move along the ground.*" (emphasis added)

Team playing is what wins a game because it uses a collective effort. Being the best player often means nothing if there is no help from the rest of the team. Besides, a leader knows that there is nothing fun about playing a game alone. Team playing makes the game fun. Team playing brings victory. Regardless of talent, playing alone makes the whole team lose. Playing as a team player means giving value to all your teammates, even those less talented.

When it comes to being a team leader, one doesn't have to be the best player on the team. We have seen sport teams in which the team leader is the third, fourth, or fifth best player. A team leader is the one who brings the team together. He earns the respect of his teammates. The team leader is not often the coach. It is usually the player that others listen to. Coaches would often use such players to help with team building.

One of the advantages of a leader being a team player is being able to do what is helpful for the team. For example, a team-player-type of leader knows when the time comes to retire from active playing. Playing effectively and at high level is limited with time. A team player realizes that his or her level of competing will diminish to the point that they would be doing a favour to the team if they retired rather than continued to play.

Sports have taught us that no matter how great a player is; time comes when his level of play diminishes. We saw that with Michael Jordan in basketball. This is the man who played in six championship finals and won all six. This is the man who won five Most Valuable Player awards. His personal achievements in basketball have made him the best basketball player of all time. But when he came back from his retirement to play for Washington Wizards, he was a different player. He was already almost 39 years old, and no longer as quick and as effective as he once was. Even though he could still play well, his level of play with the Wizards was so inferior to his level during his Chicago Bulls era. He eventually had to retire in 2003, after two seasons with the Wizards, as he would have started hurting his legacy rather than building it.

African leaders need to find a way to let others lead. Leaving at the right time helps the leader to exit with his head high. Almost every African leader who has left power at the right time and refused to be buried as president is celebrated and has entered heroic status. It is the case of President Senghor, President Nyerere, President Kenneth Kaunda, President Thabo Mbeki, and President Mandela, just to name a few.

Team playing is what builds communities. Team playing puts all the pieces together in harmony so much that what could not be achieved with individual play is achieved through team play. It is amazing what a good team of players can do together.

Canada is well known for hockey. Hockey is huge in the minds and lives of Canadians. But Canada had gone for 30 years without winning an Olympic gold medal until 2010. In 2010, Canada put a team together that was not only talented, but hungry to win together as a team.

It happened to be the time when Sydney Crosby and Jerome Iginla were young and extremely talented. These two also had a very talented supporting team. Some people would simply jump to the fact that the winning goal was scored by the superstar Sydney Crosby. But they forget that there would be no winning goal from him if it was not for the perfect pass that he got from Jerome Iginla.

Similarly, the Edmonton Oilers dominated hockey in the 1980s under the superstar, arguably the best hockey player of all time, Wayne Gretzky. But we cannot ignore the fact that the Oilers would probably not have won those many Stanley Cups if Gretzky did not have Mark Messier as teammate, with their team behind them.

A true leader must therefore value the team. You are who you are because of the team. You can go as far as you can because of the support of the team. A leader's success often depends on what kind of team he has. A good teammate must be valued and recognized. President Obama recognized the high value of his Vice-President Joe Biden that he in turn honored him with the highest civilian honor. It is said that the bond between Obama and Biden is among the strongest in American history. The two worked together as true partners. Their partnership was also enhanced with their wives working together as partners, especially in support to the American veterans.

"To know Joe Biden is to know love without pretense, service without self-regard, and to live life fully. ...My family is so proud to call ourselves honorary Bidens." (Obama) (22)

"You have more than kept your commitment to me by saying you wanted me to help govern. I can say I was part of a journey of a remarkable man who did remarkable things for this country." (Biden) (23)

This is why I am praying that people like President Dr. John Magufuli find good teammates who would team up with him to fight corruption, injustice and for good governance. I am praying that Tanzanians would buy into Magufuli's philosophy of fairness (reducing the wages of the highly paid to increase the wages of lowly paid), of hard work, of combating wasteful spending, and many other great things he is doing.

A good teammate is a partner. Every partner or team member wants the team to win. Like in basketball or American football, when a team wins a championship, every player on that team gets a championship ring. Many players would rather accept a lower pay just so they can play on a championship team.

Partnership is one of the best ingredients of success. Just as for a team to succeed, you need all the players to play their best, partnership helps a leader to reach where he could not reach by himself! Perhaps the best example of partnership in the Bible is that of David and Jonathan. Their partnership helped David escape death and eventually become king.

After David had finished talking with Saul, Jonathan became one in spirit with David, and he loved him as himself. From that day Saul kept David with him and did not let him return home to his family. And Jonathan made a covenant with David because he loved him as himself. Jonathan took off the robe he was wearing and gave it to David, along with his tunic, and even his sword, his bow and his belt. 1 Samuel 18:1-4

Jonathan said to David, 'Whatever you want me to do, I'll do for you.' 1 Samuel 20:4

But if my father intends to harm you, may the Lord deal with Jonathan, be it ever so severely, if I do not let you know and send you away in peace. 1 Samuel 20:13

The story of partnership between David and Jonathan is the highest sacrificial love a human can have for another human. Jonathan fulfilled God's command of loving your neighbor as yourself. He refused to stand in a way and be an obstacle to David's ascension to power. Instead, he willingly forfeited his right as the heir to King Saul and let David be the King as he saw David as the anointed one of the Lord. Their partnership is such an amazing love story from the beginning to the end. Look how 1 Samuel 20 concludes:

After the boy had gone, David got up from the south side of the stone and bowed down before Jonathan three times, with his face to the ground. Then they kissed each other and wept together—but David wept the most. Jonathan said to David, 'Go in peace, for we have sworn friendship with each other in the name of the Lord, saying, (The Lord is witness between you and me, and between your descendants and my descendants forever.')' Then David left, and Jonathan went back to the town. 1 Samuel 20:41-42

Partnership brings about complementarity. Each partner brings certain skills and assets to the table. When all the skills are put together, what was lacking in one partner is completed by the other partner and vice-versa, and as a result, more is accomplished.

It is reasonable to deduce that colonialism was defeated because Africa's founding leaders partnered to fight the system, and together, they won. Africans must go back to partnership among themselves. The mad pursuit for individual success is rendering all of us powerless and unable to break through.

If Africa is going to join other continents in development and possibly become the leader among others, partnership must be a way of life among African leaders. African leaders must foster this spirit of partnership in their people so that we start working together.

Consider how many Africans live in Diaspora. What if they worked together as partners for some common goals for Africa! Africa has some of the most brilliant minds in the Diaspora, but unfortunately, most of the great, super intelligent Africans have been reduced to simply being providers for their families. Imagine if they put their minds together; their partnership could achieve wonders.

I remember one time when our community in Congo approached the Diaspora to request books for a public library in Congo. We discussed the request, and we all agreed that it was a noble cause to help students, teachers and the whole community to get a well-resourced library. A committee was put together. We all worked together in such a strong partnership that we managed to get various donations of books, and others donated their own books.

We initiated contributions of money; people contributed so much! We were able to send a whole container full of books. That could not happen, or at least it would be almost impossible, if such a valuable project was to be done by one person. But a project that cost us thousands of dollars did not seem to be much of a burden, as each one contributed just a small portion of that amount due to partnership. No wonder the Bible has something to say about the value of partnership.

"Two are better than one, because they have a good return for their work. If one falls down, his friend can help him up. But pity the man who falls and has no one to help him up! Also, if two lie down together, they will keep warm. But how can one keep warm alone? Though one may be overpowered, two can defend themselves. A cord of three strands is not easily broken." Ecclesiastes 4:9-12

African founding leaders were strong in partnership, and therefore became impossible to break. As African leaders of to-day, we must work in partnership, and then we can be assured of success together. We have to resist divisions among us, as that is the best weapon of the oppressor of Africa. Our hero, Patrice Lumumba, said it well:

"These divisions, which the colonial powers have always exploited the better to dominate us, have played an important role — and are still playing that role — in the suicide of Africa." (24)

Why do coaches always emphasize team-work? It is because without it, failure is almost a guaranty. It does not matter how talented some players are individually, if they try to win individually they almost always end up on the losing side. Playing as a team makes everyone and the team better.

It is 'we' not 'me' that wins games and championships. It is the 'we' that makes impossibilities possible. You look at the vast land of Canada and wonder how could it be possible to have roads that cover it from coast to coast? How do you get a federal government that can unite its people, who are separated up to 7,000 kilometres away? It takes teamwork. Provincial governments and municipalities have to work together to make the federal government work.

For Africa to work, African countries must work as a team. It is teamwork that will enable Africans and their friends to build a just, peaceful, and prosperous Africa. African leaders must resolve not to be satisfied with their own individual countries succeeding while the rest are drowning.

When I was in Europe in June 2017, I was impressed by what their union has done to make most of Europe a good place to live. We drove in Belgium, Holland, Germany, and Denmark. The only noticeable difference to me was their languages. Otherwise, the standard of living was very similar, as if you were in the same country. African countries must build a team aspect that standardizes basic things, such as roads, from one African country to another. Individualism will render us powerless, while teamwork will make us powerful.

The biggest mistake a superstar player or a leader can make is to think that he is indispensable. As great as a player or leader may be, he is still one player, not the whole team. I know that sometimes this feeling of indispensability is not always the leader's fault alone. Sometimes it is the leader's entourage that tells him what he wants to hear and pushes his ego to the roof, because that is how they get their selfish interests met from the leader's influence. Even when you are the superstar on a team, you are still one of the players. A leader should always consider himself as one of the players, and that no one is indispensable, including himself. It is team play, not individual play that wins victories.

If you want proof of that, ask Russel Westbrook, the superstar point guard for the Oklahoma Thunder NBA Team. He used to play a selfish game. One day, he scored 54 points in a game, but his team lost. But when he started to lead his team as a team player, he helped his team and himself to achieve much. He even got to be named the most valuable player of the 2016-2017 season. Do you know why? He passed more to his teammates and played as one of them. He also made the record for finishing the season with 42 games of triple doubles.

To achieve greatness, you need the help of your team. Great players know that they need not only other top players alongside them, but average players, too. LeBron James, who is considered best basketball player in the world, after Michael Jordan, was once criticized for asking his team management to bring more players to help him. Charles Barkley criticized him because he said LeBron James already had two other all-star teammates. But Shaquille O'Neil defended James, saying that, in most cases, role players are the ones who help you win championships. He said that the superstar players do their job, but you need the role players to win a championship. And he gave examples of championships won because of good role players helping the superstar players. What is the lesson? Every player on a team is important. Again, no one should feel that they can do it alone and that they are indispensable.

Lord, help me be a team player and partner with others on the team. Help me see the value in others.

Application of Day 10

1. What does it mean to be a team player?

2. Why is team play better than an individual play?

3. In your own words, how does partnership bring about complementarity?

4. Do you agree or disagree with the statement 'For Africa to work, African countries must work as a team'? Explain why you agree or disagree.

5. Ecclesiastes 4:9 says that two are better than one. How do we think and operate as 'we' or 'us', and not 'me' or 'I'?

6. What are you personally doing to be a team player?

DISCIPLE

Disciple of Christ or Servant of Christ!

It is very important for any leader (here I am referring to Christian leaders) to know that at the end of the day, he or she is not actually the primary leader. Christ is the leader of any Christian leader. A Christian leader must never forget that he or she represents Christ here on Earth in whatever leadership he or she is involved in.

To be a servant presupposes that there is a master. To be a servant means you work for somebody. To be a slave means you are owned by somebody. As Christians, not only we are servants of God, which means God is our employer, but we are also God's slaves; which means God owns us.

Africa needs to rediscover the servant-heart. These days, everyone seems to want titles: Apostle, Bishop, Reverend, International Evangelist, President, Prophet, and Doctor (Honorary doctorates have become so easy to obtain). I remember the story of one pastor who cherished his title. His title was 'Reverend Pastor'.

One day, a church member greeted him, mentioning half of his title, saying, "Good morning, Pastor." The Reverend Pastor was very offended and said, "And Reverend, who do you leave that for?" He continued and said, "I am not Pastor, I am Reverend Pastor." No wonder why everyone wants to have his own church where he can graduate from pastor or assistant pastor to senior pastor or lead pastor.

Now you see some pastors with 20 members and they no longer want to be called Pastor, but Reverend Pastor or Bishop or Prophet or Apostle. But they seem to forget that our 'servant title' is truly our primary title. Our greatness is defined through our servanthood. One becomes a leader by serving Christ and God's people, not by having an impressive sounding title. Do you really want to be a Christian leader? Then, become and be proud to be called a servant.

Now I know that the Master may choose to call us a different title than servant, but that is up to Him. Jesus chose to call us his disciples, his friends, and that is such a privilege that He gave us, but it is also His prerogative to call us whatever name or title he chooses. But we still remain his disciples and his servants.

"I no longer call you servants, because a servant does not know his master's business. Instead, I have called you friends, for everything that I learned from my Father I have made known to you." John 15:15

Even when our Master calls us friends, we still remain his servants, as it is the best attitude we must have toward the one who loved us so much that he died for us.

When we had a servant in Burundi, we did all we could to remove the title servant in our relationship with him. We broke some barriers, such as asking him to come sit down in our living room instead of talking to us from outside the door as he was used to, whenever he wanted to talk with us. No matter how we tried to break the master-servant relationship, he still referred to us as bosses.

This attitude of servanthood is important, because when we start to deviate from it, we may end up over-estimating our status and under-estimating the greatness of God. Jesus's own attitude should serve as the right one for servanthood. Philippians tells us that Jesus, who is God, humbled himself and took the human nature.

> "*Your attitude should be the same as that of Christ Jesus. Who, being in very nature God, did not consider equality with God something to be grasped. But made himself nothing, taking the very nature of a servant, being made in human likeness.*" Philippians 2:5-7

I know having an attitude of a servant is easier said than done, because humanly, we all want to boss people around. There is a general human tendency to rule over the other and to have others serve us. But that is not leadership.

True Christian leadership is serving as Christ would. It is serving others as if we are serving our Lord and Master Jesus Christ. True leadership is realizing that even our servants are as human as we are, and of the same value as us as far as God is concerned.

When we understand that those who work for us, our servants, and us are all employees in God's kingdom, we cease to regard them as inferior to or of less value than us. When we realize that human employees and human employers, at least Christian ones, are all servants of God, then we can start to see them as equal and pieces of the puzzle in God's great kingdom. Our greatness, as far as we are concerned as Christians, is in our servant-hood. We are all employed by Christ with, as our primary job, making disciples.

As Christians, we may have different roles. Some are employers while others are employees. Some are self-employed and do not have a human employer or employee. Some work as domestic servants and others are their bosses. But all these different roles should be understood as fulfilling their particular roles so that the team can function well. The leader or the employer is needed because he provides the vision and the plan to achieve it. The worker is needed because that job must be done so that the company or organization can function well.

This is why at a country level you need a president or prime minister, ministers, teachers, police, labourers, nurses, doctors, and many others. All these people and their various jobs work together to make a country function. In God's kingdom, we must keep our focus in making disciples that will in turn make other disciples.

Before his ascension into Heaven, Jesus left us the Great Commission, which consists of making disciples that make disciples. As Christians, our primary mission on Earth is making disciples. Discipleship is an on-going process. As long as we are alive, we must be making disciples. While still on Earth, we do not graduate from making disciples.

> Then Jesus came to them and said, "All authority in heaven and on earth has been given to me. Therefore go and make disciples of all nations, baptizing them in the name of the Father and of the Son and of the Holy Spirit, and teaching them to obey everything I have commanded you. And surely I am with you always, to the very end of the age."
> Matthew 28:19-20

Discipleship is very rewarding. It is such a joy to see a disciple become a disciple-making disciple. Once someone becomes a disciple and goes further, making other disciples, it does not take long before you see a healthy group of disciples, all serving our Lord and Master Jesus Christ.

When we served as missionaries in Burundi, I started the Discipleship program. Some disciples became very committed Christians and started to disciple others. That group of disciples became so united and on fire for God that the whole campus was changed and transformed. After I left to go back to Canada, four of those disciples became the leaders and stepped in to fill my shoes.

I visited more than two years after I left, and I was encouraged to see that many of those disciples had continued to serve our Lord. Yes, they confessed that some of them struggled after I left, but the group was still there to continue building each other up.

As African Christians, we need to go back to putting emphasis on disciple making. There seems to be more focus on evangelism that is mainly preaching and having people say the prayer to receive Jesus. Not much is done to follow up and get the new converts into discipleship. Receiving Christ, while it is the most important decision for any human being, should not stop there. Discipleship must begin the very day we receive Christ, and it must continue until Christ's return. For a Christian, discipleship is an on-going process until one dies. Once you become a disciple of Jesus, you cannot retire while on Earth; it is a permanent responsibility. You must either be a disciple who is learning, or the disciple who is making other disciples.

Disciple-making is the primary responsibility of a disciple of Christ, and yet it has become for most Christians the least observed command. The Bible tells us that there is great rejoicing in heaven when one sinner becomes a disciple of Jesus:

"In the same way, I tell you, there is rejoicing in the presence of the angels of God over one sinner who repents." Luke 15:7

But many have reduced church to a social club where we go to enjoy coffee and muffins. I am a big advocate of the holistic gospel of faith demonstrated by works. We cannot limit the church to only proclamation. While it is important we make sure everyone hears the gospel, we also have to make sure people know we actually love them.

I truly think that the effectiveness of the gospel will be seen in our ability to present the gospel that preaches the message of salvation, but also the gospel that practically loves people and meets their physical needs. We have to avoid embracing one while rejecting the other.

I do not think we even need to get stuck at what is more important between proclamation and faith in action. Yes, proclamation has the life-and-death, eternal consequences, and we must make sure everyone is afforded the opportunity to make the decision to follow Christ or not. We must also make sure that we avoid hearing Christ tell us that He was hungry and we refused to give Him something to eat. Discipleship is making disciples that make disciples who practice faith in action that changes and transforms people spiritually and makes them also the agents of social change.

So, just so you do not misunderstand me, I am not equating the verbal proclamation of the gospel with social gospel, but I am affirming that once a disciple of Christ, one must also be involved in bettering his society through social gospel.

I think of so many people who are still lost in their sinful state, with no hope for the eternal joyful life. How I pray that the church will rise up and honor Jesus Christ's command to go make disciples of all nations, baptizing them in the name of the Father, and of the Son, and of the Holy Spirit. We can give as much as we have and be very generous, but all earthly gifts are temporary. Salvation in Christ is the best gift anyone can receive because it is eternal.

Social gospel must have Jesus Christ as its foundation, because without Him, it is only social but not social gospel. And I know there is much debate here, but this is my take on it; once saved in Christ, we must produce fruits. As we know, the fruits do not produce the tree. There must be a tree for fruits to be produced. The tree is like being saved. We must first be saved in Christ and then we can produce good fruits. True and meaningful social gospel begins after salvation. Any other good work is just good but not gospel. No human good can produce eternal salvation. The Bible explains clearly what salvation is and what must follow after salvation. One passage of scriptures that explains it very well is found in Ephesians:

> *"For it is by grace you have been saved, through faith—and this is not from yourselves, it is the gift of God— not by works, so that no one can boast. For we are God's handiwork, created in Christ Jesus to do good works, which God prepared in advance for us to do."* Ephesians 2:8-10

My understanding of this passage in Ephesians is that, while good works cannot save anyone, good works are evidence of one's salvation in Christ. Good works testify to those who do not know Christ that we belong to Him, that we have been saved in Christ.

This is why I believe that giving to the poor, visiting prisoners, advocating for fair wages for poorly paid workers and servants, ending the exploitation of women and children, speaking against racism and discrimination, advocating for the abolition of child labor and child prostitution, and so many other causes, is very much part of being a Christian.

To deny the value of social gospel is to be ignorant of its power. How do you expect someone dying of hunger to clearly hear the gospel? The best way is to feed him first and then preach the gospel. It is very likely that once fed, he would want to know why you cared enough to feed him. Then you can share about the love of God that compels you to care for others and give him an opportunity to receive Christ's love too.

Please understand me well; I am not equating faith or grace with works. No. I am simply saying that works must follow salvation in Christ. Yes, some people have been called specifically to be evangelists, and they need to concentrate on that. Billy Graham has faithfully served Christ through evangelism for decades. My friend Filipe Drumond of Last Harvest Evangelistic Association is an evangelist and does an excellent job of it. We all have to operate within our gifting. Some other Christians have been called into social gospel. Tony Campolo is one of them. Mother Teresa was one of them. Bishop John Osmers is another.

This is the point: even though a Christian may not be a called evangelist, every Christian must still evangelize. Every Christian must go make disciples. Even though one may not be called into social gospel, every Christian must do good works. To choose one exclusively and reject the other is just choosing to go with part of the gospel. Holistic gospel is salvation in Christ evidenced with, among other things, good works. Let us not hinder anyone from entering God's kingdom because our works could not match our claim of faith.

I know that we also have to guard ourselves from becoming too socially focussed that we never actually share the gospel. I have seen situations where the social is too emphasized and the proclamation of the gospel never seems to happen. That is wrong. You can give as much food to the poor, clothe as many people, and visit as many prisoners as many times as you want, but without sharing the gospel, you have not given enough. Giving enough is primarily sharing the gospel, and then everything else makes sense. Without the gospel, without Christ, we have nothing of eternal value. With Christ, we must now also make a difference in this world with social gospel. Therefore, being a disciple of Christ is good, not only because it assures us of eternal salvation, eternal life, but it makes us good people. Being a Christian leader empowers us to lead well and to make our communities better.

Jesus Christ, our Lord and Saviour, was an exemplary leader. He broke social barriers to lift up the oppressed and the marginalized. He gave value to children, to women, to tax collectors like Zacchaeus. He turned his unschooled disciples into leaders. He stood up for a woman caught in adultery. He challenged the establishment, the Pharisees, and teachers of the law. He demonstrated his humility by washing his disciples' feet. He was so caring and compassionate that when the crowd was hungry, he fed them, and when people cried after the death of Lazarus, he cried too. His leadership style is our greatest example of authentic and transformational leadership. This is why, even though our primary responsibility as Christians is winning souls to Christ, we must make a positive difference in our society. Leaders are responsible for doing everything in their power to leave their communities better than they found them.

I believe that the church today is at war. It is a war that has been imposed on the disciples of Christ. The world's agenda, especially the Western world, is to wipe out the church's influence. It is evident today that countries that were once predominantly Christian have replaced Christianity with extreme secularism.

Take, for example, Canada: what is really the role of the church in Canada today? What is the church's influence in Canada? If the extreme secularism in Canada continues to grow at the fast speed we are experiencing, it will not be long before we find ourselves in a state of total moral decay, where almost all evil practices will be allowed and perhaps even encouraged. The church in Canada must wake up and take back its rightful place to prevent the country from total moral fallout.

Unfortunately, moral decay is also happening in America. In America, the church still has a voice, though it is getting smaller. This is why I believe that Christians must be involved in politics. We need men and women who fear God to represent God and people in high offices. It is really puzzling to see how many Christians there are in the world, and yet their influence seems not to be felt on the world stage. There are more than two billion Christians today, representing almost a third of the world population, and yet they seem to have been silenced. With that many Christians, imagine what the church could do if we were united and determined to impact the world for Christ.

It is important to know that salvation in Christ gives us hope for eternal life, but it also makes us ambassadors of Christ here on Earth, and His agents of positive change in the world.

We cannot be passive about it. We must be active and productive disciples of Jesus Christ who make the difference in the world for Christ. We must never underestimate our value in this world. Bill Hybels is right when he says that the church is the hope of this world. We are representing God on Earth; the God who made everything. If we let Him use us, we will indeed be God's agents of hope to the world.

Lord, thank you for making me your disciple. May you use me to disciple others and to be your agent of hope to the world.

Application of Day 11

1. What does it mean to be a disciple of Christ?
2. How does being a servant help a leader lead well?
3. Why is Africa, the most Christianized continent, the most corrupt and least caring of the needy?
4. How can Christianity impact Africa for better?

COURAGEOUS

Another word for courageous is brave!

Leadership requires being brave; it requires courage. As a leader, one gets confronted by many opposing forces and discouragements. A leader is able to face those challenges and keep going. The Bible is full of scriptures that encourage and command us to be courageous.

> *"David also said to Solomon his son, be strong and courageous, and do the work. Do not be afraid or discouraged, for the LORD God, my God, is with you. He will not fail you or forsake you until all the work for the service of the temple of the Lord is finished."* 1 Chronicles 28:20

> *"Be strong and courageous. Do not be afraid or terrified because of them, for the LORD your God goes with you; he will never leave you nor forsake you. Then Moses summoned Joshua and said to him in the presence of all Israel. Be strong and courageous, for you must go with this people into the land that the LORD swore to their ancestors to give them, and you must divide it among them as their inheritance. The LORD himself goes before you and will be*

with you; he will never leave you nor forsake you. Do not be afraid; do not be discouraged." Deuteronomy 31:6-8

We know that one of the top tactics of the devil is discouragement. The devil instills fear in order to render a leader powerless. There is not much you can achieve while operating in fear. Fear has the power to suck energy and the will to do anything out of us. Fear paralyzes us. This is why God commands us not to fear:

"So do not fear, for I am with you; do not be dismayed, for I am your God. I will strengthen you and help you; I will uphold you with my righteous right hand." Isaiah 41:10

The best courage a leader can have is courage in God. When our courage is in God, we have no reason to fear. Fear comes to us because in ourselves, we cannot fight the devil. The best thing a leader can do for himself and for the people he is leading is to put his trust in the Lord his God who can fight for him. Remember, our God wins every battle!

When God tells us not to fear and not to be dismayed, we must follow his instruction. He promised to strengthen us and to help us. He will uphold us with His righteous hand. What a wonderful guarantee from the Creator of the universe. Think of even us human beings: our children find their courage in us and totally trust in us to fully protect them or to fight for them. How much more must we be courageous in God, in our Lord Jesus Christ?

The Bible tells us that He who is in us is stronger than the one who is in the world, so that we absolutely have no reason to fear. When we chose to live in fear, we make a very negative statement about God. When we fear, we elevate the devil to where he does not belong. No matter how difficult the battle is, we must be courageous in God, as no battle is too difficult for Him.

For a Christian, fear has no place. Unfortunately, the flesh always forgets the power we have in the God we have believed in. This is why when we forget to trust in Christ, we automatically put ourselves in a losing situation. Every time we forget to trust in God, we render the devil powerful.

Consider the disciples of Jesus. They were traveling with Jesus by boat, crossing the Sea of Galilee, and when storms suddenly came, they were afraid. They thought they were going to drown. But if you think about it, did they really have reason to be afraid? Would a boat carrying Jesus drown? Jesus was disappointed with them because they should have trusted that with Him in the boat, the storm is just a little powerless trouble.

> *"Then he got into the boat and his disciples followed him. Suddenly a furious storm came up on the lake, so that the waves swept over the boat. But Jesus was sleeping. The disciples went and woke him, saying, 'Lord', save us! We're going to drown!' He replied, 'You of little faith, why are you so afraid?' Then he got up and rebuked the winds and the waves, and it was completely calm."* Matthew 8:23-26

Fear and doubt are two major enemies of courage. They work in opposition. Fear and doubt are very damaging to a Christian leader. If you are leading people, your attitude of fear and doubt makes you unreliable. This is why it is crucial for any leader to be first fearless and courageous, without doubt, in order to be fully used by God. It is acceptable to be initially afraid, but it is not ok for a leader to live or stay in fear and doubt. Apostle Peter is a classic example of a leader who had to overcome fear and doubt in order to be used by God. Consider these two passages and see how he changed from a man full of fear and doubt to a fearless and courageous leader.

The first passage looks at Peter as a disciple of Jesus and as a leader in training. Fear and doubt are still crippling him, but thank God, his Master and Lord is still with him on Earth and still teaching him.

> *"Shortly before dawn Jesus went out to them, walking on the lake. When the disciples saw him walking on the lake, they were terrified. 'It's a ghost,' they said, and cried out in fear. But Jesus immediately said to them: 'Take courage! It is I. Don't be afraid.' 'Lord, if it's you,' Peter replied, 'tell me to come to you on the water.' 'Come,' he said. Then Peter got down out of the boat, walked on the water and came toward Jesus. But when he saw the wind, he was afraid and, beginning to sink, cried out, 'Lord, save me!' Immediately Jesus reached out his hand and caught him. 'You of little faith,' he said, 'why did you doubt?'"* Matthew 14:25-31

The second passage happens after Jesus has gone back to Heaven. Peter is now a graduate from the school of Jesus Christ. The Holy Spirit has now come and has empowered Peter. Fear and doubt have become the things of the past. Now, it is courage time:

> *"Then Peter, filled with the Holy Spirit, said to them: 'Rulers and elders of the people! If we are being called to account today for an act of kindness shown to a man who was lame and are being asked how he was healed, then know this, you and all the people of Israel: It is by the name of Jesus Christ of Nazareth, whom you crucified but whom God raised from the dead, that this man stands before you healed. Jesus is 'the stone you builders rejected, which has become the cornerstone.' Salvation is found in no one else, for there is no other name under heaven given to mankind by which we must be saved.' When they saw the courage of Peter and John and realized that they were unschooled, ordinary men, they were astonished and they took note that these men had been with Jesus."* Acts 4:8-13

Courage in God turns impossibilities into possibilities. Take, for example, King David. While he was still a young boy, after seeing the giant Goliath terrorizing everyone, David decided to be courageous in God and go fight Goliath. A simple shepherd boy managed to do what was practically impossible humanly. He killed Goliath, with a mere sling and stone! He told Goliath that he had come to fight him in the name of the Lord. What seemed like a terrible joke from a young boy turned into an amazing display of victory against the renowned giant!

When a leader trusts in the Lord or finds his courage in the Lord, then he must be confident that the Lord will win the battle for him. Like King David, King Jehoshaphat faced a vast army. On their own, they could not fight with such a powerful army. But again, just as David against Goliath, Jehoshaphat trusted in the Lord, refused to fear or to be dismayed, and the Lord won the battle for His people.

Courage is a must-have asset for a leader. It is like being a parent; whenever children are afraid, they run to their parents because they expect their parents to be courageous enough to deal with their fears. This is one of the reasons why being a parent is a serious responsibility because one gets to bear responsibility over his life and the life of his children.

A leader must be courageous because people depend on him or her to lead them in all times, including times of adversity. We still remember the terror of 9/11 that devastated and terrorized not only the United States of America, but the whole world. Everyone was terrified. Fear invaded the whole world. Such an extremely difficult time required strong and courageous leadership to act and to assure people that things would be ok.

The most notable courageous leader was the mayor of New York City, Rudy Giuliani. President Bush did his part at the international level, assuring people that America would win the war on terror. But it was Giuliani who took charge with amazing courage. He coordinated the work of firefighters, the police, the army forces, and the medical teams, showing support to the

families of those lost in the terror attacks, assuring New Yorkers
that they would be ok, and more. Without his courage, people
could have been more devastated and beaten up with deadly fear
and left without hope.

African leaders must regain the courage we were once
known for. Think of the Freedom Fighters. The likes of Patrice
Lumumba, Kenneth Kaunda, Kwame Nkrumah, Julius Nyerere,
Jomo Kenyatta, Haile Selassie, Michombero, and many others,
who succeeded because they were courageous enough to face any
consequences imposed by the colonial masters. They refused to
be intimidated. They acted as one to fight colonialism. And with
their courage, they succeeded. Today, we are free because of their
unwavering courage.

Let us just consider Patrice Emery Lumumba. This is a
man of unbelievable courage. During the Congolese fight for
independence, for which Lumumba was the most remarkable
leader, finally Independence Day arrived. On the list of speak-
ers, Lumumba's speech was not included. In the midst of the
colonial masters, Lumumba refused to keep quiet.

Even though Lumumba was not scheduled to make a speech,
he still jumped to the microphone and gave his passionately
famous speech. In his speech, he decided to speak the truth and
nothing but the truth that obviously angered the former masters
to the core. Here is a part of his speech, to illustrate just how
courageous Lumumba was:

"For this independence of the Congo, even as it is celebrated
today with Belgium, a friendly country with whom we
deal as equal to equal, no Congolese worthy of the name
will ever be able to forget that it was by fighting that it
has been won a day-to-day fight, an ardent and idealistic
fight, a fight in which we were spared neither privation
nor suffering, and for which we gave our strength and our
blood. We are proud of this struggle, of tears, of fire, and of
blood, to the depths of our being, for it was a noble and just

struggle, and indispensable to put an end to the humiliating slavery which was imposed upon us by force. This was our fate for 80 years of a colonial regime; our wounds are too fresh and too painful still for us to drive them from our memory. We have known harassing work, exacted in exchange for salaries which did not permit us to eat enough to drive away hunger, or to clothe ourselves, or to house ourselves decently, or to raise our children as creatures dear to us. We have known ironies, insults, blows that we endured morning, noon and evening, because we are Negroes. Who will forget that to a Black one said 'tu', certainly not as to a friend, but because the more honorable 'vous' was reserved for whites alone? We have seen our lands seized in the name of allegedly legal laws, which in fact recognized only that might is right. We have seen that the law was not the same for a White and for a Black – accommodating for the first, cruel and inhuman for the other." (25)

It is a shame when Africans of today are more afraid of any consequences imposed by the superpowers or former colonial masters. We need to be courageous enough today to chart our own course. We just have to make sure we are being courageous positively. Being courageous is not being a dictator; it is not being macho. It is about facing genuine difficulties and, with courage, overcoming them.

What kind of a leader are you? Can people depend on you to fight for them? Can your people trust in you to protect them? Can they count on you to defend them? Are you courageous enough to stand for what is right, even though it is not popular? Are you courageous in yourself or in God?

I admire people like Archbishop Desmond Tutu. This is a man who completely refused to allow fear to stop him from combatting apartheid head-on. He knew he could have been killed or jailed like Mandela, but he pressed on.

A leader is the one who values the noble cause he is fighting for and because of it, refuses completely to give in to the demands from the oppressor. We need more heroes, Africans or non-Africans, like Archbishop Desmond Tutu.

It is important that we exercise the right kind of courage. Sometimes, we have a tendency to justify our wrongdoings in the name of being courageous. When African leaders try to cover up their wrongs, in the name of standing up to the Westerners, it is not right. When you receive aid from any donor, you owe the donor a total transparency. When a leader and his inner circle use the funds that were meant to repair roads for their own personal use, they must be held accountable. Something is wrong when we receive aid and refuse to account for it. And then we claim to be fully independent and that we do not need to be accountable to anyone.

Justifying your wrong in the name of being courageous renders your courage worthless. If you want to prove your courage, then stand up for all the abused women and defend them wholeheartedly. If you want us to regard you as a courageous leader, then stand up against our enemies and fight for your country.

Courage is not justifying your wrong and then claiming to stand against imperialism. Courage is about honestly standing up for the people. Understanding the difference between wrong and right courage is crucial to striking a balance so that we can be courageous in the right way and be accountable for our wrongs, not hiding them under the carpet in the name of being courageous.

President Thomas Sankara was a courageous leader. He stood up to Burkina Faso's former master, France, in the right way. His courage was about fighting for the rights of women; he established equality between men and women during his short stay in power. That is the right courage. Sankara was courageous enough to call his people to hard work, and Burkina Faso started producing its own food in abundance. Sankara was courageous enough to fight the elite establishment, and he made sure to reduce the wages of the wealthy to increase the wages of the lowly paid. That is the right courage and worth imitating. We need more African leaders to start exhibiting the right courage.

For Christians, just as the apostle Peter stood before the Sanhedrin and defended his faith, even at the risk of being killed or imprisoned, the church must start to be courageous, stand for the truth, and defend the faith that cost the blood of our Lord and Saviour Jesus Christ. When the church allows fear and doubt to overtake it, then it has lost its identity. When Christians lack the courage to speak against evil and stand up for the truth, they are simply saying that they do not trust God enough to win the battle for them or even to fight for them.

Courage means acknowledging that the battle is difficult, but with God or when committed to God, victory is certain. So, while we will always encounter situations that make us afraid, we have to acknowledge the gravity of the problem, but then move on to courage and trust in God. What a comfort knowing that the battle is not ours, but God's! Let us simply cast our burdens, our battles, and our fears unto Him, and He will fight the battles and win the victory for us.

Lord, give me courage that overcomes fear. Help me have the right courage.

Application of Day 12

1. Why is courage a must-have asset for a leader?
2. List some of the things courage does for a leader.
3. Which of the biblical leaders can be described as courageous and why?
4. Which present day or in the recent past leader do you consider to be courageous and why?
5. Can you become courageous or is courage only an in-born quality?

6. Think of your own life today. Are you courageous? Can you use being a bit more courageous? Have you allowed fear to overtake you? Can you list some areas in which you need to be more courageous and list steps to get there?

ADVOCATE

An advocate is a defender, a helper!

Advocacy is one of the key roles of a leader. This world has many voiceless people, those who cannot defend themselves. A leader speaks on behalf of the voiceless. A leader confronts the giants and the oppressors of the weak. A leader stands in the gap between the strong and the weak, the employer and the employee, the rich and the poor, the decision-makers and those under authority, and between the masters and the servants. A leader uses well his access to the influencers and the influenced.

Bishop John Osmers has lived his adult life as an advocate for the poor, the oppressed, and the prisoners. When the Congolese refugees were in prison in Zambia in 1991, Bishop John Osmers, or Father John at that time, paid a good lawyer to defend them. He visited them every day in prison to encourage them, to assure them that he didn't forget them, and that he was doing everything in his power to secure their freedom. I remember how truly joyful he was to see them free.

One day, after seeing his dedication to advocating for the poor and all the oppressed, I asked him, "Father, why do you do all these things? Why are you so committed to helping the poor?

Why do you have to advocate for the oppressed? Bishop Osmers answered me with a story of the refugees he advocated for in Botswana. These refugees had no rights and were being treated as less than second-class citizens. So he hired a lawyer to defend them in court. This was a very difficult court case that required so much advocacy and real fighting for people's rights. In the end, these refugees won the case and had their rights upheld.

Bishop Osmers told me that he met one of those refugees one day at the post office, and when he saw Father John, his smile was priceless. Then he said, "That is why I do what I do", to put a smile on other people's faces, to see that the rights of the oppressed are given back to them or restored, and to advocate for the poor and the oppressed.

I know that not everyone is called to that high level of advocacy like Bishop John Osmers is, but we are all called to advocate for the voiceless and the oppressed. Advocacy is not reserved to only a tiny select group of people; it is to be exercised by every human being in whatever capacity they may have.

There was one time I worked for a company that hired French-speaking people for their acting production. This company would hire close to 100 people, and they would have a group of supervisors composed of about 10 members. Curiously, all the actors, except the priest, were Blacks, and the supervisors were almost all Whites. In the Black community, there were a number of actors more than capable of being supervisors. In fact, it would be an added advantage having them as supervisors because they were fully bilingual.

After working there for two seasons, we became very aware of injustice and discrimination. I took the time to evaluate the situation and to make sure I was not being too hard on the overall leader who hired everyone. I tried to give him the benefit of the doubt. But the more things happened, the more it became very clear that discrimination was happening. There was a definite establishment of superiority of Whites vis-à-vis of Blacks. When

I had collected all the evidence of discrimination, I decided to write a well-thought through letter to the company manager.

He read my letter, and I think he could not sleep. He called me very early in the morning, very upset and determined to prove me wrong and to have me withdraw what I wrote. But I asked him to calm down so we could discuss my letter and the work situation calmly. We ended up discussing it for an hour, and at the end, he promised to do better. In the end, he hired at least one African as a supervisor, gave the cooking contract to an African woman, and improved the overall conditions of service.

Yes, I lost that good-paying job because it would be too un-comfortable working with him, given how strong and truthful my letter was, but because of my advocacy, the whole system was improved and people were treated as humans. Advocacy cost me that job, but the reward for defending the defenceless is still priceless to this day.

I remember when I was a kid growing up in the Democratic Republic of Congo, called Zaire at that time, we had a young man who was a renowned bully. He used to terrorize everyone. Everyone was afraid of him. He was not that big in stature, but everyone I knew was scared of him. If he came to you and asked you to bring him bananas tomorrow, you had better bring them or be ready to suffer the consequences. If you met him at the river, he would order that all the kids wait until he was done swimming or bathing in the river before they could go in, and people would obey his orders.

But then came the best news for me; one of my cousins came to live with us. He had taken karate, and he was very good at it. I saw him ask four people to fight against him at once and he beat them. He became very popular as the newest strong young man in our area. And thank God everyone, including the bully, knew that he was my first cousin. Very quickly, I was exempted from any attempt at bullying because no one would dare have a problem with me or they would have to deal with my cousin. My cousin, even without saying a word, became my advocate, my defender, and my shield.

A leader puts himself in other people's shoes and takes on advocating for others as if he was defending his own rights. A leader makes the struggles of others his own; and that is how he can truly advocate for them, because their pain is his pain, and he shares their sufferings with them.

A Christian leader must be an advocate for the poor, the oppressed, and the prisoners. Jesus Christ our Lord, Saviour, and Master is the true Advocate, and as his disciples, we are to be advocates for the oppressed, as He is our greatest example. In Matthew 25:36, Jesus tells us that whenever we help the poor, it is Him we help; whenever we look after the sick, it is Christ we look after, and whenever we visit prisoners, it is him we visit. So it is very clear that Jesus identifies himself with the oppressed, so much that any act of kindness to them is direct advocacy for Jesus.

> *"I needed clothes and you clothed me, I was sick and you looked after me, I was in prison and you came to visit me."*
> Matthew 25:36

This knowledge changes everything, the knowledge that advocacy for the poor is advocacy for Jesus makes it clear that advocacy as far as Christian leaders are concerned, as far as all Christians are concerned, is a must-do. Advocacy for those in need and the oppressed is far from being a suggestion or advice; it is imperative. Advocating for the poor is not an option for Christians, but a command.

I remember when I was a missionary in Burundi; the local teachers came to tell me about the disparity in salaries between international teachers and native teachers. According to them, they were getting less than half of the wage that foreign teachers earned. I told them that if that was true, the gap was too big but that there is almost always an incentive to foreign workers so as to attract them. They understood that as normal.

When I had the opportunity to talk with the national director, I explained the situation to him and advocated for the increase in the local teachers' wage. He increased their wages substantially. When I travelled to attend their first graduation in June 2017, one of the teachers was still thanking me for having advocated for them.

Sometimes we think that we are doing well just because we do not oppress anyone. We also think that God will defend or advocate for the oppressed. But God has put us here on Earth to be His representatives in the advocacy for the oppressed. The problem we have is that we try to run away from our God-given responsibility.

God created us and saved us, so He can use us to make a difference in this world. We have to stop thinking that others will do it, because we are the ones to do it. A song by Matthew West says it as best as it can be said. It is a long song, but it is worth being quoted in full. The title of the song is 'Do Something':

I woke up this morning. Saw a world full of trouble now. Thought, how'd we ever get so far down? How's it ever gonna turn around? So I turned my eyes to Heaven. I thought, "God, why don't You do something?" Well, I just couldn't bear the thought of People living in poverty. Children sold into slavery. The thought disgusted me. So, I shook my fist at Heaven. Said, "God, why don't you do something? He said, "I did, I created you". If not us, then who? If not me and you right now, it's time for us to do something. If not now, then when will we see an end to all this pain? It's not enough to do nothing. It's time for us to do something. I'm so tired of talking about how we are God's hands and feet. But it's easier to say than to be. Live like angels of apathy we tell ourselves; it's alright, "somebody else will do something". Well, I don't know about you but I'm sick and tired of life with no desire. I don't want a flame, I want a fire. I wanna be the one who stands up and says, "I'm gonna do something". If not us, then who? If not me and you right now, it's time for us to do something. If not now, then when will we see an end to all this pain? It's not enough to do nothing. It's time for us to do something. We are the salt of the earth. We are a city on a hill (shine shine, shine shine). But we're never gonna change the world by standing still. No we won't stand still. No we won't stand still. No we won't stand still. If not us, then who? If not me and you right now, it's time for us to do something. If not now, then when will we see an end to all this pain? It's not enough to do nothing. It's time for us to do something. (26)

God placed us here on Earth to advocate for the oppressed. When you are a leader and you keep quiet in the face of injustice; then consider yourself to be equally as unjust as a practitioner of injustice. Many people try to justify themselves saying, "But I do not mistreat people," or maybe they say, "But I am not unjust." They do not read into Archbishop Desmond Tutu's words:

"If you are neutral in situations of injustice, you have chosen the side of the oppressor. If an elephant has its foot on the tail of a mouse and you say that you are neutral, the mouse will not appreciate your neutrality." (27)

Advocacy is a noble calling. I have so much respect for people who stand up against injustice and refuse to go along with the current trend. William Wilberforce is a great example of an exceptional advocate. While most everyone was comfortable with Whites using Blacks as slaves, Wilberforce used every fiber of his veins to fight for the abolition of slavery. His story is worth a quotation:

William Wilberforce (24 August 1759 – 29 July 1833) was an English politician, philanthropist, and a leader of the movement to stop the slave trade... He became an Evangelical Christian, which resulted in major changes to his lifestyle and a lifelong concern for reform. In 1787, he came into contact with Thomas Clarkson and a group of anti-slave-trade activists, including Granville Sharp, Hannah More and Charles Middleton. They persuaded Wilberforce to take on the cause of abolition, and he soon became one of the leading English abolitionists. He headed the parliamentary campaign against the British slave trade for twenty years until the passage of the Slave Trade Act of 1807. Wilberforce was convinced of the importance of religion, morality and education. He championed causes and campaigns such as the Society for the Suppression of Vice, British missionary work in India, the creation of a free colony in Sierra Leone, the foundation of the Church Mission Society, and the Society for the Prevention of Cruelty to Animals. His underlying conservatism led him to support politically and socially controversial legislation, and resulted in criticism that he was ignoring injustices at home while campaigning for the enslaved abroad. In later years, Wilberforce supported the campaign for the complete abolition of slavery, and continued his involvement after 1826, when he resigned from Parliament because of his failing health. That campaign led to the Slavery Abolition Act 1833, which abolished slavery in most of the British Empire; Wilberforce died just three days after hearing that the passage of the Act through Parliament was assured. He was buried in Westminster Abbey, close to his friend William Pitt. (28)

This world is full of injustice. What role do you play, as a leader, to contribute to eliminate or to combat that injustice? One of the main responsibilities of a leader is advocacy. Jesus did not keep silent when people were ready to stone the adulterous woman. He advocated for her. He challenged the self-proclaimed righteous to be the first to throw the first stone. He could have excused Himself to the prostitute, but instead He took a stand that saved her life.

Advocating for the people is a basic and essential responsibility of a leader. What is discouraging and upsetting about leadership in Africa is that, even when leaders fail completely on their basic responsibility to advocate for and defend their people, they refuse to resign. The measure of a good leader is demonstrated by his ability to admit that he has failed and therefore stop leading; let someone else come in and renew hope in the people.

A leader is a representative of the people. When people are hurting, the leader too must be hurting. That is why if a leader can no longer feel the hurts of his people or can no longer be able to advocate for them, whether willingly or not, he is no longer fit to lead.

Congolese hero Patrice Emery Lumumba is celebrated worldwide because he advocated for his people and for all the people of Africa, including being willing to be a martyr for them. We need urgently to rediscover our advocacy responsibility, as without it, one should not be a leader, even for one more extra minute.

What kind of advocacy really works? I have always been offended by injustice. I have always done whatever I can to combat injustice, oppression of the weak or poor, and inequality. But I have come to realize that I often use the wrong method in my attempt to advocate for the oppressed. We need to remember that the goal of advocacy is securing freedom for the oppressed and justice for the unfairly treated. The goal should not be to just voice an opinion in favor of the oppressed as such an opinion does not free the oppressed or improve their situation. Advocacy should be productive. After some good counsel from a friend and through experience, here is what I think works and what hardly works. I want, however, for you to keep in mind the use of these two words, 'hardly works'.

To change the situation of the oppressed or unjustly treated is not often achieved through rallying or lobbying the oppressed or the unjustly treated to join us in our fight for their freedom. When I was in grade 11 in a boarding school, I was very offended by the treatment of the students from poor families by the children of the rich families. The rich kids treated the poor kids as their servants. They sent them outside the school to buy fruits for them. They would give them their clothes to wash for them. Whatever service they could have done for themselves, they would order these poor students to do for them.

To try and defend the poor students, I decided to befriend them and treat them as equals. We would really enjoy our conversations. Then I started empowering them to fight the oppression and abuse from the rich kids. Many of them, if not all, became convinced that they did not deserve being treated like slaves by their own fellow students.

During each year, there was an election of student leaders. Leaders had some advantages which gave them privileges and power. For example, one of those student leaders would have the key to the fruit storage. The person with that key could open and close the storage at any time and would take his friends to eat bananas there. Not the right thing to do, but that is what happened, and it would give so much power and prestige to the key holder and his friends.

So I asked the poor students to be candidates on all the positions and to vote for themselves. They were the majority, and there would be no way they would lose if they applied the formula I gave them. They were all excited about the idea of taking over the student council body. Then, something happened. The rich kids suspected I was helping the poor kids plan a coup to overthrow them. By then, they already did not like me for siding with the poor. They could not put me down, as I was also one of them, status-wise, a kid from a rich family and a boarder like them.

But they were clever enough to cook something up. They went to talk to the poor students. They asked them what I told them. The poor students told them everything. Then they told the poor students that they cared for them and that what I was doing was to bring division and unnecessary conflict between them. At the end, they convinced all the poor kids to vote for the rich kids, and in turn the rich kids would be good to them. Election day came, and it was a shock for me. We started voting for president; I looked at the one we had proposed as president and he signalled to say it was ok. Election came and finished without anyone from the poor students in the council. I asked them why they did not follow through with our plan. They told me that the rich kids went to see them and told them to disregard what I told them. They told me that the rich kids assured them that they would be kind to them. Obviously, the rich kids' promise of kindness ended when they uttered those words, because their cruelty continued right after securing their victory in the elections.

When I was going to serve as missionary in Burundi, a friend of mine, advised me not to make the poor my friends. At that time, I was quite offended at his advice. I thought to myself that if I claim to be an advocate of the poor, the best way to show that was to have more poor than rich people as my friends. I thought that my friend did not care about the poor. But I was wrong, because he cared so much for the poor. In fact, today, he has built a school and a church in a deep rural area of his native country. When he took me into the village where he serves the poor, I was amazed at how much he had changed the situation of the poor in that village. He has become like a chief in the village; he is the biggest hero of that village. That taught me something; you do not have to be a friend of someone before you can help him. If you are convinced that a particular cause needs your advocacy, work at finding how to best advocate for that cause.

Now I know my friend was right to some degree. After my experience serving in Burundi, I know that you do not change the situation of the poor by lobbying the poor against the rich. The rich and powerful do not even need to fight you personally, because they have the power to influence the poor to fight you.

The best way to advocate for the poor and mistreated is to influence the rich and powerful to be kind to them. The powerful have the power to pay better wages to their workers. They have the choice to treat their servants as humans or not humans. They have the power to hire and fire. The poor and the mistreated do not have that power or even the choice, at least, as a norm; they do not take advantage of the power and choice they have. Most of them cannot afford to lose a job, even if it pays less than a dollar a day. This is why they might even hate you as an advocate, because you are trying to call them to a rebellion that is going to cost them their jobs.

Influence the rich, the powerful, and the decision makers, and you stand a chance of making a contribution to a lasting positive change for the mistreated. If you truly care for the poor and the unjustly treated, then elevate your influence and be at the level of the influencers so that they can listen to you and want to apply the change you advocate for.

There is a need for denouncing the wrongs committed by the influencers. We advocate for the oppressed by voicing our disapproval of the oppressive actions committed by the decision makers and influencers. We just need to have the wisdom to know when to advocate for the mistreated by influencing the influencers and when to speak out against the wrongs committed by the influencers.

The time has come when we need to start empowering the upcoming influencers so that when their time comes, they will be righteous, fair, and just leaders. We have too long only focused directly on the poor. While that is a valuable cause, neglecting to build on and empower the upcoming leaders for Christ will always diminish our potential for maximum positive change.

We need to graduate from the tendency that we can only invest in the extremely poor, dying with flies all over their faces. How disrespectful it is that we have to have human beings like us be so hungry, too weak to brush the flies from their faces, for us to intervene. So, let us help the very poor, but let us also invest in the obvious potential leaders to maximize our ability to make this world a better place for all. Let me clarify one thing here; while we must influence the influencers to be kind and fair to the poor; we must also be friendly to the poor. Those in power must take time to listen to the poor. The more those in position of power relate in a friendly manner to the poor, the more the poor are empowered to realize their value and the more we are able to build communities based on equality. The goal in all I am proposing is to do advocacy for the poor in a way that changes their lives for the better.

I had the privilege of being chaplain and a teacher of both Leadership and Christian Education to the Gitega International Academy students in Burundi. These students are mostly from rich and influential families, and have the privilege to master both English and French. After their graduation in June 2017, some of them went to study in North America. The fact is that they have more chances to become major leaders in Burundi. Imagine how much positive change they could implement if they truly serve as Christ-like leaders!

This is why I say to our friends in the West, who truly care for Africa and Africans that the time has come to give special attention to investing in our future leaders. Influencing them for Christ gives us hope for a fruitful return on our investment. To advocate for the poor and the mistreated is best done by influencing leaders, the employers, and decision makers to act favorably toward them. We need to influence those in positions of power, those who have to be kind and caring for the poor and the less fortunate; that is, in my opinion, the best advocacy for the poor and the less fortunate. This is a biblical model too. Positive change for the poor and less fortunate will happen when the influencers adhere to the truth that helping them is not optional, but a necessity; in fact, a must-do.

> *"Do not mistreat or oppress a foreigner, for you were foreigners in Egypt. Do not take advantage of the widow or the fatherless. If you do and they cry out to me, I will certainly hear their cry. My anger will be aroused, and I will kill you with the sword; your wives will become widows and your children fatherless."* Exodus 22:21-24

> *"Do not take advantage of a hired worker who is poor and needy, whether that worker is a fellow Israelite or a foreigner residing in one of your towns. Pay them their wages each day before sunset, because they are poor and are counting on it. Otherwise they may cry to the Lord against you, and you will be guilty of sin."* Deuteronomy 24:14-15

Advocating for the less fortunate is a must-do for every true leader. The world is a better place for us all when those in positions of power make decisions and choices that make the lives of the poor or the mistreated better. Think of your own sphere of influence and use your influence positively to influence the influencers for the benefit of those in need. At the end, it is not only the needy who win, but also the advocates. As I write this book on leadership, I cannot stop thinking of all the women and girls who continue to suffer terrible torture of rape and abuse in the Democratic Republic of Congo, even in 2017. The world is watching and remains in silence as you go to sleep, not knowing if that very night you will be the next victim of rape. I salute the heroic dedication of Doctor Denis Mukwege, who has dedicated his life to repairing your broken lives; may God bless him. How I pray that we will all join in the effort to end their misery and suffering that has been going on for years!

I think of the millions of orphans left to fend for themselves. Children twelve years old, looking after their younger siblings and being robbed of their childhood normalcy. How I pray that no child should have to take care of other children, and no child should be without parents. How I pray that leaders will establish systems that ensure every orphan child gets a new family to take care of him or her.

I think of all the migrants losing their lives trying to find green pastures overseas. I think of the Black African migrants who are being sold into slavery on their own African land even in 2017. How I pray that we can develop Africa enough for its people to find no need to leave their African countries. How I pray that we can all stand up against slavery and free the slave migrants. May God raise more African leaders who will make Africa the best place on earth to live in!

I think of many children sold for prostitution. Children who should be going to school and preparing themselves for a good future are instead forced into the sex trade, enduring torture and unbelievable abuse. How I thank God for organisations such as the International Justice Mission (IJM) and what they are doing to fight for the abused, those in sex slave trade, and the persecuted. May God raise more defenders of the oppressed like IJM!

I think of all the poor street children going for days without food, resorting to stealing, as it seems the only way for them to survive. Children who should be in school but unable to finish even the first grade of elementary school. How I pray that leaders will arise that will make education up to grade 12 free for all, including uniforms and books.

I think of all the children being used as labor and being forced to work long hours with minimal pay. How I pray that leaders will arise that will not only abolish child labor but will also punish severely those who practise it. The time has come, and it is long overdue to stand for children's freedom and rights.

I think of people with physical challenges who walk with their hands and feet, because they cannot afford wheelchairs. I think of the blind that are left to care for themselves. I think of the deaf who cannot hear and live in societies where there are no sign language services to help them be and feel included. There are many others with various physical challenges. How I pray that leadership will arise to support those who are unable to help themselves.

I think of those who are discriminated against because of their race, gender, or faith. I think of all the families that have lost loved ones due to being shot because of their race or color of skin. I think of many who are murdered because of their faith. I think of women who continue to be paid less than men for the same job. How I pray that leadership will arise that will bring equality of gender, race, or faith.

I think of all the African workers and servants making less than a dollar a day. They cannot afford to send their children to school. Their pay cannot even buy enough food to feed their families for a week. Their employers exploit them without their consciences being disturbed. How I pray that leaders will arise in Africa and establish a decent minimum wage system.

I think of the poorly paid law enforcement officers, the police, and the army in Africa. They are expected not to accept corruption or bribes, but they are so poorly paid that they cannot survive even for a week in most countries. How I pray that law enforcement officers be well paid so that they are motivated not to accept bribes.

Dear leaders, wherever you may be, the time has come and it is now that we must stand together for what is right, and stand against what is wrong, unfair, and unjust. Please read this book and apply it in your life and in your sphere of influence. Together, with God, we can make this world better. Together, with our God, we can establish the kind of leadership that will benefit all of us. Those suffering from abuse of any kind, as mentioned above, are waiting for us to act in their favor. May God bless you as you read this book, meditate on it, and take action to change this world.

This book is written to inspire, encourage, and challenge leaders to use our leadership for the benefit of us all. May God help us be the kind of leaders He created and intended us to be! May God use us to advocate for those in need.

Lord, make me an advocate for the oppressed, the disadvantaged, the exploited, and the voiceless! Like William Wilberforce, use me to advocate for those who are captives of injustice.

Application of Day 13

1. What does it mean to be an advocate?

2. What should be a Christian response to the oppressed and the abused who are unable to defend themselves?

3. Listen to Matthew West's song, 'Do Something'. When he saw the world in trouble, all the suffering, he asked God to do something to solve the problem. But God said that He sent him to do something. Are we running away from our advocacy, leaving the problem for God or someone else to solve?

4. Consider the suffering of women and girls in D.R. Congo who are raped daily, often in front of their families. Why is the church silent, doing nothing to defend these powerless and voiceless Congolese? Where are the superpowers who should be defending the powerless against the unbelievable abuse of human rights? Don't their lives matter?

5. William Wilberforce advocated for the suffering slaves in the 18th century when, at that time, slavery was seen as normal practice. Why don't we have more advocates like him in the 21st century?

6. Are you an advocate? Do you actively stand up for the oppressed, discriminated, and abused?

7. Can you think of a group of people you must advocate for?

8. I say that you can best advocate for the poor by influencing the rich. Do you agree or disagree? Explain.

BUILDER

A builder is an encourager!

A leader builds others up. A leader lifts others up. When you meet a true leader, usually, you come out built-up and feeling good about yourself. You come out encouraged, even if they had to address an issue in your life because they have such a positive way of addressing it that it does not hurt.

Unfortunately, some people, especially the self-imposed leaders, specialize in demolition. They can take a building down in half an hour that took years to build. The sad part is that they are often so wrongly confident that they are not even aware that they destroy instead of building up the people they were meant to encourage or to build.

I remember one brother in our church in Zambia. He was so convinced that he was called by God to counsel anyone going through a difficult time. He was convinced that he was gifted to build others up. But after each of his counseling sessions, the people counselled were more discouraged than encouraged, more destroyed than built up. I wish someone would have demanded he stop counselling people, because he was clearly a destroyer and not a builder.

Give that brother a bit of a break, because he was suffering from the disease of ignorance and not of the lack of the will to do good. But unfortunately, there are many others who suffer from the lack of will to do good. They find pleasure in destroying rather than building others. Such people are even in churches. For them, no sermon is good; no service done by others than themselves is good. They specialize in discouragement. They find everything wrong in others, including the non-existent wrong they clearly see. Only they are perfect. Only they can do things right.

I remember in Zambia, we had a sister who was probably the best soloist in our church. Every two months she would sing a solo in church. Everyone looked forward to her solo singing. Before she could plan to sing, people would start asking her when she would sing next. But one day, she was confronted by one brother who specialized in discouragement. He told her that her voice was terrible and that singing was not her gift. He asked her to kindly stop singing solos in church. Not only did this sister stop singing, but she was devastated and destroyed. It didn't take long before people started noticing that she was not singing solos anymore. People would ask her to sing, and she would excuse herself. One day, someone she trusted went to ask her what was really going on. It was then that she shared how that brother told her not to sing anymore in church, as she had a terrible voice. Then the church finally heard about it and was very disappointed by this destroyer specialist's behaviour. He was ordered to stop his unchristian behaviour. It took much to build up that sister to a point where she started singing in church again.

A builder or encourager builds others up. A Christian must be an encourager of others. In fact, building others up or encouraging others is expected of all Christians. Some are especially gifted in building others up and encouraging anyone who is going through a hard time, but every Christian must be a builder and an encourager of others.

"Therefore encourage one another and build each other up, just as in fact you are doing." 1Thessalonians 5:11

In the case of the Thessalonians, encouraging one another and building each other up was something they were already doing. So, the fact that the Apostle Paul still asked them to do it simply shows or emphasizes that we must continue and never stop encouraging one another and building one another up. This instruction is binding not only to the Thessalonians but to all Christians.

But before building or encouraging others can happen, a leader must first encourage himself. This world is so full of discouragements that a leader must first encourage himself in order to be able to encourage others. It is almost impossible for a discouraged leader to genuinely encourage those under his leadership. The idea of the discouraged encouraging others is as fake as a witch doctor who promises to make people rich while he himself is languishing in poverty.

We cannot give others what we, ourselves, do not have. We cannot give encouragement while we ourselves are drowning in total discouragement. King David, when faced with very discouraging defeat, first encouraged himself before encouraging his people and eventually defeated his enemies.

"And David was greatly distressed; for the people spake of stoning him, because the soul of all the people was grieved, every man for his sons and for his daughters: but David encouraged himself in the Lord his God." 1 Samuel 30:6 KJV

When you read the full story, you realize that, had David let discouragement overtake him, he could have even lost his life because his own people were ready to stone him to death. But as the great leader that he was, he chose to encourage himself in his God, and in Him he regained strength and confidence to pursue his enemies and defeat them. That victory resulted in his people being encouraged. So, if you are a leader, make sure you are first encouraged in the Lord your God, and then you can be able to build up your people; you will then be able to encourage others.

Building and encouraging are two wonderful words. They both add something of value to someone or something. When you are building, you are taking something to a higher and better level. It is like a house: when you are building it, slowly but surely you start seeing it increase in beauty and in value. The way it was when you were digging the foundation is not the way it is when you are laying bricks on top of the foundation.

I remember when I bought my first house in Edmonton, Alberta, it was not yet complete. I would go every two weeks, sometimes even once a week, just to see the progress. I would go inside to look at the walls and the floors to see what new development had been added. When it was getting close to being finished, I started seeing walls and ceilings. Then power and appliances were installed. The whole process until the day I was handed the keys of my house was a joyous ride.

After I had moved into my first, brand new house, I was highly built up and encouraged by my unofficial Canadian parents. Justice George Baynton had come to Edmonton on a work assignment, and he came with mother, Mrs. Sylvia Baynton. So, I went to visit them at the hotel where they were staying. Then I informed them that I had just bought a house. They were so overjoyed to hear that news and told me how proud of me they were. They came to see my house. When they saw that the basement was not yet finished, they sent me $2,000 to help in the finishing of the basement. Oh, I am so privileged to have them in my life.

Like that building process, and like the Bayntons who built me up and encouraged me, a leader is one who is always adding value to those he is leading. The more they meet him or her, the more they are encouraged, built up. This building and encouraging process is an on-going one. A leader does not retire from building and encouraging. The more you build people and the more you encourage them, the more they themselves get contaminated with that building and encouraging spirit that they in-turn build up and encourage others.

Do you build others up? When people have spent time with you, do they leave you encouraged or discouraged? A leader must make building and encouraging others a priority. That is the kind of leader Barnabas was. You will not find a gospel book written by Barnabas. He was one of those quiet leaders who simply let their actions do the talking for them. His ministry was encouraging others. He delighted in building others up. He is called the son of encouragement. Almost every time you hear his name mentioned, it has to do with building others, defending others, and encouraging others. Look at some of the Scripture passages that talk about him:

> "When he arrived and saw what the grace of God had done, he was glad and encouraged them all to remain true to the Lord with all their hearts. He was a good man, full of the Holy Spirit and faith, and a great number of people were brought to the Lord. Then Barnabas went to Tarsus to look for Saul, and when he found him, he brought him to Antioch. So for a whole year Barnabas and Saul met with the church and taught great numbers of people." Acts 11:23-26

> "When he came to Jerusalem, he tried to join the disciples, but they were all afraid of him, not believing that he really was a disciple. But Barnabas took him and brought him to the apostles. He told them how Saul on his journey had seen the Lord and that the Lord had spoken to him, and how in Damascus he had preached fearlessly in the name of Jesus." Acts 9:26-27

Lord, make me a builder and an encourager of others so that I can build up and encourage others!

Application of Day 14

1. Do you build others up? Do you encourage others? If yes, how do you do that?

2. Barnabas lived out his name as 'the son of encouragement'. Most times he is mentioned, it has to do with him building someone up. What must we do to imitate him?

3. What would happen if Christians fully became builders and encouragers of others?

4. Have you ever been discouraged? If yes, how did you feel after someone came to encourage you?

5. List some ways in which you can be the encourager to those who are going through a hard time.

ACCOUNTABLE

To be accountable means to be answerable to someone, to be responsible!

A leader must be accountable to someone, to the team, or to the people. One mistake leaders make is to become so big that they are accountable to no one else. They surround themselves with followers who simply agree with them, even when they are clearly in the wrong.

In the Christian context, having an accountability prayer partner or just an accountability partner helps a lot. This partner should have total freedom to speak his mind and to correct the leader when he or she is in the wrong. This partner is not to be limited to correcting the wrong; a true partner should celebrate the leader's success or a good decision made.

Accountability is needed in many areas of a person's life. It is even more needed for a leader who is in charge of an organization, because his actions affect the organization in a big way. One particular area where accountability is really needed is the area of finances. A leader must make sure that the management of finances is handled by someone else. While he may be the main fund-raiser for the organization, it is important that when finances reach the organization, another qualified person or a team of qualified personnel handle the money.

One of the things I enjoyed during my time as pastor in Youngstown is the fact I only knew how much money we had at our general meetings. Otherwise, I was never involved in the finances. My job description was clear. I received my wage that the church paid me, and that's all I knew. I have seen situations where the pastor is also the main money person, and it usually ends up in some kind of accusation of mismanagement of funds. Better to have a treasurer or a person in charge of the money, and you as a leader; remove yourself from it.

Your board of directors should be your true accountability partners. Again, in the area of finances, let the board handle it. As founder and executive director of Christian Immigrant Support Services, I made sure finances were handled by the treasurer, and he did an excellent job of it. The board should guide the direction of the organization and keep the leader in check. The board should praise what is good and correct what is wrong. The board should be fully involved in the decision making of the team or organization.

Some people think that being accountable is a sign of weakness. In fact, not being accountable is a deliberate choice to be a fool. Those who refuse to be accountable and think they are above reproach or constructive criticism often wake up too late and find themselves in irreversible trouble. True accountability partners are one of the best assets to a leader.

All leaders must be accountable. They must be under the law and not above the law. When they have done right, they must be applauded and rewarded for it, and when they have clearly done wrong, they must pay for their wrongdoings. There must be a body that, collectively, is above the leader. The leader must report to this body and receive approval or disapproval from them.

In Canada, generally leaders are accountable and their accountability pays dividends for the country. When the late Premier Ralph Klein had been in power for more than 12 years, the once very popular premier's popularity began to go down. After some time, he himself realized that his popularity was diminishing. So he went through a leadership review and got a 55% approval rate; that was a clear indication that his time as premier had to come to the end. He resigned.

I wonder how many African leaders would resign if they had a 55% approval rate. Being accountable, means that we have to make sure we ask the people we are working with if our leadership is still producing good results, or if we have fallen out their favour and we need to say goodbye. Overstaying does more damage to our legacy, and sometimes writes off even the good we did. So let us be truly accountable and react appropriately to our approval rating.

Are you a leader? Then show me one, two, or three people, a board, or a group of people to whom you are accountable. You know a person is not a leader when he is himself the pastor, CEO, accountant, treasurer, counselor, majority owner; basically everything. This is not an African problem, it is a universal problem.

I remember a few years ago in Edmonton, Alberta, a senior pastor of a large church was a 98% majority owner of the church building and premises of a church and property that was valued at 14 million dollars. As majority owner, he was not accountable to anyone. He could make all decisions alone, without needing the approval of anyone in the church.

"The Switzers follow another pattern: near-unilateral control of the church. Switzer is both pastor and president of Victory Christian Center, a non-profit corporation with shareholders, with 98 per cent control of the charity. The balance rests with his wife, who is also his co-pastor and vice-president, and associate." (29)

The church was so mismanaged that it ended up filing for bankruptcy. The property ended up being sold for less than half of its original value. The church itself went from 1,000 members to less than 200 members. The church's total collapse should serve as a lesson to every leader to realize that they need to be accountable. Accountability is the leader's friend. Leaders who think being accountable takes away their control end up losing the company or the organization; they end up not having anything to control.

Some leaders are so much a one-man show that not even one of their colleagues has a key to enter in their offices. Things that require accessing documents in the leader's office do not get done when he is not around. His co-workers have to wait for his return to access his office. I once was a victim of such an unaccountable manager (I will not call him a leader) that I had to wait for his return to access a letter that I needed as soon as possible. African leaders and leaders everywhere must learn to be accountable.

Sometimes leaders who do not like to be accountable find a way to avoid accountability by appointing a board that has no power at all over them. These kinds of boards are there just to be present in meetings, to hear the report or update from the leader, then sign their approval. In the eyes of people, it seems as if the leader is accountable, but in reality, he is not. No wonder many companies and organizations are falling apart, because they depend on one person, the leader. It is my prayer and hope that leaders will realize that being accountable is for their good and their companies' good.

Accountability is very rewarding. I am a beneficiary of the rewards of accountability. When I was studying at the then Theological College of Central Africa, which is now the Evangelical University, I had a faithful prayer partner, Pastor Victor Chaungwe. We would always pray together in the evening and we would share openly with each other our joys and our burdens. That accountability partnership was very rewarding to me. I learned a lot through that experience.

I also remember our prayer group of six people in Edmonton, Alberta. We used to meet early in the morning two Wednesdays per month. During those meetings, we would share the word of God, share about our lives, and then pray together and for each other as well as praying for other concerns. I was a regular part of that group for more than six years. Within the group, on top of our regular meetings, I also met with Daryl Reneau for more prayer, support, and accountability. Those were very good days spiritually for me.

In fact, during the same period, I had two great friends, Greg and Glenn, with whom I met quite often, and we talked and prayed together. It felt like I was part of a mini promise-keepers' group with those two groups. I think it is crucial for men and women to have positive accountability partners, especially in the Western world, where the emphasis continues to be on living or doing life alone.

Accountability is a good and helpful thing. Unfortunately, people think having someone to whom you are accountable is like having a master over you. Yes, if you think in terms of someone you have to report to, such as your boss in your workplace. But the accountability we are talking about here is one that is out of friendship or partnership. It is not based on hierarchy. It is the kind of accountability that is built in the relationship of trust. It is in this kind of relationship that one feels free to share everything and still feel understood, loved, and accepted.

Accountability can help a person avoid making wrong decisions. Sometimes when we act on our own self-made decisions, without bouncing ideas off someone else, we deprive ourselves of the advantage of having someone else's ideas or opinions that could be helpful. Sometimes we are too involved in the situation that we cannot see clearly, and are therefore unable to make well thought-through decisions. We need the input from an accountability partner who can speak the truth to us without partiality.

An accountability partner can be your spouse, your relative, your friend, or someone you look up to. But either way, we all need one or more to navigate this difficult thing called life. Having had a few accountability partners throughout my life, I know everyone needs at least one. My dad can tell you about the vacuum he experiences after the passing of my mother, as she was his best accountability partner. To be a good leader, one must have the support of an accountability partner. And while your spouse should be your accountability partner, you need other partners not related to you.

It is my prayer that every human being, especially anyone in a position of leadership, would cherish having accountability partners to help them in the decisions and the plans they make for their people and communities. Because as humans we are limited, we need the help of others, especially our accountability partners, to help complete us where we are lacking. If you are a leader and do not have an accountability partner, I would encourage you to find one.

Find an accountability partner who will speak the truth to you and not one who just wants to please you by telling you only what you want to hear. There is nothing worse than having someone who deliberately lies to you to make you happy. Take your time to evaluate if your accountability partner is being truthful to you or is about preserving whatever selfish interests you offer him or her. Make sure you inform your accountability partners right from the start that you want them to speak the truth to you. Let them know that you would rather get the truth, even though it may hurt. Let them know that telling you the lie that they think you would like to hear is not an option. Hopefully, when you are straight forward from the beginning, and once in a while you review that with them, they will tell you the truth.

Lord, make me accountable and transparent so that I can be open to others' input and corrections!

Application of Day 15

1. In your view, what is accountability?

2. What is its value in a leader's life?

3. Who can be an accountability partner and why?

4. When it comes to an accountability relationship, who is above the other: the leader or his accountability partner? Explain why.

5. What are some of the ways that you can ensure that your accountability partner does not just tell you what you want to hear, but tells you the truth?

GRATEFUL

To be grateful is to be thankful! Grateful living is a life of contentment!

Gratitude is a leader's friend. It is always good to be thankful. The lack of gratitude is offensive. Ungratefulness denies the giver the recognition he deserves. Even Jesus was offended by ungratefulness. When he healed ten lepers, only one came back to say thank you. Jesus then wondered why only one was grateful enough to come back to say thank you:

> "When he saw them, he said, 'Go, show yourselves to the priests.' And as they went, they were cleansed. One of them, when he saw he was healed, came back, praising God in a loud voice. He threw himself at Jesus' feet and thanked him—and he was a Samaritan. Jesus asked, 'Were not all ten cleansed? Where are the other nine? Has no one returned to give praise to God except this foreigner?'" Luke 17:14-18

Gratitude is defined as:

> "The quality of being thankful; readiness to show appreciation for and to return kindness." (30)

I like this definition with its emphasis at the end 'to return kindness'. As Christians, we are grateful to God for what He has done for us, and in return, we worship Him to show Him our appreciation.

In the Bafuliiru Tribe in the Democratic Republic of Congo, we have a very good practice of gratitude. We have the custom of giving a cow to someone very special. If someone gives you a cow, it usually means that he values you highly. I saw this practice also in Burundi. And although it is not conditional that you also give them back another cow, most people do give back a cow in appreciation. Giving back a cow shows that the receiver values not only the gift itself, but the friendship it represents. Giving back a cow is a way of solidifying the ties, and really is the ultimate way of practically showing gratitude. It also encourages generosity in the community.

Sometimes, receiving back that cow comes at a point of need for the first giver. There is a story of a generous man who had given away half of his cows. He had 300 cows and gave away 150 cows. But when calamity hit and he lost all his cows, his friends gathered and decided to give him cows so he could have cows again. To his surprise, he received double the 150 cows he gave. This is why giving and gratitude go hand in hand. People who are grateful know how to bless the givers.

King David is a great example of a grateful person. After his best friend Jonathan died and David had become the king of Israel and the most powerful person, he refused to forget the kindness of his friend, really his brother, Jonathan. He decided to show gratitude to Jonathan by being kind to anyone of Jonathan's descendent.

> *"David asked, 'Is there anyone still left of the house of Saul to whom I can show kindness for Jonathan's sake?' Now there was a servant of Saul's household named Ziba. They summoned him to appear before David, and the king said to him, 'Are you Ziba?' 'At your service,' he replied. The*

king asked, 'Is there no one still alive from the house of Saul to whom I can show God's kindness?' Ziba answered the king, 'There is still a son of Jonathan; he is lame in both feet.' 'Where is he?" the king asked. Ziba answered, 'He is at the house of Makir son of Ammiel in Lo Debar.' So King David had him brought from Lo Debar, from the house of Makir son of Ammiel. When Mephibosheth son of Jonathan, the son of Saul, came to David, he bowed down to pay him honor. David said, 'Mephibosheth!' 'At your service,' he replied. 'Don't be afraid,' David said to him, 'for I will surely show you kindness for the sake of your father Jonathan. I will restore to you all the land that belonged to your grandfather Saul, and you will always eat at my table.'" 2 Samuel 9:1-7

Gratitude should be taught to our children from a very young age. We are living in a time when children have become the bosses in their homes and the parents have become servants to their children. In some homes, this reversal of roles and positions is so confusing that it is very hard even to be a witness. You see parents giving gifts to their children, and it does not even remotely occur to their children to thank their parents for it. I have seen children getting gifts from their grandparents, and it has to take mom or dad to pull them aside and ask them and sometimes beg them to go say thank you to grandma and grandpa.

One day, our then 6-year-old son Joshua wanted to play his games on my phone. I gave him my phone and he just took it without saying thank you, and it seemed to me that he did not seem to appreciate the fact that he did not deserve to have it because it is my phone and not his. I asked him to give it back and I told him that he had lost the privilege to play on my phone for that day. He was very sad and apologetic. I accepted his apology, but I still maintained the decision to not allow him to play on my phone that day. From that time on, he makes sure to say thank you for anything he receives as a gift or privilege. Once in a while he forgets, but generally he has gotten better at being grateful.

I thank God for our experience as missionaries in Burundi. There, our children saw the suffering they had never seen in Canada; extreme suffering. Experience has taught my children the value of gratitude because they always remember not to take for granted the good life they enjoy in Canada. The three oldest, who were old enough to understand what was going on at the time, have developed a thankful attitude.

Ungratefulness establishes in us the attitude of 'I deserve it'. It is as if the giver owes you something. This attitude makes a person an ungrateful receiver. For the ungrateful, the simple words 'thank you' are difficult to say. The lack of gratitude also has power to deprive a person of extending kindness to others. Often, when people develop the ungrateful attitude, they think that they can continually receive, but they do not have to give anything to anyone. They receive mercy, but when it is their turn to also be merciful toward others, they refuse to offer mercy.

That is what happened to the unmerciful servant. Forgiven a debt that he would otherwise never be able to pay back, yet he refused to forgive a small debt owed to him. It is such a practical lesson why ungratefulness is a terribly selfish way to live our life. Consider the unmerciful servant's extreme lack of gratitude:

> "The servant fell on his knees before him. 'Be patient with me,' he begged, 'and I will pay back everything.' The servant's master took pity on him, canceled the debt and let him go. But when that servant went out, he found one of his fellow servants who owed him a hundred silver coins. He grabbed him and began to choke him. 'Pay back what you owe me!' he demanded. His fellow servant fell to his knees and begged him, 'Be patient with me, and I will pay it back.' But he refused. Instead, he went off and had the man

thrown into prison until he could pay the debt." Matthew
18:26-30

Gratitude must become our lifestyle. We must be thankful
to the one who has done good to us. Think of what God has done
for us. He loved us so much that He offered His own Son to die
for us. How can we not be grateful to Him?

> *"He who did not spare his own Son, but gave him up for us
> all—how will he not also, along with him, graciously give
> us all things?"* Romans 8:32

Gratitude is often very rewarding, while the lack of it can
hinder us from receiving any other kindness from the giver. One
day, I learned the value of gratitude. A distant friend bought three
apples and gave one to each of the three of us. I said thank you,
but for some reason my thank you was a quiet one that he did
not hear it. He was offended by that, and right away he asked me
to give him back his apple. I asked him why. Then he said that it
was because I did not say thank you. I told him that I said thank
you. Thank God the other person heard me say thank you, so he
confirmed that I had said thank you. So the giver apologized and
did not take his apple back. An apple in those days in Africa was
a rare and expensive fruit. While I was glad there was a witness
to confirm that I had said thank you, and therefore I got to keep
the apple, I learned to always say thank you loud and clear.

Almost every one of us, if we are truly grateful, has a long
list of people who have been so good to us that they deserve a
proper thank you. Throughout my life, I have encountered people
who have been so good to me. Some have loved me and cared for
me like I was their own son or brother. This is why I dedicated 12
pages of my first book, *Africa, It's Time!* to express my gratitude
to them. It is very important to say thank you.

I think of two families that gave their money to pay for my
education. One family paid for my tuition and another paid for
my books. All I had to pay was my living costs, which I easily

paid with my part-time jobs while studying. It is not that these families could not use that money for their own needs, but they chose to sacrifice their needs for the sake of helping me. Many others have been good to me in various ways. I cannot pay them back, but at least I owe them my gratitude. We have to develop a lifestyle of gratitude.

The least I can practically do in way of thanking them is helping someone else or others in need. We deserve nothing, so we must be appreciative for everything we receive. Even doing well in school or work or business is a gift from God, and we must thank Him for everything.

Are you grateful? Do you say thank you to those who do acts of kindness to you? Are you showing a good example to your children of what it means to be a grateful person? Do you teach your children the value of gratitude? Being grateful helps us in our workplaces, in our marriages, and in general shows us how to be a good, appreciative person. The world can use our gratitude; let us give it every time we have an opportunity to be thankful.

Grateful living is a life of contentment. Contentment is essential to purposeful, joyful, and simply put, meaningful living. To be content is to be joyful, regardless of the circumstance. Contentment helps a person to live a meaningful life because it focuses on the goodness of God rather than on needs and wants. To be content is to be free from envy and jealousy.

Contentment frees us from unnecessary competition. A content person is happy with what he has, and it is not in comparison with what another person has. A life of contentment is really a life of freedom, in which there is nothing to prove to anyone. There are many people who are miserable today, not because they are not blessed, but because they are constantly trying to prove something, trying to compete with someone else, and trying to outdo everyone else. The problem with that is that you will almost certainly find people who are better than you in some or many areas of life. You will do yourself a favour when you stop trying to be better than someone else. Being yourself is what God designed you to be, and the sooner you are content in being you and performing to your own best ability and giftedness, the more you will be at peace.

Being content is truly a statement of gratitude to God, saying that we are thankful for who God made us to be and the abilities He gave us. It is acknowledging that God did not shortchange us, but that in making us, He gave us His very best. We have then every reason to be content and to thank God for who He made us to be.

Contentment does not mean laissez-faire. It is not an excuse for mediocrity and a false sense of happiness. It is rather satisfaction that comes out of doing one's best, even when that best ends in a loss or failure. It is about doing your best and then happily living with whatever comes from it. After all, it is not about living up to other people's standard of what is best, but rather one's own best. As I have often said, the best competition is competition with oneself. Contentment says, "I have done my best and that is what matters." It is ok to imitate the good in others, but it is not ok to live your life trying to outdo others, or you will soon crash from realizing that there are those who will outperform you, even at your very best.

When I was a young teenager, I had a distant relative, my age, who I tried to compete with. His family was richer than ours, even though we were also rich in comparison to many other people. He would work for his dad on weekends and make much money. As a young person, he would buy new clothes all the time. I had many clothes, yet anytime he bought a new style of clothes that I did not yet have, I would look for ways to get similar styles of clothes. But I got to a point where he made more money and bought more new clothes that I just could not keep up competing with him.

I had to come to my senses. I looked in my closet and found that I had more clothes than I even needed. I thought about many others, boys and girls my age, whose only clothes were the ones they were wearing. Then I realized how ungrateful I was because of my lack of contentment due to unhealthy competition. That day, I decided that I was going to be content with whatever I have. That experience and realization has since helped me in my journey to contentment. While I still desire things, I can now say like the Apostle Paul:

> *"I know what it is to be in need, and I know what it is to have plenty. I have learned the secret of being content in any and every situation, whether well fed or hungry, whether living in plenty or in want."* Philippians 4:12

Like the Apostle Paul, we need to learn the secret of contentment in all situations. Contentment gives us inner peace; it makes us grateful and satisfied. It helps us appreciate the beauty and goodness around us. It makes us better people. It protects us against greed.

The lack of contentment puts us in so much trouble. If the lack of contentment is not controlled or overcome, it has the potential to drive us into bankruptcy, kill our marriage, and make us unreasonable and ungrateful. The lack of contentment makes us joyless.

We must do everything we can to be content. We must ask God to help make us content so that we can truly appreciate what God has done for us. Contentment will help us in our personal life, in our marriage, in our parenthood, in our work, and in our leadership.

Lord, you are good to me; help me live a life of gratitude, thankfulness, and contentment!

Application of Day 16

1. What is the value of gratitude or of thanks?
2. Why is it wrong not to be grateful?

3. Ten lepers are healed but only one comes back to say thank you. Describe the attitude of the nine others. Describe the attitude of the grateful one.

4. King David was a grateful leader. Even after his friend Jonathan was dead, he still cared for Jonathan's family. What can we learn from his gratitude?

5. What is the value of contentment? What are the problems the lack of it can cause?

6. Why should we teach gratitude to our children?

7. How about you - are you grateful, thankful, and content?

8. Can you think of the ways you can be more grateful, thankful, and content? Can you resolve to follow through to better yourself and your ministry?

DEVELOPER

Two other qualities to go with developer are enricher and equipper!

A leader must be in the business of developing others. A true leader is one whose work continues to flourish in his absence. A leader develops others so that they grow and mature to be able to take over from him. A leader continually puts himself out of the job he started. The leader's greatest achievement is seeing his students developed and equipped enough to take over from him and actually advance the company or the organization further than he left it.

One of the major problems we have in Africa is that most leaders prefer to hold on to their powerful seat until they die. It seems like they deliberately refuse to develop other leaders who could succeed them, so they claim that they have no one ready or equipped to take over from them. But there is no way you can justify that in a country of millions of people, and after 10 or 20 years in power, you still do not have someone to take over. Leadership is about developing others and then passing the mantle to them.

Africa is the only continent in the 21st century where we find a number of leaders staying more than 30 years in power.

Are we trying to turn African countries into kingdoms? There is an end to everything under the sun. Presidencies are not marriages that they should be going on until 'death do us part'. There is time to be the main leader, and there is time to let others lead. The baton is not for the runner to keep to himself, he must pass it on to the next person. Africa will do better when that baton is continually being passed on successfully. If Jesus Christ trusted mere men to take over the baton, who are we not to follow his example? He left the key to Peter who had denied Him three times:

> *"I will give you the keys of the kingdom of heaven; whatever you bind on earth will be bound in heaven, and whatever you loose on earth will be loosed in heaven."* Matthew 16:19

He knew that He had developed Peter and the other disciples enough for them to take over from Him. Today, the gospel has gone all over the world because that baton Jesus left to Peter keeps being passed on to the next person until Jesus comes back to take His church.

I must say that this problem of holding on to the baton for too long or until we die is not only a problem of African government leaders. We see it also in the church. Some church leaders are holding on to their batons for too long. It is important even for church leaders to realize that the time comes when we can no longer function efficiently; at that time, we should let others take over. In fact, an effective leader does not wait until he can no longer function efficiently; he makes sure he develops other leaders and lets them take over while he is still able to help them in their transition. This is really an area where African leaders need to improve.

A true leader must continually work at developing himself so that he is equipped to develop others. You cannot teach what you do not know. You cannot give what you do not have. As a leader develops others, he must make sure to be learning also so that he is continually a step ahead of those he is developing. A leader must keep growing. A leader must keep getting better in order to continually better others.

I have seen the value of personal development with the writing of my book *Africa, It's Time!* I published the first edition in 2015. But, by the time I published the second edition of the same book in 2017, I had learned more, so much that the second edition is much better than the first edition.

To enrich others is to make them better than they are. It is the leader's job to make others even better than the leader himself. What a joy it is for any leader to have his students succeed far beyond the leader's own success! Africa needs this kind of mindset in its leaders. Make others bigger and better. Don't make them so small that they have to depend on you for the rest of their lives. It is a shame when a leader is intimidated by the rise of his students.

For the team members to do well, a leader must equip them. Any student needs proper skills, tools to be able to successfully face the challenges of the job ahead. It is possible to have talent and skills, but if they are not developed, they diminish and could get to a point where they are at a standstill or lost. This is why even best players need a coach to develop their skills.

A leader studies his students or those under him, discovers their skills and then finds a way to develop those skills so that the student can perform even at a higher level. It is the leader's responsibility to make everyone around him better.

The problem we have in Africa is that those who know do not want to develop or equip others. Some die with their knowledge without having helped others. This is why most rich people in Africa, when they die their riches die with them because they had not developed anyone to be skilled and equipped enough to take over the business.

A parent wants to see his children succeed more than he did. I remember a Medical Doctor telling my mother one day that the joy of a good parent is raising children who end up more successful in life than he ever was. If you completed a grade 10 education as a parent, your child should have a diploma as a minimum. If you got a diploma, your child should get a bachelor's degree as a minimum.

Obviously, it is not always easy to beat your parents' record. If you are Dr. Martin Luther King's daughter or son, how do you beat his record? If you are Nelson Mandela's child, how do you beat his record? People like Mandela or Dr. King reached the very top of human achievement that it would be unfair to expect their children to do better than their parents did. They had set the standard so high that it is almost impossible to beat it. But still, it should be every parent's desire to equip and develop his children to succeed more than he ever did. It is always very sad when you see a parent who is offended at his child's surpassing success.

Developing and equipping others is really multiplying yourself. You cannot do everything alone, even if you live a long life. When you have equipped, enriched, and developed others, whether you are alive or dead, your work continues. Dr. Martin Luther King's Civil Rights Movement is still alive and well many decades after his death. His work has produced the first Black President of the United States of America.

So, it is important that every leader continually asks himself these two important questions:

Am I developing myself or standing still?

Am I developing someone else or others?

If the answer is no to both questions; not only is the leader in trouble, but the community or organization he is leading is in trouble too. I wonder sometimes if we, Christian leaders, do take time to study God's Word and learn from it. Because if we did, there are plenty of examples we would find that will demonstrate the value of developing and enriching others.

Jesus developed 12 disciples. In fact, the Bible also shows a group of 72 disciples of Jesus. It is not clear how much time Jesus spent with them or how much He invested in training them. But Luke tells us that He sent them out on a mission.

> *"After this the Lord appointed seventy-two others and sent them two by two ahead of him to every town and place where he was about to go. He told them, 'The harvest is plentiful, but the workers are few. Ask the Lord of the harvest, therefore, to send out workers into his harvest field. Go! I am sending you out like lambs among wolves.'"* Luke 10:1-3

Elijah developed Elisha. Moses developed Aaron and Joshua. Paul developed Timothy. The question to you and me is; who are we developing? Like Elijah, who is our Elisha? Like Moses, who are our Aaron and Joshua? Like Paul, who is our Timothy?

In fact, developing others and ensuring their growth is really one of the key responsibilities of a leader. When you develop others, you are helping them expand their knowledge, skills, and talents. You are helping them grow from beginners to intermediate and eventually to the advanced level in whatever area they are involved in. Harvey Firestone put it so well:

> *"The growth and development of people is the highest calling of leadership."* (31)

It is the leader's responsibility to equip those under his leadership. The problem we have today is that, often, the leader is less equipped than those he is leading. You see some pastors who go to preach or teach without having prepared. No wonder you hear some of them repeat the same slogan over and over, "We have to go higher." "You guys need to go deeper." "Don't stay at the same level." "Go higher; go deeper." One fellow pastor told me that he does not prepare the sermons. He goes on the pulpit and the Spirit tells him what to say.

I agree with him partly, because the Holy Spirit can change our message and give us the message He wants to communicate on a particular day or circumstance. But we are still expected to prepare the message. Just because the Spirit can choose to change our message on a particular occasion, does not forbid us from continuing to equip and develop ourselves in order to develop, enrich, and equip the people under our leadership.

As a leader, you are the standard setter. The level of development or equipment your people will get depends on how far you can take them. After washing his disciples' feet, Jesus then told his disciples to do likewise. He had to set the standard for them to follow. After He did it, they were left without any excuse. Now that they had seen how their Master did it, they were also equipped to do it toward one another.

People under your leadership are not going to go deeper and higher because you have repeated the slogan so many times. When you yourself are still stuck in the shallowest place, you are depriving your people of the possibility of going deeper. People under your leadership will go higher when they see you go higher, because then they have an example to follow.

The church should never be a place of mediocrity. We are to show ourselves approved as the Apostle Paul urged us to do, as ministers of the gospel. The church must lead the world, and it cannot do that if its own leaders do not make equipping themselves a priority. The apostle Paul, who knew the value of personal development for a leader, urged his young mentee Timothy to do exactly that:

> *"Do your best to present yourself to God as one approved, a worker who does not need to be ashamed and who correctly handles the word of truth."* 2 Timothy 2:15

Being an ambassador of Christ on Earth is an extremely high calling and requires us to be equipped, enriched, and developed enough to bring honor, not shame, to the name of our one and only Lord and Saviour.

Our Lord Jesus Christ left us the model that we should follow. He, who was human and yet divine, spent three and half years developing his disciples. This was a full-time discipleship development. He equipped them enough that, after He left, they became true ambassadors of Christ.

They were now able to write the gospels and epistles in the Bible. With the indwelling of the Holy Spirit, they were empowered to preach the gospel fearlessly. We, the Christian leaders of today, must also be equipped in Christ and in His Word and empowered by the Holy Spirit, just like the first disciples of Jesus Christ, in order to equip and develop other leaders and believers in Christ.

It is very sad what is happening in Africa today. It seems as if the pastorate has become everyone's profession. You find new converts, and three or four months after salvation, they are already pastors. I have preached in some churches in Africa and in the congregation where a quarter or more of the members are all pastors.

You see that phenomenon even among the African Diaspora here in Canada and the West. Everyone wants to be a pastor. People do not want to sit under a leader and be equipped first. The small knowledge they get causes them to split the church and take away some members of their church and go form their own. Some hide themselves in the scripture that says where two or three are gathered, God is there with them. They stick there to justify having a church that goes for two, three, or four years with only three members, just to keep their pastor title. Some go as far as calling themselves bishops, with a single church with less than 30 people. No wonder politicians can feel justified to do all wrongs, because they see the church failing to do better.

When a developer of others is not himself developed, trained, or equipped, he becomes a liability to those under his leadership. And I do not mean that a pastor, for example, must be necessarily more knowledgeable than every member of the congregation. No. In some churches you might have members who are theology professors who know more than the pastor. But the pastor must be knowledgeable enough to earn the respect of even the theological professors.

Let me not be too hard on Africans as they are not the only ones affected by this syndrome of everyone wanting to be a pastor. Someone I know, who is married to a Filipino wife, was telling me that it is exactly the same within the Filipino community. Everywhere they go, they form multiple churches. They do not seem to serve under a leader for a long time. Everyone wants to start their own church.

I hope the church can start having bodies that regulate and offer credentials, so that you have to pass a test and other conditions to become a pastor. Let us face it, being in charge of a congregation should not be given to everyone just because they slept and woke up convinced they should be pastors. Such bodies will spare the church of false teachers and ill-equipped leaders.

Obviously, in every rule there are exceptions. For example, there are people without formal education who self-teach themselves and perform as well as the ones who have gone through formal training. There are churches that are led with capable self-taught leaders, and they are healthy and thriving. Formal education or training is not a guarantee for good leadership. It helps limit the damages that can arise out of the lack of it. But again, even for the self-taught, there must be a body that can examine and approve or disapprove their knowledge.

Lord, help me use all the knowledge, skills, gifts, and anything you have given me to build, enrich, and equip others! Help me continue to develop and equip myself so that I can be equipped to develop, enrich, and equip others.

Application of Day 17

1. Why is it important to develop and equip yourself before developing others?

2. What is the value of a leader developing others?

3. What are the advantages of passing on the baton to someone else? What are the disadvantages of holding on to the baton?

4. Do you agree that developing and equipping others is really multiplying yourself? Explain why you agree or disagree.

5. Some people do not want to enrich, equip, or develop others because they want to keep everyone else ignorant so that they can keep reigning. What do you think of that approach? Are such people truly leaders?

6. If you are a leader right now, who are you developing, enriching, and equipping? If you were to die today, who are the people who would keep your legacy going?

DOER

A leader is a doer, is a hard-worker, and is tenacious!

A leader acts. He is a doer and a hard-worker. He leads by example. Jesus didn't just teach his disciples about foot-washing; he washed their feet and then challenged them to follow his example. A true leader doesn't just command others to do; he works alongside others. Just like Jesus, a leader is the example or the standard-setter. So you want people to work hard? Then be the first to work hard.

It is unfortunate that Africa is being bombarded by the prosperity gospel that preaches miraculous riches without hard work or without work altogether. Africa will not develop with just prayer. Africans will not wake up rich with day dreaming. Work must be put in to propel Africa to the so-needed development.

Hard work pays off. It is hard but rewarding. I remember the time when I was working three jobs. Thank God I was young and single. I worked so hard, and my work paid off. I was able to buy myself a new house. I bought new vehicles, one at a time. I had money saved in the bank. I was able to help many people in need. I afforded myself trips to Africa and the U.S. I could treat myself well anytime I wanted.

Now you meet many Africans waiting for a Western sponsor. They have good causes, but they want money before they can even start. Simon Gillebault, a long time missionary in Burundi, was sharing his own experience with African Christian believers with good causes, but they asked him to give them money and then they would do their God-given mission. But he said that you are to start first with whatever resources you have.

In fact, in most African cultures, if you need help with things like getting married or building a house, you have to work hard first to raise enough initial money or to build the foundation of your house before you can ask your family for help. Why have we become so lazy and irresponsible that we are expecting everything to be handed to us without our contribution?

Jesus Christ our Lord is against doing everything for us; He wants us involved. He always wants us to participate in what He is doing. Not that he needs our help, as if he is limited in power to do whatever he wants, but he wants us to be His co-workers. This is why, when He wanted to multiply fish and bread, He asked for the human contribution. He used a small boy's lunch to make more out of it and feed the multitude. When He wanted to raise Lazarus, He asked people to remove the stone.

The time has come for Africa to start providing at least the few fish and bread. The time has come for Africa to start removing the stone. We thank God for our Western friends, partners, and supporters, but we should be the ones at work. It is very unfortunate when we get our Western friends to come paint our churches or community building walls.

When I was launching my book *Africa, It's Time!* in Zambia, I asked my fellow Africans if it was all right that our friends should be flying thousands of kilometres or miles to come paint our walls. Many of them had never thought about it, but when confronted with that question, many realized how abusive we have become towards our generous friends. But our friends too need to let us do what we can, and help us with what we cannot do. Let me clarify here, that there is room for working alongside the local people. So, it is ok if partners come to join the locals in what the locals are already doing, be it painting or building. Whatever project needs to be done and which involves partners, it must be done in partnership with the locals and not be left for partners to do on their own. That is how true partnership should work.

Partnership is about doing things together, sharing the work. Partnership is not about doing for others what they can do themselves or what they can also participate in doing. I tell our children that it is ok if they need help with what they cannot do for themselves, but what they can do, they should do.

I think that our Western friends have also contributed to making Africans dependent on them, which I think is unbiblical. Seriously, why would you fly thousands of miles or kilometres to go paint walls? Why would you fly from far away to hand candies to children? It is very sad that our African children have come to know that being White means candy-giver. I know that from experience because anytime I drove in Africa with my wife (who is White) in our van, children would scream "*Muzungu, tupe bon bon*", which means "White person, give us candies."

This is why I am advocating for a new paradigm of partnership between Africans and Westerners. For example, if you go volunteer your services in Africa, work alongside or with the people on a basis of equality. If you have some expertise that the local people do not have, teach them the skills so that they will continue to do the work after you leave. Do not make people dependent on you. Do not give them fish, but teach them how they can catch fish themselves, as that is true empowerment.

Having said that, I must also say to my fellow Africans, please graduate from total donation dependency. There is nothing wrong with receiving help, but we must prove to ourselves that we can first work hard. We must do all we can on our own first. I call on African leadership to pioneer a culture of hard workers. A leader must be a hard worker. You want to change the culture of laziness in your community, then be the first to work hard.

Africa is suffering, partly because leaders are preaching the message that they themselves do not practice. They go by the saying, "Do as I say, but not as I do." That is recipe for disaster. People are not going to be changed by what you say as much as they would be by what they see you do. You cannot develop a community, later on a country or a continent, by pronouncements, although there is room for them. You have a better chance of developing your community by what you do. So, do not just preach the message, live it by example; do not just tell people to work hard, let them see you working hard, as that is the best way you can help change your people for the better.

Not only does a leader need to work hard, he must also be tenacious. Without tenacity, you can give up on the work you sweated on for so long that was about to yield great results. A leader is not one that gives up easily. Sometimes the going becomes tough; a leader needs to be tenacious to keep going. Tenacity is truly a mark of a leader. You can work very hard, but if in the end you lack tenacity, you can multiply all your efforts and hard work by zero. A leader is not a quitter. The story of John Stephen Akhwari, the marathon athlete from Tanzania, demonstrates the value of tenacity:

> *"While competing in the marathon in Mexico City, Akhwari cramped up due to the high altitude of the city. He had not trained at such an altitude back in his country. At the 19 kilometre point during the 42 km race, there was jockeying for position between some runners and he was hit. He fell badly wounding his knee and dislocating that joint plus his shoulder hit hard against the pavement. He however continued running, finishing last among the 57 competitors who completed the race (75 had started). The winner of the marathon, Mamo Wolde of Ethiopia, finished in 2:20:26.*

Akhwari finished in 3:25:27, when there were only a few thousand people left in the stadium, and the sun had set. A television crew was sent out from the medal ceremony when word was received that there was one more runner about to finish. As he finally crossed the finish line a cheer came from the small crowd. When interviewed later and asked why he continued running, he said, 'My country did not send me 5,000 miles to start the race; they sent me 5,000 miles to finish the race.'" (32)

John Akhwari's example should inspire everyone. Hard work is often validated by tenacity because the combination of the two tends to always produce victory and success. Michael Jordan is considered the best modern basketball player, not only because he worked hard in his practices and games, and not only because he won six championships, but because he was also tenacious. It is that tenacious mindset that made him the only player in basketball history to win six championships in six tries.

The opposite of hard work is laziness or sloth. The Bible tells us that the lazy person should not eat. Sloth is defined as the 'reluctance to work or to make an effort. It is synonymous to laziness.' For Africa to join other continents in development, we have to put an end to sloth or laziness. To develop ourselves, we must work hard.

It is also important that we do the right work. Work must be able to provide for our family. True, we cannot work all the time; we need time to relax too. But we cannot let relaxing take all our time. In fact, relaxing must come after productive work. There is no such a thing as doing work to kill time. That is still laziness.

I know someone who used to spend at least six hours every day of his holidays and weekends playing checkers. Imagine what he could achieve if he used that time, or even half of it, doing something productive. If he had that much time on his hands, why not use it to do good for someone else or volunteer his time and services to help out in his community? The good thing at least, is that he was doing it on his holidays and it did not affect his regular job. But what he was doing was wasting a considerable amount of time that could have been used to make a huge difference in his family and in his community. What he was doing was being a sloth, lazy and unproductive. I like John Hardon's definition of sloth:

> "Sloth is the desire for ease, even at the expense of doing the known will of God." (33)

Wasting time is one of the areas we need to change and improve on, as Africans. We have to be at work. Wasting time is going to guarantee a state of poverty to anyone or any community that practices it. The reason why China will soon overtake the United States of America is not just the large population; it is mostly because of hard work. The reason why Japan is one of the most powerful nations on Earth is hard work. Africa needs to do better, work more than everyone else, if we are going to join other continents in development. Jesus knew the value of work that He ordained that we must work while it is day.

> "As long as it is day, we must do the works of him who sent me. Night is coming, when no one can work." John 9:4

To truly lead, we must be doers. We must be hard workers. We must imitate Jesus by working while it is day. We must imitate God by working six days a week like He did in creation. That is how we can expect the African continent to start becoming the head and not remain the tail.

Lord, help me be a doer of your word, a hard worker, and be tenacious enough to hold on up to completion of the mission you have given me!

Application of Day 18

1. Why is it wrong waiting for others to do for us what we can do for ourselves?

2. Why is Africa the poorest continent of all when it is probably the most blessed with resources?

3. What can we learn from John Stephen Akhwari?

4. Who should set the standard for hard work in a society and why?

5. What are some of the advantages of hard work?

FAIR

Being fair is also being just!

Aleader treats all people fairly. Africa can use this quality. The poor need to be treated fairly. I know fairness is a problem everywhere in the world, but in Africa it is a huge problem. The law does not apply equally between rich and poor. The poor get treated like they are less human. We must specifically address this problem in Africa.

In my first book, *Africa, It's Time!* I ask the question, who is the better boss, the Colonial master or the fellow African? It is unfortunate that the poor in Africa are treated more unfairly today than they were during colonialism. Is that not a shame?

A leader must be fair. A leader must be just. A leader must treat everyone equally. If you are a leader, do not pick and choose who to treat with respect and who to push aside. God created all human beings equal and they all deserve fair treatment. James warns us against the practice of favoritism.

"My brothers and sisters, believers in our glorious Lord Jesus Christ must not show favoritism. Suppose a man comes into your meeting wearing a gold ring and fine clothes, and a poor man in filthy old clothes also comes

in. If you show special attention to the man wearing fine clothes and say, 'Here's a good seat for you,' but say to the poor man, 'You stand there' or 'Sit on the floor by my feet,' have you not discriminated among yourselves and become judges with evil thoughts?" James 2:1-4

I have sometimes seen a committed member of the church lose a child. The church announces the loss casually and the pastor, the church leadership, and most members do not show up to comfort such a member, just because this is a poor person. But when a non-committed member of the church loses a child and he happens to be one of the top rich people of the church, the announcement in the church is forceful and very appealing for the whole church to comfort the rich brother. The pastor and the whole leadership go to visit the family every day till the day of the burial to truly show their support. The members of the church go in big numbers to show their sympathy. But they all forget to wonder how the poor and yet active member of the church would feel seeing the support that his fellow and non-committed brother receives for the same kind of loss.

We all need to improve our ability to be fair. Even in the Western world, it is sad that women in some countries still earn less than what men earn for the same jobs and tasks. Leaders in the Western world, where this unfair practice is still happening, must wake up and change it immediately. Some people in leadership positions hide behind the fact that much has been improved in terms of equality between men and women. When it comes to fairness, we must go all the way. 80% fairness does not cut it. Anything less than total fairness smells injustice. We can all agree with Martin Luther King that,

"Injustice anywhere is a threat to justice everywhere." (34)

The level of unfairness in Africa is unbelievable. To have people still earning less than a dollar a day in the 21st century, is not only primitive and unjust, but a total shame to the so-called embracers of *Ubuntu*. *Ubuntu* believes in the common good. *Ubuntu* believes in fairness. Many of our leaders, including Christian leaders, are so unfair that their own consciences have stopped bothering them with issues of injustice and unfairness. To pay your worker or servant pittance, less than a dollar a day, you truly have to subdue your conscience to justify such an ill treatment, especially when you could easily afford to do better. Unfortunately, most of our leaders pride themselves on abusing their people so much that being unfair to those they think pose no threat to them is something they do without remorse. They are only concerned with their tiny inner circle that do all they can to protect their boss and their own positions.

Let me openly thank countries, such as Zambia, that have introduced a minimum wage system to ensure that every citizen is protected by law; so no employer can pay his employee less than the minimum wage required by law. This is a commendable act. We need the whole of Africa to introduce the minimum wage system to combat the exploitation of Africans. We need to go even further in doing more study to make sure minimum wages afford everyone the ability to feed their families decently and afford their children at least a high school education.

Being a leader is like being a parent. When you have children, you must continually work at ensuring fair treatment for all your children. It is very damaging to a child to feel that he is less loved by his parent than another sibling. In our parenting, we make opportunities to enjoy as a family, but we also spend time with each child out individually. It is during such a personal time with your child that you make him or her feel special. When you do that for each child, they all feel loved and see that you are being fair to all.

There is a temptation to categorize your children. Some children, as we all know, are easier to love than others. Some are more obedient and respectful than others. Some are so challenging that it feels as if they were the opposition parties. Some are just happier than others. Some are grumpy and there seems to be nothing that will cheer them up. But, regardless of the make-up of the people you are leading or children you are parenting, you must make every effort to be fair to them all. The moment the grumpy one feels that you are unfair to him or her, and if nothing is done quickly to remedy the situation, you will likely lose that child or person. This is why taking time as a parent to do a one-on-one date with your child gives you the opportunity to build up and reinforce the relationship with your child. It is important to make sure your child knows he or she is special. Otherwise, you will find yourself, knowingly or unknowingly, favouring one child over the other, which is a terrible thing you can do to your children. Favouring one child over others makes him feel superior to his or her siblings and creates dysfunction in the family relationship.

Sometime back, I stayed with one family that had 3 children. The unfair negative treatment they showed to their middle child was very disappointing. The boy was like a stranger and a beggar in his own family. His siblings could do no wrong, while even his best intentions were almost always wrong in the eyes of his parents. Sometimes, certain children or people seem easier to love more than others. But as a parent or as a leader, one must make efforts to love and care for everyone fairly. What makes a leader is not responding positively to only those who seem easy to love, but loving everyone, including the difficult ones, equally.

Being fair is a must-have quality for a leader. A leader must guard against being misguided by the inner circle so as to give privileges to a few people while being unfair to the majority of the population. There is truly much work to be done in Africa to establish fairness. You look at issues such as the servant quarter housing in most African cities, and you wonder how people's consciences do not reproach them and urge them to improve the living conditions of their servants. You find someone having an eight-bedroom house, but happy to have a servant in servant quarters too small to fit a decent bed. Most of the time, servants are not even given a bed. They sleep on a mat. Where is our *Ubuntu?* Come on Africans, we can do better.

What has happened to our African human consciences? What has happened to our sense of fairness? When we sleep in our mansions while our servants sleep in a room smaller than a kitchenette, does it occur to our minds that they are as human as we are? Have you really forgotten that the Christ who died for us is the same who died for them and that He would want us not to despise those He valued enough to die for? Have we totally forgotten that when we oppress the less privileged, we are waging war with God? Who has bewitched us that we abuse women, children, the poor, and anyone in a desperate situation without any remorse?

I know we may wonder about how we can truly be fair. Can we truly be fair? The simple answer is yes. Yes, we can be fair. Is it easy to be completely fair? No, it is not easy, but it is doable. It is one of those things that require effort. Beyond effort, we need to humbly ask God to help us be fair. We have to constantly put ourselves in the shoes of the less privileged and ask ourselves how we would want to be treated if we were them. You have heard of the golden rule:

"Treat others the way you would like to be treated yourself."
(35)

In fact this golden rule is actually borrowing from the biblical command:

"So in everything, do to others what you would have them do to you, for this sums up the Law and the Prophets."
Matthew 7:12

Imagine if we lived out this command! Imagine if we served people the way we would want to be served! Imagine if we treated them the way we want to be treated! Imagine if we paid people the wages that we wanted them to pay us if we were working for them! Imagine what our community would look like if we treated people the way we would have them treat us! May God help us in our efforts to treat others as fairly as we would have them treat us!

Lord, help me be fair with everyone. May I treat everyone with respect and without favouritism!

Application of Day 19

1. What does it mean to be fair?

2. Why must a leader be fair?

3. What happens when a leader or a parent is clearly unfair to some and so good to others?

4. If the church is to take her advocacy seriously, should she not advocate for the establishment of decent minimum wage for the exploited workers?

5. Everyone has a role to play to ensure fairness. How will you personally implement and advocate for fairness?

PRINCIPLED

A principled person is someone with high ethics or high morality!

A leader needs to be principled. When it comes to issues of corruption and bribery, when a leader's integrity is on the line, principles must prevail.

A principled person has values. A principled leader is an ethical one. When you are principled, you do not allow even friendship to take you away from your values. For a principled leader, nothing is worth giving up principles for.

I remember one day, I bought a very good African gospel music CD. A good friend of mine liked the music so much that he asked me to copy my CD. I told him that where I bought the CD, there were still many copies that he could go and buy his own copy. But he argued that he did not need to spend his $20 to buy a CD when he could make his copy from mine. So I insisted that I could not let him make a copy from mine as that was stealing from the gospel choir that produced the CD. He was very upset with me. But, even though I love my friends, the principle was more valuable than the friendship.

A principle helps a leader and any person to have a clear stand on what is right or wrong. I remember whenever

I was being confronted with the issue of corruption or bribery in Africa, it was very clear in my mind that it was wrong and we must do everything to stop condoning the practice by not participating in accepting to bribe anyone.

Sometimes I would share my experience with my students but their naïve answers would make me realize how much we have allowed corruption and bribery to be part of us. For example, some of them would say, "Are you saying that you cannot afford 5,000 francs, the equivalent of $3 USD?" To them, the only issue is how large a bribe is being asked. If the amount is too small, then why not just pay it?

The good thing is that those kinds of situations made for opportunities to teach good ethics with tangible situations. The more practical issues like that came up, the more opportunities I had to teach my students about ethics, principles, and values. Thank God, even before I left, many had developed good principles so much that they were capable of questioning some wrong practices that were already being accepted in the culture as normal, just because the majority of the people do it.

A principle helps you stand with your people. One of the practices that African leaders must put an end to is the whole issue of African leaders always going to seek medical treatment outside their countries. Why is it that when African leaders are sick, they have to go to the West for treatment? What do such actions say about their own leadership? There are some basic structures that every country must build to ensure self-dependency.

A leader must make sure structures such as hospitals and schools are adequate enough so that no one needs to travel abroad to get a good education or quality medical treatment. Dr. Aaron Motsoaledi challenged African leaders with these words:

"*We are the only continent that has its leaders seeking medical services outside the continent, outside our terri-*

tory. We must be ashamed of that. This is called health tourism. We must promote our own." (36)

Think of the cost of your medical treatment in the Western hospitals. What if you used that money to invest in building hospitals in your own country? Think of the cost of education abroad for your children and those in your inner circle? If that money was invested in your own country, you could probably build good schools with it.

When are we Africans going to truly be independent? Why is that we are failing so badly in our principles test? I think that if you are unable to build quality health care centers in your own country; then accept to suffer the consequences of it just like your people. If you truly want good quality healthcare for yourself and your family, then build the infrastructure in your country. If you want quality education for your children, then build good schools in your country. Principles require that you enjoy the good and suffer the consequences of failure with your people. This trend of educating your children abroad and receiving medical treatment abroad is contributing to the continuity of the neo-colonialism. And unfortunately, it is deliberately selfish on the part of those who are the representatives of the people.

A principled leader does what is right and not necessarily what is convenient or popular. Sometimes, being principled makes us unpopular with some friends, but if it is for the good of our people, then it is worth it, regardless of the consequences. African leaders must make decisions based on what is good for their people, and not based on what will be pleasing to their Western partners.

Take, for example, Burkina Faso under the leadership of the late President Thomas Sankara. The country, through their president, banned the importation of food and clothes. Then they started manufacturing their own 100% cotton clothing. Sankara redistributed the land so that everyone had a portion of land to produce food. In four years, they were self-sufficient with their own food.

When you think about it as a neutral observer, you have to ask yourself what is of great gain for the country: depending on imported second-hand clothes or creating their own clothing manufacturing companies. Imagine how it felt for the Burkinabe to produce and depend on their own food! That is decision-making based on principles. The good thing about Sankara is the fact that he led by example. He wore clothes made in Burkina Faso. Consider what is said about his revolution:

> "In 1984, Sankara renamed the country Burkina Faso (land of people of integrity). Sankara purged corruption from the government, slashing ministerial salaries and adopting a simpler approach to life. Journalist Paula Akugizibwe says Sankara 'rode a bicycle to work before he upgraded, at his Cabinet's insistence, to a Renault 5 - one of the cheapest cars available in Burkina Faso at the time. He lived in a small brick house and wore only cotton that was produced, weaved and sewn in Burkina Faso.' In fact the adoption of local clothes and local foods was central to Sankara's economic strategy to break the country from the domination of the West. He famously said: 'Where is imperialism? Look at your plates when you eat. These imported grains of rice, corn, and millet - that is imperialism.' His solution was to grow food - 'Let us consume only what we ourselves control!' The results were incredible: self-sufficiency in 4 years. Former UN Special Rapporteur on the Right to Food Jean Ziegler says that a combination of massive land distribution, fertilizer and irrigation saw agricultural productivity boom; 'hunger was a thing of the past'." (37)

This quotation mentions just a few of Sankara's achievements, but he did more than that. No wonder why people in

Burkina Faso are still in love with Sankara these many years. His record might take long to beat.

Being principled helps a leader defend his opponent, even when such truth could hurt him in the votes. Senator John McCain is one great example of a principled leader. During his campaign for the presidency of the United States of America, he was challenged by a lady who alleged that the then Democratic Presidential Candidate Barack Obama was an Arab. John McCain refused to score cheap points, but instead defended Obama, his opponent:

> *"He is a decent family man, a citizen that I just happen to have disagreement with on fundamental issues."* (38)

African leaders must be principled. And I am not inviting them to become arrogant as if they are waging a war with the West. No. African leaders must be able to make decisions based on what is best for their countries. To be pleasing to others is good, as long as it does not throw our principles out the window.

Being principled will help African leaders collaborate with their Western counterparts on an equal basis. For example, if another country is giving you aid and they impose on you conditions that undermine your principles, you must be able to refuse such help.

Are you a principled person? Are you a principled leader? What do you do when you are given a bribe: do you refuse it or accept it, even when you know it is illegal and wrong to take a bribe? Do you compromise your values just because you do not want to offend people or your friends? Do you corrupt people to get what you want? Do you do the wrong you know to be wrong just because everyone else does it? Are you principled enough to do the right thing even when the whole community does the wrong thing? Do you get medical treatment in your country or abroad? These are important questions a leader must ask himself.

For us as Christians, we are called to be imitators of our Lord, Savior, and Master Jesus Christ. Our Lord was a principled person. Even after 40 days of prayer and fasting, He remained principled so that he could not give in to the devil's temptation. Let's not forget that He took upon himself flesh like us. So, as human, He must have been extremely hungry.

The devil had tempted Him at his exact point of need. After all, He had not eaten for 40 days. Asking Jesus to turn the stone into bread was a well-calculated test. I am sure the devil was saying to himself that there will be no chance of failure in his temptation, because anyone that hungry would jump at the opportunity to get food and eat.

Jesus, being as principled as He was, would not allow Satan to have victory over Him. The principle to remain true to who He is was far more valuable than giving in to Satan's temptation to turn the stone into bread. By the way, if He wanted to, He could turn the stone into bread. So, the reason Jesus did not do it is not because He was unable to perform such a miracle, but rather, He would not do it because He would have surrendered victory to Satan.

We can imitate Jesus Christ by living a principled life, and in so doing, we will live a truthful life and a life obedient to God and His truth. Principled living will help us stand for what is right. Principled living will help us stand up for a just and fair society for all. Our world today urgently needs principled people. I hope you can join us in this adventure of right living. The hope of Africa and the world depend on throwing away relativism and embracing principled living.

Lord, make me principled enough not to compromise on your Word.

Application of Day 20

1. What does it mean to be principled?

2. Why must a leader be principled?

3. What are the advantages of being principled?

4. What are the challenges of being principled?

5. What do you think about my story of refusing to let my friend copy my music CD? What would you have done?

6. What do you think of Senator John McCain, who refused to go for cheap votes, but defended his opponent Senator Obama at that time?

7. Are you principled? How can you be more principled?

RELATIONAL

A quality similar to relational is friendly!

Jesus' ministry was so effective partly because He was relational. He did so much with his disciples. He called his disciples his friends. Jesus valued relationships. He related to everyone, including the outcasts of society. This is why the Pharisees and teachers of the law questioned his authority, because they had expected Him to be so kingly and authoritarian that He would not be easily approachable. The fact that He was so relational and friendly did not fit their criteria for a king or someone in authority. Jesus related to all people and gave value to everyone He encountered.

For example, Jesus not only called Zacchaeus from the tree, he also decided to dine in Zacchaeus' home. Zacchaeus, a tax collector who was seen as oppressive to the people, was saved by Jesus' grace over him. He ended up acting in repentance and decided to give back the money that he had overcharged people or stolen from people through his tax collections. Jesus' relational approach changed and transformed not only Zacchaeus but those he had offended.

Jesus was relational with the Samaritan woman at the well. He broke the barrier of hostility between the Jews and the

Samaritans and chose to be friendly and accepting toward the Samaritan. He also broke the barrier of gender and chose to be friendly to a woman. That approach brought salvation not only to the Samaritan woman but to many from her village.

> *Many of the Samaritans from that town believed in him because of the woman's testimony, 'He told me everything I ever did.' So when the Samaritans came to him, they urged him to stay with them, and he stayed two days. And because of his words many more became believers. They said to the woman, 'We no longer believe just because of what you said; now we have heard for ourselves, and we know that this man really is the Savior of the world.'* John 4:39-42

Jesus shocked everyone when he let a prostitute pour perfume on him. He forgave her sins and praised her for her kind actions toward him. For Jesus, the prostitute was as valuable as anyone else, and He was happy to relate with her as He did with everyone. We can learn from Jesus' actions that everyone is special, regardless of their past. Just because people have made errors in the past, we must not stop relating with them and being friendly to them.

A leader must be relational. A leader must be friendly. When a leader thinks he is so powerful that he cannot reduce himself to relating with everyone, he ceases to be a leader. One way of being a good leader is being able to be friendly with everyone, including the ones considered the least valuable in society.

Being relational and friendly often pays dividends for a leader. President Pierre Nkurunziza became popular because of his ability to mix with everyone. He is famously known for playing soccer/football with people in rural areas and in the cities. He is known for going out on the streets to participate actively in the community cleaning that happens every Saturday morning. President Nkurunziza became more popular because he was able to be friendly and relational with everyone.

President Obama is appreciated worldwide for being relational and friendly. Being president of the United States is considered the most powerful leader in the world. But Obama did not let the power of the White House turn him into a world dictator. From the beginning of his first term presidency, he signalled that he would forge partnerships and not dictate solutions. That is one of the reasons Obama is very popular all over the world.

> *Obama the Humble declares there will be no more 'dictating' to other countries. We should 'forge partnerships as opposed to simply dictating solutions,' he told the G-20 summit. In Middle East negotiations, he told al-Arabiya, America will henceforth 'start by listening, because all too often the United States starts by dictating.'* (39)

One of the acts that have made me appreciate President John Magufuli is when he noticed a woman who was demonstrating in the audience and the security personnel was harshly escorting her out. Magufuli ordered that she be brought to him and asked her to plead her case. She told her case to the president, and he acted right there in her favour.

> **Widow disrupts meeting attended by Tanzania's President Magufuli, gets his empathy.** *Narrating her complaints, the woman reportedly said she has been blocked by dishonest members of the Judiciary, police and private advocates from securing the right to gain control of property left by her departed husband, Mohamed Shosi, who died in 2012. ...The president ordered the judges to speedily listen to her case. He also directed the chief justice, who was present, to give the woman his phone number so that she can follow up with him on the case's progress.*

Mr. Magufuli also ordered the police boss to ensure that Ms. Shoshi gets full protection. (40)

What kind of leaders are we? Are we relational? Are we friendly? Can people feel free to approach us? When we refuse to be relational or friendly, we impose fear in people so much that they cannot talk to us. We become isolated from the very people we claim to lead. Then we surround ourselves with those who pretend to be our friends, and yet the only reason they are friendly to us is because of the privileges they get from us. Relating to everyone as Jesus did allows the leader to know if he or she is doing well or not because people will be free to express their opinions.

A leader must start this journey of friendliness and relationship in his or her own home. Often, we want to be heroes outside our families when we are like roaring lions in our own families. Before we can be relational and friendly to the whole world, we must start within our families. Once we have established good relationship within our homes, we then must also make sure we are relational and friendly with everyone else.

A leader must know his people. To know his people, a leader must relate to them. He must walk, talk, and eat with his people. You become united with your people when you relate to them. In my tribe, Bafuliiru, we say, *Ubuguma kulyanwa*, which means 'Oneness or unity is eating together'. Jesus walked with people. He ate with people. He would have conversations with people. That is how He got to know people very well; yes, because He was God, but also because He valued interacting with people. A leader must, like Jesus, relate well with people.

Relating well with people or simply being friendly can help establish great relationships. I remember meeting George and Sylvia Baynton for the first time at church in Saskatoon. It was in September of 1996. I had just been two weeks in Canada. We greeted each other, and I thought it would just end there but we continued talking. They were surprised to see that I was wearing a heavy coat in September. Coming from Africa, the September cold felt like winter. One thing that stuck with me about them was their friendliness. Right there, they asked me what I was going to do for lunch. I said I was going back to my apartment to make lunch.

They invited me to go to lunch with them at a restaurant. At the restaurant, we visited for quite some time, and then they took me back to my apartment. Soon after, they invited me into their home. I look back today in 2017, more than 21 years ago since we first met, and realize that they have become family to me. I live in Lloydminster now, but I still remember that the Bayntons are the ones who first introduced me to Lloydminster in 1997. My story with them is a long and wonderful one.

But the lesson is very clear: relate well to everyone and just be friendly, because you never know all the good that can come out of it. There are many people out there who are lonely, without anyone to talk to or to befriend them. Relate to them.

Relating to the lonely and depressed can help prevent suicide. This is exactly what happened to me some time back in Zambia. I had gone to visit a family friend. But I noticed that one of the daughters, a mature lady, was under the tree alone. It did not look right, especially because it was already dark. This lady and I did not relate much. She was not one of my friends in their family. She had been divorced, so she came back home to live with her mother and father and her siblings. She had a job but later lost it. When she had a job, she was loved and respected as she contributed financially. But when she lost her job, she became the outcast in her family. Everyone put her down. She looked for other jobs and could not find one. The more she was unemployed, the more she was the laughing stock of the family.

Life became too unbearable, and she thought it would be best for everyone if she ceased to exist. Where I found her that night, under the tree, she was planning her suicide. At the beginning of our conversation, she was quite guarded; she did not say much to give me a clue as to why she was under that tree alone at night. But the more we talked, the more she started opening up and sharing about her life.

We talked for a long time. At the end, she revealed to me her suicidal plan. I offered to pray for her. Then after, I asked her to go tomorrow to look for work again. She first said that she had gone everywhere and could not find a job, and that there was no point going again. I encouraged her not to give up, but to keep trying. She told me she would go out of appreciation for me taking my time to be friendly to her. She went the next day, and the first place she went to offered her a job. She was overjoyed and came back running to tell me the news. Life completely changed for her that day. This is what being relational and friendly can do for people. Let us do our part, which is relating well with everyone, and then God will do his part.

Our unfriendliness, just as our friendliness can make a difference for eternity. Did you know that it is said that Mahatma Gandhi once considered becoming a Christian but our unfriendliness pushed him away? It is said that Gandhi had come to admire Jesus and often quoted Jesus' Sermon on the Mount. One day, a missionary by the name of E. Stanley Jones asked him why he quoted Jesus often and yet rejected becoming Jesus' follower. In response, Gandhi said:

"I like your Christ, I do not like your Christians. Your Christians are so unlike your Christ." (41)

Apparently, Gandhi, in his search for Christ, had gone to attend a church, but he was not allowed to worship in that church. He was instead chased out. How sad and tragic! Our Lord is relational and friendly, and we, His followers, must imitate Him in relating to people.

It is very un-Christ like when even Christians fail to relate to others who may be different than them. You find Christians who are racist or discriminatory toward those who are different than them. How can you be a Christian and a racist at the same time? Is that not terrible? You see some churches full of only White people or only Black people and yet the community around them is totally multicultural. How can you justify that in the 21st century?

One time, I was part of predominantly White church and quite involved there. Once in a while there would be a Black person who came to visit. People, often someone from the leadership in the church, would ask him, "Have you met Charles?" Then, I would see someone coming to introduce this new Black person to me, saying, "This is Charles." After a few times of that happening, then I understood that the church had informally made it my responsibility to be a friend to every Black person who visits the church.

I asked to talk to the chairman of the board. Then I told him how it was not good that all Black people should be sent to me. He said that they thought that the Black people might want to relate to me because I was one of them. I explained to him how, if a Black person wanted to find other Black people, there were many churches of predominantly Black people for that. I told him that people make their own choices to worship where they want, and if they choose a predominantly White church, then they should make friends with anyone whether White, Black, Asian or anyone else.

As the church of Jesus Christ, we should be relational and friendly people, because that is who our Lord was and still is. But when we, who should know better, pick and choose who to relate to, who to be friendly to, we are at that time living in contradiction to the Christian faith.

We have to avoid stereotyping people. A friend of mine, a Black African who studied in China, went to attend a Chinese church in Edmonton one day. That church was meeting in the gymnasium of another church. The usher started telling him, "You have come to the wrong place; you need to go to the main church in the main sanctuary." He tried to explain that he was indeed coming to attend the Chinese church service, but she was too busy pointing him to the mainline church. Then, he asked her in Mandarin, "Is this not the Mandarin-speaking church?" She was shocked and then she said yes and ushered him to a seat, actually a prominent front seat.

A story is told of a rich man who was in need for some change to pay for parking downtown. He saw a beggar and tried everything to avoid him. But the beggar had noticed that he checked his pockets for the money to pay his parking and could not find the money, so he went to give him money to pay for the parking. As he tried to ignore him and continue on his way, the beggar called him and handed him the money to pay for the parking. That day, his view of beggars changed. He realized for the first time that they were just as human as everyone else, and that they too were a blessing to humanity.

When I had just come to Canada, I had heard stories about the Indigenous people. They were not uplifting stories, to say the least. But I was fortunate to go to seminary with an Indigenous person, Ray Aldred. I quickly realized that he was the most intelligent student among all of us. He was also the leader of his church community. That gave me a totally different picture of the Indigenous people. Ray has served in many leadership roles, including Assistant Professor of Theology at Ambrose Seminary in Calgary, Alberta. He is a very influential leader and one of the key voices for the Indigenous people.

Then later, I was introduced to Pastor Randy Ermineskin of the then Hobbema Native Gospel Church, who later became the Chief of the Ermineskin Cree Nation in Maskwacis Reserve. His church was one of our great supporters in our mission in Burundi. But my high respect for him and the church in Maskwacis is not based on their support for us; it is based on discovering that the stories I had heard about the Indigenous people were unfair and untrue. Pastor Randy and his assistant Pastor Sandra are very intelligent people and great people, and so are their people too.

I have met other great Indigenous people. We just need to start relating to each other outside the stereotype. In God's eyes, no human being is inferior or superior to another human being. As Christians, we should be exemplary as far as relating well with every human being, because everyone is valuable and deserves to be related to by everyone else.

It is very unfortunate when even Christians get caught up with stereotyping and the failure to relate to people who are different from them. Ask yourself some questions: how many friends outside your community do you truly relate to? If you are a White person, how many friends do you have from the Black community, the Indigenous community, the Asian community or the Arab community? If you are a Black person, how many non-Blacks friends do you have? If you are Indigenous, how many non-Indigenous friends do you have? If you Asian, how many non-Asian friends do you have? If you are an Arab, how many non-Arab friends do you have? We will not make a better world if we cannot even be free to relate to people outside our community. Even within our community, how many of those considered outcasts do we relate to? Going forward in building a better community requires that we imitate Jesus, our Lord, in relating to everyone, including the ones that look different and the ones that society has deemed outcasts.

Relating well with everyone almost always pays great dividends. Inclusion and integration are always the best ways to build a better community. Exclusion and isolation are not the ways to build society. When people feel excluded, not accepted, they often become a liability to society. Now, I know that sometimes people have willingly allowed evil to enter their hearts; for those ones, it does not matter how much you try to include them, they exclude themselves. But it is the responsibility of leaders to put in every effort to relate with everyone and to include everyone.

Sometimes, we make errors in the name of empowering every community. I saw, for example, the approach that the City of Edmonton had of empowering every community to be somehow self-reliant so that they can solve their own problems. I think that was their best attempt to show respect to each community. But that is a wrong approach. I actually had opportunities to discuss the whole empowering model with some of the city officials. I showed them that their approach was an excluding one and not empowering the communities they intended to empower. They totally got it. If you really want to empower the communities, instead of funding them to do their own thing, why not hire them to work with you or among you. The best way to empower people is to live all aspects of life on an equal basis. Then everyone can relate with everyone and not have to be confined only to their community.

Unfortunately, this exclusion system is happening in the church. Again, in the name of empowering 'the other', denominations are helping create various cultural churches. Once people have their own churches, their own community organizations, their own cultural businesses such as restaurants and cultural grocery shops, what is left in common with other Canadian communities different than them? I can understand the need to have cultural celebrations in which communities showcase who they are. But when they have their own government-funded cultural associations, own cultural churches funded by the denomination they belong to, and their own cultural businesses, there is not much that makes them want to be part of the general community.

Again, relating to brothers and sisters in the Lord from different backgrounds will be better if we hire them and have them as full integral part of the church. Helping them form their own cultural churches is a way of excluding them. I believe that the church of Jesus Christ is a multicultural, multi-background, and multiracial church. It should never be 'us' versus 'them' because it must only be about 'us'.

The reason why I understand a bit more what is considered Canadian culture is because when I arrived in Saskatoon, most people I related to frequently were non-Africans. Non-Africans helped integrate me into the Canadian system and culture.

Relating to only your culture limits you to knowing just your culture, while interacting with other cultures opens your worldview and increases your knowledge and experiences much more. Please do not get me wrong, I am of the view that each person's culture is important and must be celebrated. I am proud to be of Congolese background, but I gain more knowledge by knowing something about other cultures.

I think that while there is value in our Canadian mosaic system, we have to work hard as Canadians of various kinds to build unity among us. We need to emphasize the inter-relations among various cultures and backgrounds in order to build what can be known as typically Canadian. I do not think that it speaks well of our country that we can hardly define what is typically Canadian. I think the church should work hard to establish true inclusion and serve as an example of what it means to truly be Canadian. Churches in other countries can also set the example of what it means to be inclusive so that we can truly live-out Paul's message of unity in Christ.

> There is neither Jew nor Gentile, neither slave nor free, nor
> is there male and female, for you are all one in Christ Jesus.
> Galatians 3:28

May God help us know how to relate well to one another and build a world based on the love of God and not on prejudice, exclusion, and stereotypes!

Lord, make me relational and friendly so that I can be able to relate with everyone!

Application of Day 21

1. If Jesus is our example and we know how relational He was toward everyone including the outcasts, why do we fail to relate well to people as He did?

2. Make a list of the outcast people Jesus related to. What can you learn from that?

3. When we invite people to follow Jesus but we fail to be friendly to them, how is that not a contradiction?

4. Make it personal; how many non-Christian friends do you have? How are you doing with stereotyping? Do you relate to people who are not from your community? List some ways we can relate better to everyone.

OPTIMISTIC

Optimistic and hopeful go hand in hand!

The world is full of pessimists. Many people go on in life without hope; no wonder they condemn themselves to mediocre, hopeless and mere existence. A leader must not be one of them. Unfortunately, many of our African friends have decided to go the pessimistic way. Some simply believe that Africa will always be behind other continents. Thank God that some Africans are strong believers of a future prosperous Africa.

Hope keeps us positive even in the midst of present suffering. Optimism says if we do the right thing now, a better and prosperous future is just a step away. Hope gives us energy and joy enough to motivate us to do better and to work towards achieving our goals. When you are optimistic, you refuse failures or to let the past dictate the outcome. Hopeful people refuse to quit. They keep working on their convictions, and eventually, they succeed. Hope and optimism can be the difference between success and failure.

Often pessimists fail before failure can even appear. They fail because they do not even try. Pessimists convince themselves of the worst. Their pessimistic approach deprives them of the joy and energy to do anything worth doing. Pessimism is a terrible state to live in. Pessimism sucks life out of anyone so much that it buries people even before they are physically dead.

One day, I was talking to a fellow well-educated African. I asked him what needs to be done for Africa to join other continents in development. He simply and quickly answered that we must forget about Africa ever joining other continents in development. He said that Africa will always be behind. To him, we should just be grateful that we have a chance to live in the West, but Africa, according to him, is cursed and will continue to go from bad to worse.

Another day, I was talking to another African who told me that he would like to go back to Africa and establish himself there. He dreamed of having a better life in his native country of Cameroon. So, I said, "Well, if we start going back to Africa, we can go make a difference, and sooner or later, we will have a great continent where it will be good for everyone to live."

He seemed shocked by what I said. He told me that there was nothing that can be changed in Africa. He was going to make a good life for himself and his family and that was all for him. I said, "What about your contribution to the betterment of Africa in general and Cameroon in particular?"

He said, "No, there is nothing you can do for Cameroon or Africa. You just have to build yourself your own empire." According to him, you cannot fight corruption, so you might as well keep quiet about it, do not try to point out the wrong, live quietly, and just make a life for yourself.

The pessimistic approach is very unproductive and sometimes selfish too. Pessimists are not even willing to try to make things better. They adhere to the saying that, "If you cannot beat them, then you must join them." But how can you join them when they are in the wrong and you know it?

Is not corruption wrong, even though it is practiced by the majority? Must we all become corrupt because we seem to be unable to beat corruption? Should not the Diaspora contribute

to building a corruption-free Africa even if the majority is corrupt?

I felt so bad to see that Africa's children have lost hope in
the continent that gave them birth. Thank God I have talked to
many other Africans who are optimistic that Africa can be the
best place on Earth to live. These hopeful, optimistic Africans
are now starting to make their contributions into building a better Africa. We need to be optimistic and hopeful if we are to
build a better Africa.

I am inviting all fellow optimistic Africans and friends of
Africa to join forces to lead Africa to heights never seen before. I
hope you understand that I am not just daydreaming; this is doable. The more we are optimistic, the more we will contaminate
the pessimists, and before long, they will join us. But even if they
choose not to join us, we will continue being optimistic, and
sooner or later, Africa will be the place where everyone wants
to live.

Leaders must provide reason for optimism and hope.
The African Diaspora must contribute to build optimism and
hope. The advantage of the Diaspora is that they have seen how
things work in Africa versus how they work in the West.

Optimism is knowing that we can solve the problems of
this world by solving one, or two, or three, depending on what
we are capable of. An optimistic person knows that every child
freed from permanent hunger is part of the solution to the whole
problem of hunger. Optimism is about giving your very best contribution, knowing that every little bit is better than nothing
and contributes to building a better world for all.

Optimists do not just let the fact that they cannot solve all
the problems stop them from making their contributions. They
solve those problems that they can solve, and that is their contribution to the betterment of society. Pessimists, on the other
hand, do not even do the very minimum. They do not even
start. Pessimism is a very negative state of mind. It is damaging
not only to oneself, but to the entire community in which it is

operating. Pessimists have the power of being contagious toward others so that nothing of worth can be achieved.

I sometimes wonder why people would choose to lock themselves in pessimism and hopelessness. How depressing life would be if we convince ourselves that life will always be miserable, that there is no hope for us, that Africa will never be a place where all children go to bed with a full stomach.

Hopelessness and pessimism are both very depressing. We need leaders who inspire people with hope and optimism. Leaders need to work on building a better society and therefore give their people reason for hope and optimism. Africa and the whole world can truly use such leaders.

Optimists and pessimists have existed together for centuries. It is part of life that people can look at the same situation or obstacle and some will believe that they can overcome that obstacle, while others will convince themselves that they cannot overcome it. The Bible illustrates this typical characteristic of optimists versus pessimists:

> *"They gave Moses this account: 'We went into the land to which you sent us, and it does flow with milk and honey! Here is its fruit. But the people who live there are powerful and the cities are fortified and very large. We even saw descendants of Anak there. The Amalekites live in the Negev; the Hittites, Jebusites and Amorites live in the hill country; and the Canaanites live near the sea and along the Jordan.' Then Caleb silenced the people before Moses and said, 'We should go up and take possession of the land, for we can certainly do it.' But the men who had gone up with him said, 'We can't attack those people; they are stronger than we are.' And they spread among the Israelites a bad report about the land they had explored. They said, 'The land we explored devours those living in it. All the people we saw there are of great size. We saw the Nephilim there (the descendants of Anakcome from the Nephilim). We seemed*

*like grasshoppers in our own eyes, and we looked the same
to them.'"* Numbers 13:26-33

What kind of a leader are you? Are you an optimist like
Caleb? Are you hopeful? Are you a pessimist? Do you trust in
God? To lead people, a leader must be hopeful and optimistic.
The people you lead depend on you to see hope for a better future. If you cannot be optimistic and hopeful, do yourself and
your people a favour; quit leading, because you are taking people
nowhere.

The best optimism is in trusting God that, with Him on
our side, we are more than conquerors. Humanly, we are often
powerless to overcome difficult obstacles on our own. There is
nothing wrong with admitting that. Admission of that fact does
not mean being a pessimist. But we cannot stop at admitting
that fact. Optimism says that yes, the situation is difficult, but
our God is more powerful and we can trust Him to win the
battle for us. The difference between pessimism and optimism is
in the fact that pessimism stops at the fact, but optimism trusts
in God to go beyond the fact.

The world is already full of hopelessness and hopeless
people. The statistics are already big enough. You do not need
to add yourself to the stats. Instead, find a way to renew hope
and optimism in our world and people today. Do not burden
yourself with how big the world's problems are. You are not the
one to solve all of them. But you can surely solve some. You can
educate one poor child. You can volunteer your services. You can
advocate against the abuse of women and children. You can be
a good husband, a good wife, or a good parent. You can be the
best employer. You can combat corruption and bribery. You can
inspire hope in a young person. You can be a mentor or a coach
to someone. Everyone can do something to bring hope and optimism to our hopeless world. When you do your part, you can be
at peace with that.

Lord, make me more and more optimistic and hopeful so that I can contaminate people around me with this hope and optimism!

Application of Day 22

1. What does it mean to be an optimist? What does it mean to be hopeful?

2. Why is pessimism wrong?

3. What can optimism do for a leader?

4. What are the disadvantages of pessimism?

5. What are the advantages of hope?

6. Why is it that many Africans are not hopeful about Africa's future?

7. Think of yourself: are you an optimist or a pessimist?

PERSON OF CONVICTION

To be a person of conviction means to be of strong persuasion or strong belief!

A leader must have conviction. Conviction makes you do things that you would not ordinarily do without it. It makes you endure any hardships, discouragements, or challenges that a leader faces.

Patrice Emery Lumumba was so convicted about Congo's full independence that he was willing to die for that cause. Martin Luther King's strong conviction about fighting for equality in America propelled him to go all the way, including dying, for that cause. Both men knew that they could be dead anytime, but not even the imminent threat of death could stop them from fighting for their noble causes.

Thomas Sankara was a man of strong conviction. He was convinced that men and women are equal and must be treated as equal. He fought for that equality in Burkina Faso. He was convinced that his country's resources must be shared fairly. He was doing all he could to reduce the wages of top earners and increase wages of the bottom earners. He himself gave so much away that he lived and died as though he were poor. His strong convictions led him to fight for community welfare more than personal gain.

Mother Teresa's strong conviction about alleviating poverty took her to Kolkata (Calcutta) to spend the rest of her adult life and old age helping the poor. Her conviction has led her to become one of the greatest humanitarians to have lived on Earth. Who is the Mother Teresa of Africa? We certainly have a few, but we should have many more.

Where are the men and women of conviction in Africa today? Where are Africans with strong convictions that are willing to die for a cause today? Where are African leaders willing to do all they can to end violence against women and children? Where are leaders with conviction who must stand against inequality of wages between men and women?

Where are African leaders with strong conviction to provide solutions to end the massive overflow of street children? Where are African leaders with conviction to end the epidemic of corruption? Are there African leaders who can end the abuse of African employees by African and non-African employers? Can African leaders be sympathetic enough to people with physical challenges and provide them all with wheelchairs? Can Africans take care of their orphans and not always leave these orphans to be supported by Westerners?

I thank God that, at least the young people I have interacted with, are developing strong convictions to make a difference in their communities. During my Africa, It's Time! book tour, in June 2017, I met Divine, a very remarkable young person. Divine is one of those quiet girls that do not say much but she has strong conviction that is rare for young people her age. After I talked about my book, she came to see me and asked me if she could buy my book. I thought she was not serious enough when she asked me that question.

I told her that I was remaining with only four copies and that the book might be expensive for her. She asked me how much. I told her that it was $20 USD. She asked me to please let her buy one copy. I gave her my book to go read for about two hours and then make up her mind if she still wanted it. After reading it for two hours, she told me that she must buy a copy.

I wanted to know why, of all the students who loved the book, she was the one so determined to have a copy. Then she told me her story. She wanted to start her own organization to help children whose families cannot afford to educate them or send them to school. I asked her how she planned to do that. She told me that she was going to start right away by working during summer holidays to start saving money for her organization. She told me that she does not want to see any child not attending school. I was amazed by such conviction from such a young girl.

On graduation day, June 17, 2017 at Gitega International Academy, her mother came. Then she brought her mother and told me that her mother had brought the money to buy a copy of my book. I gave her an autographed copy, and she had such a huge smile on her face. I was even more impressed to see that Divine, who did not have an educated mother as her mother could not speak English or French, had such passion and conviction to educated the less fortunate children.

For someone from a family where her mother cannot even speak any of the modern languages to be that determined to make a significant difference in the lives of underprivileged children is something amazing.

If Africa can invest in people like Divine and others like her through mentoring, teaching and coaching, these young people will be remarkable leaders of the future. It is this kind of conviction that we hope can start penetrating into adult Africans' consciences. If Africa could have more leaders of Divine's conviction; it would not take us long to build the kind of Africa that is just, peaceful and prosperous for all.

I have been privileged to meet these young Africans who love Africa with everything in them, and it gives me hope that the continent of Africa will soon become a head and cease to be a tail. But, we must make sure that this hope does not turn into unrealistic or wishful thinking.

These young people need leaders with conviction to start mentoring and developing them. We need to train and equip them fully so that when their time comes, they will be ready to pick up the baton and run with it to the finish line. The young people I had the opportunity to equip and develop at Gitega International Academy, and many others like them in Africa and throughout the world, can be used by God to lead Africa to the Promised Land.

We must make sure we light the fire in the young people. We must continue to help them grow in those strong convictions so that when their time to lead comes, they would have reached a place where to retreat or to surrender will no longer be viable options for them.

For Africa to emerge out of the mess of poverty, corruption, injustice, exploitation, abuse of public funds, extreme selfishness, and other evils, we need leaders with strong convictions who will combat these evils head on. Africa desperately needs leaders that love their countries and their continent enough to the point of death.

African leaders must now develop strong convictions so that they can start doing away with the pursuit of selfish success. True leaders are the ones who focus on community success. Success must be enjoyed by many not just one person. It is my prayer that our African leaders will be able to read this book and apply it in their efforts to build a just, peaceful, and prosperous Africa.

I am not against personal development or personal success because it is the collective of those personal achievements that can lead to community success. We have to avoid the pitfall of socialism or communism that discourages personal success. People tend to achieve more at a community level when they have had to overcome challenges at the personal level. When we each use our God-given skills and talents at a personal level,

we can then use our personal success to the benefit of our community.

Even in the area of strong convictions, it starts with an individual convicted to make a difference in his or her life, not
only to his benefit alone, but to the benefit of the community. If
I am strongly convicted to contribute toward ending corruption
in my community, I have to start at my personal level to resolve
not to be corrupted. When I can clearly overcome that, then I
must also speak against it so as to influence my community to
join me in the fight against corruption.

I think of great Africans, such as PLO Lumumba, and the
great work they are doing personally to affect continental and
even global change in this area of corruption and other evils
of this world. PLO Lumumba is such a great ambassador that I
believe God is using to speak to our generation about revitaliz-
ing our good, moral, and strong convictions to help our African
continent especially to seriously deal with our problems.

What has happened to us Africans that we have become
enemies of our own consciences so much that we subdue them
and refuse to listen to them? What has happened to us that we
have become so selfish that the suffering of millions around us
does not bother us anymore? What has happened to us that we
have ceased to have convictions that move us to actions that
make a positive difference in our communities? What has happened to us that we have now locked ourselves in the beggar
mindset?

**The beggar mindset is an evil way of life that cripples
us with greed.** It makes a person pursue extreme selfish gain at
any cost. The beggar mindset sees everyone as a threat. It makes
people desperate to make more, to gain more and to acquire
more. People with the beggar mindset are willing to steal even
from the poor to add more to their over-abundance that they
never even enjoy because they are too busy chasing for more
selfish gain.

This beggar mindset is killing Africans. I am not talking about politicians only. I am talking about most of our leaders. Obviously, politicians and government leaders are the ones who have more access to the community goods. But in general, it is about all African leaders. I remember when former Prime Minister Brian Mulroney was on trial for allegedly accepting bribery worth $300,000 CAD from a citizen. He spent many days going through the trial. He was found innocent, but I could not be more proud of Canada and our justice system. I thought for a moment, what could have happened if Mulroney was an African leader? We are talking not even half a million dollars.

Our African leaders become millionaires within a month or two in power, but a former Canadian Prime Minister went on trial for $300,000. It is clear that, while Canada is not perfect, we can be proud of ourselves for the level we have reached in terms of making everyone, including top leaders, accountable. Africa desperately needs to get rid of its beggar mindset. African leaders must start championing causes that make a difference in their communities. We have become the only continent that is going backwards, from bad to worse, and we seem not to be bothered by it. Let us wake up. Let us be moved by what moves God. Let us search our hearts and find those hidden or buried convictions that will help us reverse the trends and start moving forward.

Let us see any begging mother on the street as if she was our mother. Let us look at street children as if they were our own children. Let us put ourselves in the shoes of the poor servants who have to take care of their families with less than a dollar a day. Let us put ourselves in the place of the defenceless mother that is raped in front of her own children. Let us put ourselves in the shoes of children who have to work 12 hours a day in the mines and be robbed of any chance of education and normal childhood. Why are we leaders when we cannot stand up for our people that we claim to lead? Oh, Africa, what has happened to you that you have sealed your conscience to never feel the unbelievable pain and everyday torture of others? Decide today to revive your conscience and the strong convictions in your heart and act. You can do it. We can do it.

The world is desperately looking for men and women of strong convictions who will be willing to pay whatever price it takes to be used by God to bring deliverance from bondage. Leaders have chosen to subdue their consciences so that they cannot act.

Think of the whole issue of gun control: what will it take to make a decision to establish strong and firm gun control laws? How many people have to die before it has to be obvious that gun control must be put in place? Haven't we lost too many people? After the Vegas mass shooting in October 2017, the same rhetoric surfaced that this is not the time to talk about gun control legislation. And many victims are asking, when will it ever be time, as it never seems to be the right time?

Think of racism and discrimination: what will it take for leaders to rise up and put an end to it? How many innocent people have to die or lose their jobs for leaders to take firm actions? Is it really that difficult to see that racism is totally wrong and that it must be fought by any decent human being? How can anyone justify hating a fellow human being?

God is calling for leaders who will stand up to do the right thing, even when it could cost their lives. In fact, it is surprising that even Christian leaders have forgotten that living for Christ is very much about picking up our cross and following Him. It is about fighting to establish God's righteousness on Earth. It is not Christian to see injustice and decide to be silent. A leader must speak up and defend a cause, even though it may cost him his position or his own life.

Consider the story of John the Baptist. When he saw the wrong that King Herod did by marrying his brother's wife, he spoke against it. He knew it could cost his life, but telling the truth was more important than living. The world needs men and women of such conviction as John the Baptist. This is why

Martin Luther King's statement is celebrated, because he was true to it:

> *"If a man has not discovered what he is willing to die for, he is not fit to live." (42)*

We, especially leaders, are not here on Earth just to show presence. It is not as if it is enough just for people to see us around, to see that we exist. No. We have been put on earth to make a difference in our lives and the lives of others. Each one of us must discover something we can champion, something we can live for and something we can eventually be willing to die for. That is what it means to have conviction!

Lord, make me a person of conviction so that I can make a positive difference in this world and to your glory!

Application of Day 23

1. What does it mean to be a person of strong convictions?

2. Who among world leaders, past or present, had or has strong convictions? Explain why you picked them.

3. What can happen to our world if we have more young people with strong convictions like Divine?

4. Are you a person of strong convictions? What are you standing for or against?

INTENTIONAL

Intentional means to be purposeful in word and in action!

When one wants to truly help others, to make a tangible difference, he or she must be intentional. Things do not just happen because we wish they would. Being intentional is going beyond just wishing or hoping. Intentionality is a step of decisiveness and a deliberate choice to do something.

You can be intentional about many different things. For example, you can be intentional about the kind of friends you want in your life. Some people just want anyone in their lives because they feel so alone without having someone as a friend. Some have married the wrong person just because they just wanted a wife or a husband. A friend is someone very important in someone's life. It is best to be intentional about who you spend time with, because friendships have the power to determine your future. It is said that people can show you your future simply by looking at your friends. So, friendship is one area which we cannot, especially leaders, take lightly; we have to be intentional in who we embrace as friends. If you want to be successful, you have to find a way to make friends with successful people.

I remember a cousin who was poor, but all his friends were rich and very successful. People used to wonder how such a poor person would be able to make such successful people his friends. They did not know that he was very intentional about becoming rich himself. One day, he managed to become a friend to the owner of the sugar company in our area, called Sucrerie de Kiliba. The owner gave him a contract to be the middle person, so that people who would buy sugar would buy it from him. In a matter of months, he became very rich, even more successful than all his rich friends. His intentionality paid off, and he got what he wanted out of it.

We often get what we intentionally want. If you want to be a good person, you have to intentionally surround yourself with good people. The Bible is very clear that bad company can turn you into a bad person. Hence, the need to intentionally avoid and to actually flee from bad company!

"Do not be misled; 'Bad company corrupts good character.'" 1 Corinthians 15:33

How intentional are you in the way you live your life? There are many areas of life that require intentionality. Purposeful living requires being intentional in the way we live our life. To be intentional about helping the poor is to find the poor and tangibly make a difference in their lives. To intentionally love your children is to clearly communicate and do things that demonstrate that you truly love them. We, Africans, need to be intentional about changing what is wrong and enhancing what is right in our society.

We must ask ourselves, what in our society needs our help? We need to sometimes ask ourselves, who needs our services? We need to be intentionally concerned about the interests of others and not just our own interests.

As Africans, we need to intentionally graduate from the over-pursuit of accumulation of things, the material stuff, often non-essential stuff. There are many people who serve as examples that come to mind. Let me mention a few:

President Thomas Sankara: President Sankara was the President of Burkina Faso for four years. He was very intentional at fighting for Africa's total independence and self-sufficiency. He was the poor's friend, as he himself was one of them. He drove a small Volkswagen. He died poor. He stood up for the oppressed and the marginalized. He defended and established women's rights.

Bishop John Osmers: This man has worked hard all his life. He left New Zealand to serve as priest, and later as bishop, in Africa. He constantly lived in small houses and drove beaten-up vehicles while spending all his money sponsoring the education of many Africans.

Dr. Ernest Schmidt: This man was a gynecologist at a main hospital in Canada for many years. With his wife Leona Schmidt, they lived modestly all their life together as missionaries in the then Belgian Congo and in Canada. They decided the best way to spend their money was supporting various causes, rather than spending it on themselves.

Retired Deputy Chief Justice George Baynton and his wife Sylvia Baynton are two very intentional people. They spend their money funding many causes, such as supporting missionaries, orphans, children campers at Lakeview Bible Camp, and others. They are a true testimony to what being a Christian truly is.

Why are many Africans focused on simply satisfying self-interests? Go ask many leaders of orphanages, "Who are the children's sponsors?", and you will discover that it is almost exclusively Westerners. Can we as Africans go back to our *Ubuntu*? Can we give birth to intentional living and intentional caring of others?

I am calling on each of us to become intentional about solving our African problems and intentional about building an Africa that is the best place on Earth for all to live in. To build that kind of Africa, we must be intentional. Tough problems like the ones we have in Africa require intentional leaders to solve them.

Some problems require extra effort, real intention, to properly and effectively deal with them. Even Jesus, knowing that some problems require more than just casual prayer, told His disciples in Matthew 17:21 that some kind of demons only go out by prayer and fasting. The disciples were to put in extra effort. African leaders must put in extra effort to truly solve the difficult problems of Africa.

To be effective, a leader must be intentional. A leader must be intentional in the way he relates to people. He must be intentional in the way he listens to people. He must be intentional in the way he puts his team together. He must be thoughtful and purposeful. A leader knows that the consequences of his decisions and actions impact his whole community. He must be intentional at making the kind of decisions that will benefit his community.

What does it mean to be intentional? It is to be purposeful in word and action. It is about living a life that is meaningful and fulfilling. It is about making thoughtful choices. It means actively interacting and engaging with one's life.

Leaders are responsible for improving the conditions of living for their people; so they must make decisions and plans that are intentionally in the best interests of their people. It is one thing to make decisions and actions that only affect you as a person, and it is another thing when the consequences of your decisions and actions will impact the entire community.

For example, when the Prime Minister of Canada decides to reduce or increase taxes, like when Stephen Harper reduced GST to 5%, it affected everyone. So a leader cannot make decisions lightly. Great leaders are intentionally positive and make decisions based on what is good for the people and not necessarily themselves.

Selfish leaders make decisions based on their self-interests. Intentional living is living with a purpose. It is having a cause to fight for. It is living as if every minute and every second matters. Intentional leaders do not waste time but use it to make a positive difference in their communities.

Is it not sad when you see people living every day without a purpose? For them, every day comes and ends, every week begins and ends, every month begins and finishes, and every year starts and ends without any purpose to it. They live with no intention to make something, to change any situation, or to be involved in any noble cause.

They exist on planet Earth for their 70 or 80 years and go to the grave with nothing to show for their time. They leave a very big question mark for those who have to put a message on their tomb stone, as no one knows what to truly say about them. The only viable option is to write that they existed on Earth for 70 or 80 years. How sad is that?

Have you ever intentionally taken time to ask God which causes you can champion? Are you living for yourself? Do you care about the suffering of others? You are not on planet Earth by chance. God intentionally designed you with a purpose. His will is that you live an intentional life. It is God's intention that you fulfill His mission for you on Earth. God wants you to discover what you are here on Earth for so that you can intentionally work hard at accomplishing His designed purpose for you.

Mere existence is not a viable option for any human being. Human life matters so much that we must be intentionally involved in making it count for eternity. So, find out what He wants you to do for Him and His people. You do not want to go to Heaven and when God asks you what you did with the gifts He gave you; all you can say is that you buried your gifts and left them unused.

Doing nothing with the gifts God gave you is deciding to be pessimistic, lazy, and disobedient. God gave you not only talents and gifts, but He also gave you the ability to make use of them. All you need is intentionality. You must decide to use what He gave you and you will be able to add to or multiply your gifts. When you do nothing with what He gave you, you are guilty of disobedience and laziness. That is what happened to the man who was given a talent and refused to use it to make profit:

> *"Then the man who had received the one talent came, 'Master', he said, 'I knew that you are a hard man, harvesting where you have not sown and gathering where you have not scattered seed. So I was afraid and went out and hid your talent in the ground. See, here is what belongs to you. His master replied, 'You wicked, lazy servant!...You should have put my money on deposit with the bankers, so that when I returned I would have received interest."*
> Matthew 25:24-27

It is very clear from this passage above that God has given us talents to use to produce something. Like in business or investment, we are to make profit. And there is no exception; everyone has received talents. So, when you do not use the talents God gave you, you are wasting his resources He invested in you.

Here is something to think about. There is something that should have been done that is not yet done because it is waiting for you to do it. God has your specific assignment that keeps waiting for you to be intentional about taking charge. Do not be like Jonah, who thought he could get away from God's plan in his life. Find out your own God-given mission on Earth and be intentional about fulfilling it.

There may be a specific orphan child waiting for you to adopt him or her. There may be a specific poor child waiting for school fees from you. There may be a poor mother waiting for a micro-loan from you to start her business. There may be lost people waiting for you to share the gospel with them. There are farmers waiting to learn from you the best farming practices.

There is no shortage of causes; all that is missing is you being intentional at resolving to do that which God has specifically created you to do. My prayer for you is that you become intentional at finding that specific God-given mission for you, and then be intentional at fulfilling it.

Lord, make me intentional in the way I live, the way I talk to people, in my plans, and in all I do!

Application of Day 24

1. What does intentional living mean?

2. Why is mere existence not an option for a human being?

3. What is your life's purpose?

4. What is the one thing or one cause you intentionally care about that you want to make a difference in, even though it could cost your life?

5. Why have today's leaders become so intention-less?

6. Are you intentional? Do you love your spouse and children intentionally? Do you intentionally make a difference in the lives of the poor, the mistreated, the oppressed, and the disadvantaged?

FINISHER

To finish is to complete whatever assignment, task, or project we started!

Aleader does not just start something; he makes sure he reaches the finish line. A mission must be complete before a leader can move on. Our God is a finisher. Before He would rest, He finished creating. He worked six consecutive days before He took a day of rest. But today, people want to rest before even starting. Rest comes after work, not before work.

Jesus Christ, our Lord and Master completed the saving mission He came to do on Earth. He was born a baby in a manger. He grew up just like any one of us. He trained twelve disciples. He preached and taught the gospel to many. He was crucified and died on the cross. On the cross, He proclaimed *"It is finished."* He was buried in a sealed tomb. He rose again after three days, as He had promised. He ascended to Heaven to reign forever.

Jesus was pleased with Himself, not just by starting his mission, but by finishing it. He was pleased that in finishing or completing His mission, in fact His Father's mission, on Earth, He had brought glory to His Father. This is why He was proud to be able to say:

"I have brought you glory on earth by finishing the work you gave me to do." John 17:4

The human tendency is to keep starting something new that appears appealing, without having finished what was started before. A leader must resist the temptation of jumping on to new things while he still has unfinished business. Jesus completed his mission on Earth, and then He left the next phase of the mission to the Holy Spirit, who would use the disciples to carry on the mission. So, a leader must then decide to finish what he started before starting something new.

It is important to note that a leader can have a number of projects in his plan, but he must have a prioritized schedule in which to accomplish those projects. Most projects require being accomplished one at a time. This means then that a finisher type of leader, even though he may have many projects in the plan, would have a sequence, a schedule in which to finish the first project, the second, the third, and then the fourth. The key is to finish the first project before starting the second one.

It is important to know that just finishing should not be the ultimate goal. The goal instead must be finishing well. So yes, we must finish what we started but we must finish well. The goal is not only to reach the end, but to end well. Finishing a project means it is 100% completed. There are times when we are quick to claim victory when we have only done part of the job. Getting to 99% completion is not full completion. To finish means to fully complete the job that was assigned.

As a leader, it is important to know when to finish or call it quits. Sometimes, leaders keep going when the people under their leadership have already put an end to their leadership. I remember a pastor whose congregation was already done with him, but he kept going on and on. The church went from about 150 people to less than 30 people, but he kept going. Members were too embarrassed to tell him that he was finished and he should now leave. But you would think that he should have seen that himself, because that is what the congregation was hoping he would realize, but he did not.

This happens a lot with political leaders as well. We all know many African leaders who could have been heroes if they had stayed half their time in power. But they overstayed, and we know how some of them ended up being forced out in the most demeaning manor. I will not go into much detail here, but if you are interested in more details on the issue of overstaying, you can read my first book, *Africa, It's Time!*

In the West, leaders usually can tell that their approval rating has gone down and decide to resign before everyone is calling for them to step down. Sometimes, leaders in the West will conduct a leadership review to gauge where they stand in terms of their leadership approval; if it is too low, they step down. Sometimes they end their careers even when they could still perform at a decent level. As I said before regarding accountability, former Premier of Alberta, Ralph Klein, resigned when his approval rating went down.

In Africa, we still have a lot of work to do in that regard. I understand that sometimes things are complicated, and there may be genuine reasons for a leader to continue a little bit longer to finish what he started. We have to be able to accommodate exceptions. But as a rule of thumb, when people no longer want you, know that your leadership there is finished; it is done. It is time you move on to something else. Overstaying almost always damages your record and your reputation. Finishing and leaving when people are still speaking well of you can often put you on the list of great leaders. President Julius Nyerere left at the right time and today, even after his death, his legacy still lives on and he is regarded as the father of the nation of Tanzania.

A leader must aim at finishing whatever assignment God gave him 100%. God wants our loyalty to complete the mission 100%. The Bible tells the story of King Saul's disobedience due to incompletion. God gave him an assignment, and he did a part of it, but deliberately refused to fully complete the job. He thought this would be enough for God as well; he was wrong.

> "Now go, attack the Amalekites and totally destroy all that belongs to them. Do not spare them; put to death men and women, children and infants, cattle and sheep, camels and donkeys. So Saul summoned the men and mustered them at Telaim—two hundred thousand foot soldiers and ten thousand from Judah. Saul went to the city of Amalek and set an ambush in the ravine. Then he said to the Kenites, 'Go away, leave the Amalekites so that I do not destroy you along with them; for you showed kindness to all the Israelites when they came up out of Egypt.' So the Kenites moved away from the Amalekites. Then Saul attacked the Amalekites all the way from Havilah to Shur, near the eastern border of Egypt. He took Agag king of the Amalekites alive, and all his people he totally destroyed with the sword. But Saul and the army spared Agag and the best of the sheep and cattle, the fat calves and lambs—everything that was good." 1 Samuel 15:3-9

Sometimes we initiate a project, and at the beginning, we are so excited about it. But as we continue working on it, we realize that it is either not a good project or we find out that we are completely unable to finish it. In that case, a leader must be willing to end that project.

One of the problems we have in Africa is starting projects and not finishing them. You go to the D.R. Congo, and you will find roads that the government started building and three and four years later, they are actually in worse condition than they were before they started.

The road from Uvira to the border with Burundi is less than 20 kilometres long. People were promised the building of a good road. The worn out, old road was ripped out. People waited for the new road but it was not built. Years later, the road is worse than before they ripped it out. We drove through it in June 2017. The road had become so dusty that when you travel it by motorbike, you reach the destination covered in dust.

Leaders must refrain from starting a project that they have no means or will to finish. A leader must do his homework first to make sure what he is about to start he is able to complete. The Bible urges us to count the cost first and see to it that what we start we will finish:

> *"Suppose one of you wants to build a tower. Won't you first sit down and estimate the cost to see if you have enough money to complete it?"* Luke 14:28

Let me make a bit of a clarification in regard to planning properly before you start. Proper or adequate planning is very important, but over-planning can be damaging. Some people live in the planning phase but seem never to go to the next step, the execution of the project. It is important to plan sufficiently, but after that, one must move into execution. Once you have adequately planned then you need to move to the execution phase so that you start moving toward the finishing line.

The tendency to over-plan can sometimes work as procrastination. Do not lock yourself in the planning stage, or you may never get started doing the actual project. Prepare, but once you have done that, get started on the project. Some people live their lifetime in a planning stage, and no wonder at the end of their lives, they have nothing to show for their over-planning. Over-planning can easily make you miss the opportunity, as some opportunities require quick action to take them or they are gone. John Wooden says it well:

> *"When opportunity comes, it's too late to prepare."* (43)

Getting to the finish line can be very rewarding and full of joy. I remember when I started writing my first book, *Africa, It's Time!,* I sometimes wondered when I was ever going to finish.

After I completed the manuscript and sent it to the publisher, the publisher returned it with so many corrections to be made. The whole process was long, and to be honest, sometimes tiring and discouraging. But the day I held my book in my hands, I was overjoyed. The work I put in, very hard work, was worth it. That work paid amazing dividends. I learned from the book writing process that hard work, endurance and patience can be challenging, but when we get to the finish line, the joy and the sense of fulfillment outweighs the pain endured in the process. Brian Tracy says it well:

> "Whenever you complete a task of any size or importance, you feel a surge of energy, enthusiasm, and self-esteem. The more important the completed task, the happier, more confident and more powerful you feel about yourself and your world." (44)

What kind of a leader are you? Do you finish what you started? Are you the type who keeps starting? Do you start and finish one project at a time, or do you try to start and finish too many projects at the same time? I know it is tempting to start on a new and interesting project without finishing the first one.

Right now, as I am getting to the finish line on this book, I am already thinking of another book that I would like to write. The subject is very appealing to me as I see it to be as relevant as the book I am about to finish. But I must discipline myself not to start a new project without finishing the one I am working on. Jesus finished his work on Earth, at least in his human-divine nature, and then He sent the Holy Spirit to take over. A leader must start and finish one thing before starting another.

Do you work with a priority list? Do you value doing proper planning before you embark on a project? Do you over-plan so much that you live in the planning and never get to execute the project? These are important questions that we need to ask ourselves when planning to do a project.

I have learned this truth: planning is very important, but over-planning usually does more harm than good. A leader is one who starts a project and makes sure he gets to the finish line. A good beginning is a prerequisite to a good finish, but a good start is meaningless if there is no good ending. So do not just start, but make sure you finish and finish well.

Poor leaders have no respect for time. That is why, even after 30 years in power, they are still trying to finish the plan they started 30 years ago. It is also one of the reasons why some of them want to stay in power for 40 years or until they die. When you plan and execute without delays or procrastination, you are likely to finish on time or ahead of schedule. Finishing the task or completing the plan on schedule is a leader's best friend. Starting and finishing leads to success.

Lord, give me all I need to finish what you have allowed me to start.

Application of Day 25

1. God worked for six days straight and then rested on the 7th day. Why is it that we work five days today and rest for two days?

2. God always finishes what He starts. What is happening to humans today that we seem to be always starting and never finishing?

3. Can you explain why both under-planning and over-planning will damage your project?

4. Do you finish what you started?

5. What can you do to make sure you are not constantly starting new projects before finishing others?

6. How can the tendency to over-plan work as procrastination?

DEPENDABLE

Two similar qualities to dependable are reliable and trustworthy!

When you lead people, you must be dependable. Your team must be able to know that they can rely on you. People want to know if you are dependable enough for them to follow you. Dependable means you do not change with every wind. A leader must be trustworthy, because without people trusting you, you are simply imposing your power on them.

Leaders who are Christians must depend and rely on God to help them lead well. Trusting in God as your leader is truly a prerequisite to successful leadership. We already know that leading people is one of the most difficult jobs anyone can have. Depending on our human strength and abilities will soon prove insufficient for us to lead well.

Dependency on God is therefore the greatest asset a leader can have. You can have as much trust, reliance, confidence or dependence in yourself but when you face serious difficulties in your leadership, trust, reliance, or confidence in yourself will often disappoint you. Only dependence, trust, and reliance in God will always prove to be sufficient. It is only when a leader depends on God that his people can also depend on him or her. And this is the fact: your people have to trust you for you to be dependable enough to lead them. You cannot lead people who do not trust you. The last thing you want to do is to force people to trust you. They have to see in you good reasons for them to trust you and to see that you are dependable and reliable.

To be dependable and trustworthy means that what you said you will do, you will do, and complete it on time. Things may happen beyond your control, and it is possible that you may not be able to deliver the service you promised to deliver on the agreed time. A delay can be acceptable with good reason. But I have seen tailors or mechanics that promise people they will get the job done in three days, and three weeks later, it is still not complete.

Some people have sealed their consciences so that, even when they clearly broke their promise, they do not feel guilty or bad about it. Instead, they start making excuse after excuse. They lie as much as they breathe and are not bothered by it. They want people to give them business but they do not care about their negative actions that push their customers away. They do not realize that when they completely lose people's trust, they will suffer for it, as people will one-by-one stop giving them business. A leader must make every effort to be dependable, reliable, and trustworthy. Trust earns you a better reputation and, consequently, more business. Dependability makes it easy for people to follow you.

One of my cousin-in-laws was an expert tailor. He would make clothes that fit so well that he started getting more and more business. When he started getting more business, he refused to know his limits and started taking orders in big numbers, and he could not finish in due time. I remember giving him materials to make me a nice jacket. He promised to finish it in two weeks. The two weeks turned into months and a year, and I realized he would never finish it.

One day, after more than a year since I gave him the material, I went to his house where he also had his shop to ask him to give me back the materials if he could not make me the jacket. When he saw me from far away, he went to hide in the bedroom. He thought I did not see him. Then when I arrived at his home, my cousin (whom I call my sister in our culture), his wife lied to me to protect her husband and told me that he had gone out to a funeral. Knowing that he was there because I saw him, I stayed for a long time until he could not hide any longer.

He came out of the room and his wife pretended she did not know he was in, and said, "I thought you had gone to the funeral." And then he said he had a headache and decided to take a rest. That day, I stopped thinking of him as someone I could consider to make my clothes. Others discovered this too and, one by one, stopped giving him business until he lost everything.

It is always in a leader's best interest to be reliable and trustworthy. People you are leading must know that they can depend on you to protect them against any attack of the enemy. When your people cannot depend on you to protect them, you have ceased to be their leader. A leader must protect and defend his people, as they depend and rely on his leadership to do so. When a leader cannot be depended on by his people, then he must call it quits.

True leaders know that when they have lost people's trust, they must vacate their positions. It is not leader-like, when people do not want you, to remain in power by force. If you cannot defend your people, if you cannot be trusted to protect your people, then ask yourself a question: why do you still think you are their leader?

Take, for example, the people of Beni in North East Kivu, in the Democratic Republic of Congo. They get killed every day. Their mothers and daughters get raped every day. Even in 2017, they are still enduring unbelievable torture every day, terrible crimes against humanity that they have endured for more than a decade and yet they have a so-called government. If you are a government that cannot protect your people, leave office and give a chance to a new leader who can protect people and in whom people can depend and rely on.

What is wrong with us Africans that we can never admit we have failed and consequently do the right thing, to resign? How many people have to die before we admit we have failed in our leadership? I think that being truly powerful is being able to admit when we have failed. To do otherwise is fooling one self, and is very detrimental to leadership.

Late President Mobutu was honoured for a long time during his long presidency for his ability to defend and protect his people. He won every war until the last one. People could rely on him to protect them and that helped him to maintain a measure of popularity for some time.

Even though the collapse of the economy and his dictatorship drastically brought down his approval rating, his ability to defend and protect his people for so long, over many wars, remains his greatest legacy. We will remember that when he could no longer defend his people, he could no longer maintain himself in power.

African leaders must be courageous and powerful enough to give up power when they lose people's dependency. It is by admitting that you have failed that you truly becomes victorious and powerful; otherwise, you are fooling yourself, not the people. As a leader, it is important to have a few true friends or partners that you can rely on to tell you the truth.

Once in a while, ask them for feedback. Ask them how they see your leadership. Ask them if they find you reliable, trustworthy, and dependable. Ask them what people think you are. It is important for you, as a leader, to know what people think of you. Jesus is God, and yet it was important for him to hear what people said He was. He also wanted to know what his disciples thought of Him.

"When Jesus came to the region of Caesarea Philippi, he asked his disciples, 'Who do people say the Son of Man is?' They replied, 'Some say John the Baptist; others say Elijah; and still others, Jeremiah or one of the prophets.' 'But what about you?' he asked. 'Who do you say I am?' Simon Peter answered, 'You are the Messiah, the Son of the living God.' Jesus replied, 'Blessed are you, Simon son of Jonah, for this was not revealed to you by flesh and blood, but by my Father in heaven.'" Matthew 16:13-17

People want a leader they can depend on. The moment they know that their leader can no longer defend them, that leader ceases to be their leader, at least in their hearts. King Saul's leadership encountered trouble when his people could no longer depend on him as much as they could depend on David, who was not yet a king at that time.

"When the men were returning home after David had killed the Philistine, the women came out from all the towns of Israel to meet King Saul with singing and dancing, with joyful songs and with tambourines and lyres. As they danced, they sang: 'Saul has slain his thousands, and David his tens of thousands.' Saul was very angry; this refrain displeased him greatly. 'They have credited David with tens of thousands,' he thought, 'but me with only thousands. What more can he get but the kingdom?' And from that time on Saul kept a close eye on David." 1 Samuel 18:6-9

Wisdom requires that when people can no longer depend on a leader, that the leader should call it quits and find someone else to take over. When Saul realized that people no longer depended on him as much as they depended on David, he should have approached David and found a way to hand over the leadership to him. Saul should have known that planning to kill David only made David more popular. The story of David and Saul is a great lesson to leaders who overstay their welcome.

When people have stopped depending on you to lead them, you should leave before it is too late.

Do not cling to power when everyone wants you out. This is particularly important for African leaders. Why overstay when people no longer trust you and no longer find you dependable? You may still be holding on to power, but in reality, you are no longer the leader. To be a leader, you need to have people who want you as their leader. When they clearly do not want you, they do not trust you. The sooner you leave the better.

To hold on to power when you have lost people's trust is forcing people into a relationship, and as we know, forced relationships do not work. When your husband or your wife does not trust you, such a marriage is standing on sand and not on firm foundation. The smallest wind will blow that foundation away. You remove trust, dependence, and reliability in any relationship, and you can be assured there is really nothing left.

African leaders must continually remember that there is life, good life, after their current leadership role. Imagine all you can still do after the presidency or any leadership role you are clinging on to! Please know that the seat you are holding on to is not the only thing you can do. There is so much you can do after you peacefully leave your seat. You can be an advisor to your successor and to other leaders. You can find a cause to support and advocate for. You can be a consultant to aspiring leaders.

Lord, make me a reliable person and a leader that others can depend on, the kind of leader people can trust!

Application of Day 26

1. Why must a Christian leader first depend on God?

2. Why is it important for a leader to peacefully leave when his people have ceased depending on him?

3. What lessons do we learn from King Saul overstaying in power and trying to kill David, who was God's anointed one?

4. What are the advantages of leaving on time?

5. What does it mean to be dependable and to be reliable?

6. Ask yourself, "Am I reliable?" Do people trust you?

MOTIVATOR

Two other titles for a motivator are cheerleader and fire-lighter!

A leader is a motivated person. A leader motivates people. A leader cheers the team up. A leader is a fire-lighter; he lights the inner fire inside others. A leader cheers everyone on the team, including the less talented. A leader celebrates everyone's success. A cheerleader builds your morale. This is why in most sports, teams win more on their home courts than when playing on their opponents' grounds. At home, they have their crowd to cheer them on. They have even paid cheerleaders to cheer them on. This is why sport teams fight throughout the season to secure their home court advantage. Not that the home court advantage would guarantee them a championship, but it at least gives them an added advantage. There is power and energy in being cheered for.

A cheerleader gives a boost that can help you overcome the giant. What a fire-lighter does is empower you. They pump you up. They bring out the best in you that you could not see by yourself. When someone tells you genuinely that you are capable, that you are smart, and that you can do it, suddenly you start believing in the power inside you. And when that happens, the sky is the limit on what you can achieve.

Motivation gives people energy. It re-energizes the one who was about to give up. Motivation has the power to give birth to new hope, new belief, and new possibilities in a person. When motivated, a person becomes stronger than he would otherwise be without it. Motivation has the power to instill in someone confidence to succeed in what seemed difficult.

This is why a parent's influence on his/her child is second to none. When we speak positively to our children, we cheer them up. When we light the fire in them, we enable them to be achievers. Motivating children is one of the primary responsibilities of parents. It is reasonable to say that motivating your children is as important as feeding them food.

One day, my daughter Savana surprised me. She showed me her favourite book, the story of Sojourner Truth. Sojourner Truth is a remarkable Afro-American former slave who fought against injustice in the 19th century. But that was not the only surprise I got from Savana. She also was reading another story of a 6-year-old Afro-American who changed an entire White community's attitude.

I had not talked to Savana much about racial discriminations or injustice. But she was still able to see that advocacy for the oppressed and discriminated in my everyday life. She imitated it and started developing her own advocacy. When she was in grade five, she noticed one classmate who was unpopular. This particular girl was not doing as well in school as other students. Other kids picked on her. She was an outcast among her peers. So Savana decided to be her friend. She started spending time with her and playing with her. She decided to be her advocate and to include her in all activities. She refused to join any group that would only want her and not her new-found friend. And because Savana was one of the top-performing students in her class, her friends were forced to accept her friend because she would have nothing to do with them if they rejected this girl.

One day, her friend thanked her for being there for her and for having cheered her up and motivated her. On her birthday, Savana was one of the select few friends she invited.

Savana has always been that kind of a person, one who cheers up and motivates others. When we served in Burundi as missionaries, Savana had a close friend who was also our neighbour. This particular girl was also in the same class with Savana in school. When she came to our house the first time, she just sat in one spot and would not move. There was no smile on her face. But Savana quickly invited her into her room, and started making games and plays that, slowly but surely, made her friend start to smile. Savana initiated her into play, as she would lend her clothes to her friend and they would play dress-up. It was amazing to see the transformation in her friend after Savana took so much time to cheer her up and to be her fire-lighter.

A leader must make motivating others a priority. This world is full of beaten-up people without anyone to cheer them up. God has put us here on Earth to bring joy to others, to cheer people up. We may never know how many suicides, depressions, or diseases we have prevented by simply cheering, fire-lighting, and motivating people.

If you are a leader, ask yourself these questions: Do you have someone or a group of people you are cheering on? Who are you fire-lighting? Who are you motivating? What about your family, your children; do you cheer them up? Do you light the fire in them? Do you motivate them? What about yourself, who motivates you? Who cheers you up? Who fire-lights you? Everyone needs a motivator, someone to cheer them up and to lift them up. A leader must also have a motivator, a cheerleader, a fire-lighter, to refill his tank and keep him moving forward with strength and confidence.

Children especially need parental motivation. Children who are motivated, lifted up, and cheered on by their families tend to feel good about themselves and, consequently, their ability to perform well increases. It is unfortunate sometimes that the parents who are supposed to be cheerleaders, fire-lighters, and motivators to their children are the direct opposite of it so much that the children are happier when mom and/or dad are away. It is very sad when the absence of parents means party time, so much that the children wish the parents stayed away forever.

This is similar to workplaces where the boss is the opposite of a cheerleader, fire-lighter, or motivator. Everyone at work is praying for the boss to go on never-ending business trips. It is like we say in French, and I am paraphrasing it:

"A l'absence du chat, la souris dance en paix!"

which means,

"In the absence of a cat, the mouse dances in peace!"

What a tragedy to be a leader whose presence is not wanted or needed! It is every leader's responsibility to boost the morale of his employees or his people. The fact is that, when people are motivated by the leader, they produce more and the leader and his company benefit from it.

The same goes for any leader too; if a leader is motivated, fire-lighted, and cheered for, his confidence, self-esteem, and energy go up, and he performs better than if he did not get such motivation. This is why when a leader has his wife as his primary cheerleader, fire-lighter, and motivator; he is most likely going to succeed in whatever project he embarks on. Obviously, that is not the only ingredient for success, but such support is probably the biggest one for success. Without the support of your spouse and those close to you, it becomes very difficult to succeed in any endeavour. But let us be those who cheer, fire-light, and motivate others, as their success depends on it.

However, I need to clarify a misleading assumption that when a person is motivated, cheered on, or fire-lighted, then success is automatic. We have to recognize that we are humans, and humans are limited in what they can achieve, even with the highest motivation. To disregard reality and expect your children to reach anywhere you want them to reach is damaging to your children. It is important to be realistic and know what your children can or cannot do so that you maximize your motivation on what they can do and stop wasting time on what they cannot do.

You see that misunderstanding on today's talent shows, where someone who obviously cannot sing goes to compete for a singing competition. Many of these terrible singers claim they are great singers because that is what their parents or families told them. Even after terrible auditions, they cannot believe their singing is believed to be so poor. Their families and friends do not realize that it will be more devastating to their loved ones when they finally learn that they were lied to.

As parents, we must motivate our children. We must cheer them on, but in their areas of strength. Even in organizations, it is important to place people in their areas of strength so that motivation will add value to what they are already good at. Doing the contrary is simply a recipe for disaster and does more harm than good. This is why it is important to know your people, their strengths, and their weaknesses, so that you can know how to properly and effectively motivate them. A leader must motivate others, but he must do it within the realm of reality.

Motivation has the power to empower others. When you are fire-lighted, you feel enabled to do even what you were scared to do. This is why you must be your children's best cheerleader. A parent must speak positively to his or her children. It is not good that your children should be told that they are beautiful or smart or good people the first time by a stranger. The first time they hear those kind words should be from their parents.

I have seen what motivation can do. I remember the first time I was teaching my daughter Savana how to ride a two-wheel bicycle. She was struggling to catch on the concept, and she seemed to have no confidence. So, I made some kind of a chant, "Confidence, confidence, confidence", and then she really liked the chant and she began to chant confidence, confidence, confidence. And her confidence grew, and her smile came on, as well as her joy. The fear she had had disappeared, and in a matter of minutes I saw her ride on her own for 20 meters. And she kept saying to herself, "Savana, confidence, confidence." She came to me and said, "Dad, did you see that? I did it." She was laughing as she kept saying confidence, confidence. From that day, confidence became the word we used with all our children when learning how to ride a two-wheel bicycle. And it works every time.

It is very unfortunate when parents or leader are the de-motivators for those under their leadership. They become what leadership expert John Maxwell calls "the fire-fighters". Not only they do not fire-light those under their leadership, they even go as far as fighting the fire they found burning. They become op-position parties to those God intended them to motivate, cheer, and fire-light. And when their children end up failing in life, they blame the children for it as if they did not contribute to that failure.

A true leader must intentionally choose to motivate others. He must start with his own family. Motivation goes a long way in the process of building people up and giving them the con-fidence to believe they can do it. We all can use the boost that comes from being motivated, cheered on, and fire-lighted!

Lord, help me cheer, fire-light, and motivate others so that they are energized to succeed!

Application of Day 27

1. In your own words, what does it mean to be a motivator, a fire-lighter, or a cheerleader?

2. What happens when you are motivated or fire-lighted?

3. Are you motivating others? Do you cheer others up? Do you fire-light others? Or are you a de-motivator and a fire-fighter to those God gave you to motivate?

4. Do you motivate your spouse and/or your children?

5. Do you have cheerleaders, motivators, and fire-lighters in your life? Reflect on and write down what they mean to you. Share with them what you appreciate them for.

6. If you do not have fire-lighters, cheerleaders, and motivators in your life, can you work at finding some?

MENTOR

A leader is a mentor, coach and teacher!

A leader makes sure that he mentors his mentees under him. A leader coaches the team or players. A leader teaches his students. The most tragic thing for any leader is going to the grave without having mentored someone, without having coached somebody, and without having taught anyone. The worst place to take our knowledge is to the grave. We must use the gifts and leadership qualities God gave us for the benefit of our communities. It is such a waste when people die without having used their gifts. They die without having shared their knowledge. We must die empty, as Myles Munroe put it.

> Don't die old, die empty. That's the goal of life. Go to the cemetery and disappoint the graveyard. (45)

We must make sure that we leave successful successors who will carry on our legacy. When a leader dies empty, his legacy lives on and produces many fruits. Myles Munroe died, but his mentees, players, and students are all over the world. This is why he was mourned like a superstar, because he had produced so many successors.

When a leader dies empty, it often makes the succession much more easy and peaceful. When Myles Munroe died, it didn't take long to find his successor to lead his ministry. The one he mentored, trained, and taught for years succeeded him successfully and peacefully.

When Elijah was taken to Heaven, there was no need for a meeting or consultation to find his successor. He had spent a long time mentoring, coaching, and teaching Elisha, that when he was gone, Elisha successfully took over.

Jesus mentored, trained, and taught his 12 disciples so successfully that when it was time for him to leave them, the disciples were fully equipped to carry on the mission. In the case of Jesus' training of the disciples, He went a step further; He sent his disciples the promised Holy Spirit. The Holy Spirit empowered them to operate in the supernatural. Jesus gave his disciples everything they needed to succeed in the ministry.

Here are important questions every person has to answer: Who are you mentoring? Every leader should be mentoring someone. Who are you teaching? Every leader must be teaching someone. Who is mentoring you? Everyone should have a mentor. Everyone should have a mentee.

Mentoring someone is so rewarding when you see the difference it is making in your mentee. One of my former students, someone I personally led to Christ, and mentored wrote to me a wonderful thank you. These were Andy Karl's words:

> *"You have been more than a friend for me. You have been a mentor. Pastor Charles, it was a blessing to know you. You helped me know Christ better, and for me, that is a big gift you can give to somebody."* (46)

I was glad to hear that my mentoring helped Andy Karl as well as it did for many other students. Mentoring young students at Gitega International Academy is something I truly enjoyed. I think I developed the passion for mentoring because I was myself greatly mentored by Mr. John Goodbrand.

When I went to Youngstown as a young, single pastor to lead the Gospel Chapel of Youngstown, it was not an easy assignment. The church was all White people, and I was the only Black person. Most of the congregational members were farmers. I had no experience in farming. I remember that, during my first few months, I had trouble understanding their conversations. Even though they spoke English, they used farming technical words, such as 'branding', 'combine' and 'calving'. They used miles to measure distance, even though Canada has used the metric system since 1970. Unlike in the city, where you have to call someone before showing up to their house, Mr. Goodbrand told me to just show up for visitations. He was right, and that brought more people to the church that had not been coming.

Mr. Goodbrand came to take me out every Monday, except very few Mondays when he was away. We would visit, and he would educate me on the culture of the people in Youngstown and in the church. I gave him permission to critique my messages, which he did with much love. He became a true father and a real mentor to me. Mr. Goodbrand had served God for a long time, so I could also learn from him in the things of God. So, when I think of what his mentoring did for me, I feel that I am indebted to mentor others.

All leaders should have mentees. They should all mentor others so that when the time comes for them to move on, they would have qualified, trained people to take over. Would it not be great if, when you retire as president, you see your mentee take over from you and actually do a good job, perhaps better than you did? Was not President Arap Moy proud to see President Uhuru Kenyatta, whom he mentored, also become president? We all saw how President George Bush Senior was proud to see his son, President George Bush Junior also become president.

The greatest legacy for any leader is to see his mentee excel in life and do exceedingly better than him. That is what I told

Andy Karl. I told him that I keep praying for him and that I look forward to him becoming a great leader (which I have no doubt he will). I encouraged him to never forget the call of God, and that many people's lives will be made better because of his leadership.

Everyone should have a teacher or a student or both. Who is your coach? Sports have taught us that any player, regardless of their talent and skill level, needs a coach. Sometimes we wonder why a player like Michael Jordan would need a basketball coach! We wonder why Tiger Woods would need a golf coach! The simple answer is that we can all learn something to better our game and performance.

Are you putting your coaching skills to use? It is always a waste of resources and a detriment to society when someone called a coach does not actually coach. Coaching is one of those gifts God gave us to be used until we die. The apostle Paul knew the value of teaching and coaching; he instructed Timothy to continue the training process. The book of Proverbs emphasizes the value of training children. Let us look at two passages:

"And the things you have heard me say in the presence of many witnesses entrust to reliable people who will also be qualified to teach others." 2 Timothy 2:2

"Train a child in the way he should go, and when he is old he will not turn from it." Proverbs 22:6

It is clear that training has a long-lasting effect. The context here in Proverbs is that of training children. But the principle applies to any age. We can all use mentoring, coaching, and teaching because we can always learn something at any stage of our life.

If Africa is to join other continents in development, we need to develop a culture of mentoring, coaching, and teaching. When African leaders do that, then we can expect smooth transition of power and power will be in the hands of those who have successfully been mentored, coached, trained, or educated. One of the major problems Africa faces is the lack of this process of mentoring, coaching, and teaching so much that people get into power unprepared.

You may be a highly intelligent person or a very talented one, but without someone to show you how things are done, or to train you on the new equipment, or the culture of the organization, you are still doomed to fail. Training is very important. It combines your natural ability and the know-how.

Teachers, mentors, and coaches have the power to shape the destiny of a person. Most people have a teacher, a coach, or a mentor that has had a lifetime influence on them. It may be an advice, a lesson, or a training day that spoke profoundly into their lives and helped change their entire course of life.

For me, it is not one person, but many who made a lasting impact in my life. One of those people is my late mother. She taught me how to lead people without being too pushy. Whenever she gave me advice or counsel, she gave me her reasoning for it, but left me the free will to choose to follow her advice or not to follow it.

My grandparents Ibrahim and Sarah were my impactful informal mentors. I learned what love is from seeing them love each other, love their children and grandchildren, love their dogs, and love all people. I learned from them the value of humility in leadership.

My unofficial father, Bishop John Osmers, taught me how to work hard for the sake of community success. I learned from him how to debate and discuss about the big issues of life, such as faith, injustice, politics, social gospel, and gender equality. I still remember his hypothetical question:

"If Jesus came to do his ministry on Earth today in the 21st century, would He choose all disciples as men or would He choose men and women, considering that there is more

gender equality today, which was not there 2,000 years ago?" (47)

Obviously, it is a question in which the answer would have to be speculative, because no one knows what Jesus would do today, whether He would still choose 12 male disciples or He would pick males and females as per current societal structures. But through him, I learned to debate tough issues. I learned from him the value of advocacy for the powerless. I also learned from him that if you want to be a leader, you have to be prepared to carry people's burdens.

I have been blessed to have been trained by amazing leaders, extremely smart people. I think of people like Mr. and Mrs. George and Sylvia Baynton. Both were university graduates. Mr. Baynton is a renowned lawyer who became a judge and the Deputy Chief Justice. I have learned a lot from them through every conversation I have had with them. Their knowledge and life experience make every meeting with them meaningful. I learned so much from them that I would need more pages to talk about it.

People like the late Dr. Ernest and Mrs. Schmidt, also both university graduates and highly intelligent people. They taught me Canadian culture. I remember one day, while I was spending a night in their home, Dr. Schmidt was tired after our long usual late night conversation. So, he said, "I think I am going to hit the sack." I wondered what made him so upset that he was going to hit the sack, because after all, we had a wonderful conversation prior to that. So, I asked what he said again just in case I did not hear him right. But, being as smart as he was, he understood that I did not understand the expression. So he explained that he meant by that expression that he was tired and was going to go to bed. There are many things I learned from them, too many to mention them all.

There are many other people who have contributed to my knowledge and to the person I am, and I thank God for all of them. I believe that we are not necessarily born leaders; we are made leaders through our own efforts, through the contributions of others in our lives, and most importantly, through the grace of God in our lives. I do not really believe in self-made leaders. Just like my former professor at the Theological College of Central Africa, Gerry Schoberg, in answering my question "Are we righteous?" would answer "We are made righteous", so also we are made leaders. This is why mentoring, coaching, and teaching are very important for shaping us into the leaders we become.

In order to become leaders, we have first to be followers. We have first to be players in need of a coach. We need first to be students that have to be taught. And while the learning process never stops, we need the initial training, to cover the basics and the requirements of our responsibilities before we can begin to lead.

A leader must first be mentored, coached, trained, and taught before he officially begins his leadership. It is a tragedy when people wake up one day, self-proclaim themselves leaders and begin leading people. How does the untrained train others? My prayer and hope for Africa is that leaders will take the time to first be trained, mentored, and coached before they try to lead others. And once mentored, taught, and trained, a true leader must now focus his energy on training and mentoring others. There are many young people with great potential that are not utilized because they have no one to train, mentor, and teach them how to become leaders. May God open the eyes and the hearts of today's leaders to invest in tomorrow's leaders, through mentoring, teaching, and coaching!

Lord, help me coach, mentor, and teach others so that they gain more knowledge and skill to best do their mission on Earth!

Application of Day 28

1. What is the value of mentoring, coaching, and teaching?

2. Do you agree that everyone needs a mentor, a coach, or a teacher? Explain your answer.

3. Do mentoring, coaching, and teaching have power to shape someone's destiny? Explain your answer.

4. Why must leaders have mentors and mentees?

5. Do you have a mentor or a coach?

6. Are you mentoring, coaching, and teaching someone?

SELFLESS

Selfless is community-focused, giver, or generous!

You know a leader by their focus. A true leader focuses on community needs more than his own needs. It is natural that, under normal circumstances, we always take care of our own needs first. This is why, because it is already that automatic to us, humanly speaking, a leader must then focus on his community's needs. A true leader is a giver, a generous person.

A leader refuses to be consumed with focusing his attention on his needs only. A leader makes sure the community is first taken care of before thinking of taking care of himself. A leader is like a parent. When you are a parent, you make sure your children's needs come before your own. A real parent feeds the kids first. A parent wants his children to be more educated than himself.

When a leader is all about himself, his personal gain, his personal success at the expense of community gain or community success; everything goes wrong. We have many leaders who put their personal interests above their community's interests and all of them leave a negative legacy. But I will not talk about such leaders; instead, I will talk about community-focused leaders. I find that we often waste so much time talking about the negative instead of the positive.

In the Christian church, you see leaders who have developed expertise on demonology. They see demons everywhere. They hold seminars and conferences on understanding the devil and how to chase him and his demons out. They forget that if only God is glorified, the devil and his demons will flee. When we let God arise, his enemies have no other choice but to be scattered. It is important that we start talking more on positives rather than negatives.

May God arise, may his enemies be scattered; may his foes flee before him. Psalm 68:1

Community-focused leaders are a pleasure to see. Take, for example, the late Burkina Faso president, Thomas Sankara. He is said to have died poor, because his focus was not amassing wealth for himself or even his family, but his countrymen and countrywomen.

Jesus Christ, who is God, didn't leave any palace or any house to himself but lived his entire life on earth focused on community welfare, not his own. That is why even the Pharisees and the general population were confused, because they expected Jesus to reign as king on Earth, to have servants and to live in luxury and self-sufficiency. But He himself said, referring to himself, that He had no place to lay his head:

"Foxes have dens and birds have nests, but the Son of Man has no place to lay his head." Matthew 6:20

Jesus, who had power to feed 5,000 people and catch so many fish that the nets had trouble holding them all, lived an ordinary life. Why can we not imitate Him in being content with living an ordinary life? There is need for Christians of the

21st century to start focussing more on doing God's will than pursuing material gain.

Jesus' focus was doing the will of the Father. Doing the will of the Father meant forgiving the accused, such as the women caught in adultery, noticing Zacchaeus and actually going to dine with the tax collector, and looking for Peter after Peter's own betrayal of him. He met everyone at their point of need.

A number of us lived with Bishop John Osmers in the early 1990s. This man is legendary as far as community focus is concerned. He was living in an ordinary house and neighborhood. Whatever resources he had he used them to help others in need. He was living such a simple life that, if he was living in Canada, he would have been considered poor.

I remember one day, he showed up with new-to-him furniture, as our old furniture was already too old that we had to cover the holes with extra cloths. But it turned out that one day he had gone to visit his bishop of the Lusaka Diocese. At that time he himself was still a priest, not yet a bishop. So his bishop had bought new furniture and was throwing away his old furniture.

Father Osmers asked the bishop what he was going to do with his old furniture. The bishop told him that he was going to throw them away. But Father John Osmers asked the bishop to give him the old furniture. The next day, we were using the bishop's old furniture as our new furniture.

But Bishop Osmers paid for the education of so many student refugees and paid for lawyers to defend refugee prisoners and asylum seekers whose refugee status had been denied. He helped all the poor that came to beg at his house. He cared for community interests and not self-interest. When I went on my *Africa, It's Time!* African book tour in April 2017, I stayed with him in his house in Zambia. He was living in a very small house with four other people. I thought the house we lived in with him in the 1990s was small, but it looked like a mansion in comparison to the one he was now living in.

This is a retired Anglican bishop, with a pension from his native country of New Zealand. He could choose to live in a bigger house, drive a nicer vehicle, and enjoy some luxuries. Instead, at 82 years old, he was still finding his joy, not in satisfying his own needs, but in helping others.

My grandparents Ibrahim and Sarah Runyeruka are also among the most selfless people I have ever seen. My grandpa was a respected chief. He and his wife could have died rich if they wanted to, but they shared everything they had with the community. Their home was like a boarding school with so many guests. They helped everyone. They lived well, but shared so many of their resources with others. They deliberately denied themselves the luxury they could have afforded in order to help those in need in their community.

Leaders must be the enforcers of Ubuntu, **the togetherness.** A leader must not be satisfied with having taken care of his or her needs only. A leader should not go to the grave with the legacy of only having taken care of his or her immediate family. Those are the kind of leaders that when they die, they have no one to mourn their passing. Their life on Earth is considered a waste of time, even though they appear to have been personally very successful.

My mother was so kind and caring for her community wherever she was. My friends would visit her and she would offer them anything. She helped people and she would not talk or brag about it. It was at her funeral and after it that we heard of so many people that she helped. No wonder we had close to 2,000 people for her funeral. People came from all over the place to pay tribute to her. Her funeral was such an expression of gratitude to a life of the hero that she was to everyone who knew her.

While the world is getting more and more selfish, there are people who are living extraordinary lives by being community focused and not self-focused.

Take, for example, Pastor Francis Chan. When he came face-to-face with poverty, he decided to give up his luxurious house and live modestly. He also decided to take less from his salary and donate most of it.

Another example is that of Bill Gates. Many people just know him as the richest man on Earth, but they don't realize that he donates so much of his wealth to the welfare of our global community. This is the same with Facebook founder and CEO, Mark Zuckerberg, who is donating almost all his wealth.

There are many of these generous wealthy people in the West. We need to see this kind of philanthropy in the rich of the rest of the world. Poverty on Earth could be eliminated, or at least greatly reduced if we all became generous. It is said that there is enough food on Earth to feed everyone. So why are so many people going to bed hungry almost every day?

One day, I asked my friend, who is a leader of a major Non-Government Organization (NGO) in Africa, how many children in his organization's orphanages were sponsored by local wealthy people. His answer was none. With about 80 children in the orphanage, none of these orphans were sponsored by an African. They were all sponsored by people from the West. Where are all the rich Africans in terms of being true caring leaders in their communities?

Being a giver or a generous person is one of the best qualities a human being can have. Giving helps others. Now, it is important to understand that giving or being generous is not limited to giving money. There are many ways in which we can be givers. We can be generous with our time, by physically helping others, praying for others and mentoring others. We can be givers of love. We can be generous in our consideration of others, especially the less fortunate ones. We can give our services. And yes, we can also give money.

Being a giver is very rewarding. Sometimes we make the mistake of thinking that when we give, we lose, because we gave what belonged to us. But giving can be very rewarding. Show me a true giver who shares what he has with others and I will show you someone who is blessed. God Himself is in the business of rewarding a generous person. Sometimes God rewards generosity in ways that blow our minds. This is exactly what He did for Tabitha, who is called a disciple. She was so generous that when she died, those she helped pleaded for her to return back to life, and God honoured their request. Look at her amazing story below:

> *"In Joppa there was a disciple named Tabitha (which, when translated, is Dorcas), who was always doing good and helping the poor. About that time she became sick and died, and her body was washed and placed in an upstairs room. Lydda was near Joppa; so when the disciples heard that Peter was in Lydda, they sent two men to him and urged him, 'Please come at once!' Peter went with them, and when he arrived he was taken upstairs to the room. All the widows stood around him, crying and showing him the robes and other clothing that Dorcas had made while she was still with them.*
>
> *Peter sent them all out of the room; then he got down on his knees and prayed. Turning toward the dead woman, he said, 'Tabitha, get up.' She opened her eyes, and seeing Peter she sat up. He took her by the hand and helped her to her feet. Then he called for the believers, especially the widows, and presented her to them alive. This became known all over Joppa, and many people believed in the Lord. Acts 9:36-42*

We can all agree that a true giver does not give in order to receive back, and yet, almost every time we give we receive more back. I can personally testify to that. Anytime I have obeyed an urge to give to someone in need, I have always received back four, five, or ten times more than I gave. It happened to me in Bukavu, D.R. Congo, and in Lusaka, Zambia.

I remember one day as I was going to school, I felt the urge to give some money to a young boy who looked like he could use a little help. First, I tried to dismiss the idea of helping him, because I was a student on a limited budget. But I finally convinced myself to give him some money. Then I discussed in my heart how much I should give him. Once I settled how much, I went ahead and gave him some money. He was shocked and thanked me immensely. Later, that same day, a first cousin came from Uvira. He was a big businessman, but he liked to drink. He said to me, "Charles, I just want to bless you with some money before I go drink it out." He gave me more than 10 times what I had given the boy that same day.

A similar situation happened to me in Lusaka, Zambia. As I was walking through the suburb of downtown Lusaka, I saw a blind mother with her crying baby, begging for help. Again, I tried to dismiss the idea of giving her some with the excuse that I was a poor person myself at that time. I passed by her and walked a few meters. But the voice inside my heart was so strong and urged me to go back and give her some money. I obeyed the voice and started going back to give her something. On my way there, I debated how much to give her. I settled for the higher amount, which convinced me would be sacrificial on my part. I felt so much peace after that. I went home and someone came that day to my home and told me that he had felt the urge to give me something that day that he could not resist it. Again, he gave so many times more what I had given the lady in need. Yes, while it is true that we should not be giving expecting to be given back, it is also true that we cannot out-give God, as God is in the business of rewarding generous givers.

In fact, when we give, we have already received back because when we give, we have already improved someone's situation and God has already made a note of it. When we give, we have already contributed to the solution of a particular problem. When we give to the poor, it is God we have given to, the God who owns everything. Just by the fact that God has noted our giving, we have already received. The Bible goes as far as telling us that when we are kind, generous, or gracious to the poor, we are, by that action, lending to God; imagine that!

> *"Whoever is generous to the poor lends to the LORD, and he will repay him for his deed."* Proverbs 19:17 English Standard Version

The interesting thing is that God rewards even non-Christian givers. Givers are blessed even they don't do it out of obedience to and love for Christ. This is why many wealthy people in the West continue to be blessed financially; because they give. In fact, we need to realize the beneficiary of an act of giving is the giver. Yes, the receiver benefits greatly, but the giver benefits even more. You do not give so that you can receive back, but God has a way of giving you back more than what you gave; that is what the Bible tells us:

> *"Give and it will be given to you. A good measure, pressed down, shaken together and running over, will be poured into your lap. For with the measure you use, it will be measured to you."* Luke 6:38

Often, givers receive back from those they once helped. During my book tour in April 2017, I visited my cousin Bishop Peter Mphande in Zambia. This man had helped many people to succeed in life. He himself used to be a big business man. He had a shop in which he sold electronics. He used to go buy merchandise in Dubai, Hong Kong, South Korea, and other places. He made lots of money when he was still among the few that brought in such products. He was and still is truly selfless. Unlike other people who would keep the secret to themselves, he introduced and trained others in the same business he was doing. He took them to all the places he would go buy merchandise. Some he helped with small capitals. He was also very generous to the work of God and supported many Christian leaders.

Sometime later, with competition and other challenges, he lost almost all his money. Life started getting tough for him and his family. He could no longer afford to travel to go buy the merchandise. He lost his shop, as he could not even afford the rental payment. Then some of the people he helped, who had become quite wealthy, got together to discuss how they could reward him for what he did for them. They decided to contribute a large amount of money, thousands of dollars, and gave him all that money so that he could stand again on his feet. The money from his friends was enough for him to open a shop and start going to Dubai again. I saw his shop, and it looks as if he never went down. That is one of the ways generosity benefits the giver.

Obviously, giving finds its full meaning in one who is a Christ-follower. For Christians, giving is not optional, but a must-do; it is a requirement. While some have the gift of generosity, every Christian must exercise generosity. We must imitate our Father in Heaven, who gave us His own Son as a ransom for our sin.

> *"He who did not spare his own Son, but gave him up for us all—how will he not also, along with him, graciously give us all things?"* Romans 8:32

Giving is not to be limited to the rich. Everyone can give, whether they are rich or poor. I used to think that you had to be rich to give, but I was educated by a friend that anyone can give. In fact, some of the most generous people are the poor. The Bible tells us of the generous widow whom Jesus commended because she gave all she had. What do you have? If you can't give money, you can give your time. You can give your services. You can give your kindness.

Giving or being generous is part of being a Christian, at least in response to God's giving of His own Son. God commands us to give. Giving was an important part of faithful living for the Israelites under Mosaic Law. The Jews were required not to harvest their land without leaving something for the poor and the needy. They were to make sure they left something in their farms for the stranger and the poor to get some food from it:

> *"When you reap the harvest of your land, do not reap to the very edges of your field or gather the gleanings of your harvest. Leave them for the poor and for the foreigner residing among you. I am the Lord your God."* Leviticus 23:22

Selflessness is a great quality for a leader. When a leader thinks of the betterment of others and decides to be generous, everyone wins. Kevin Durant, the 2017 NBA Finals Most Valuable Player exemplified that selfless spirit. He willingly took a nearly $10 million USD pay cut in order to keep his team together. Being one of the top players in the NBA, the 2017 Finals MVP, the 2013-2014 regular season MVP, several-time season scoring leader, and so many other achievements; Durant deserved to be one of the two or three highly paid basketball players in the world.

Instead he chose to be selfless in order to allow other players on the team to be paid better. By keeping the team together, they gave themselves a stronger possibility to win a back-to-back championship. That's leadership! Listen to what he said about his decision to take a pay cut:

> *"I want to keep this thing going and looking at Andre and Shaun (Livingston) and Steph (Curry) — they all should make the most money that they can make and get what they deserve. Because they were all underpaid and I knew at some point they'd want to get what they deserve. So I just took a step back and let the chips fall where they may. Then I took it in my hands. I wanted to keep the team together and I thought it was going to help the ownership bring all the guys back."* (48)

One way to really understand selflessness and generosity is to compare these two similar terms to their opposites, which are selfishness and greed. Selfishness and greed are all about satisfying self at any cost or expense. These two have the ability to render a person so unreasonable to the point of killing innocent people. That is exactly what happened to Naboth at the hands of the extremely selfish and greedy couple of King Ahab and his famous wife Jezebel.

King Ahab wanted to get Naboth's land. Naboth could neither exchange nor sell his land to King Ahab because it was his family inheritance. He explained his valid reason to the king, but greed and selfishness would not allow King Ahab to be understanding to Naboth. With the help of his wife Jezebel, they killed Naboth and took his farm anyway. Take time to read this fascinating story in 1 Kings 21.

The lesson we can all learn is that we must do everything not to fall into the sins of selfishness and greed, as they have the potential to literally destroy a person. Anyone who is a leader or aspires to be one must avoid these two deadly sins. Selfishness and greed only offer temporal and fake pleasure, but in the long run they rob its practitioners of any contentment and joy. When life has been reduced to just making more personal gain, one ends up being a slave to his own very possessions.

A leader must be generous; he must be a giver. His giving must be done cheerfully. Don't give out of the need for recognition. Don't give with wrong motives. Don't give just to show off. Give secretly, because that is the kind of giving that God rewards. If you give and make it a show, Jesus would say that you have already received your reward; so do not expect another one from God. Give joyfully. Give cheerfully. God loves the cheerful giver, the Bible tells us.

Lord, help me be selfless and make me a community-focused leader, a giver, and a generous person who looks at the needs of others as if they were my own!

Application of Day 29

1. What kind of a leader or even just a person are you?

2. Are you selfless? What are the advantages of being selfless?

3. Are you generous? Why is it good to be generous?

4. Are you focused on the needs of the community or just your own needs?

5. Do you have a testimony of giving and receiving more back? Please share.

6. What are the disadvantages of greed?

7. How can you and I become more selfless?

PERSEVERER

Grit, resiliency, and tenacity are qualities in the same category as perseverance!

Since I have already talked about tenacity in Day 18, I will only talk about what it means to be a persevering, gritty, and resilient person.

Perseverance is a *"steady persistence in a course of action, a purpose, a state, etc., especially in spite of difficulties, obstacles, or discouragement."* (49)

In a Christian context, perseverance is continuing to be in a state of grace up to the end result, which is eternal salvation. It is the ability or courage to endure adversities or obstacles and not give up.

Grit is not a well-known or frequently used concept, and yet it is very powerful and makes the difference between successful people and unsuccessful ones.

> *"Grit in psychology is a positive, non-cognitive trait based on an individual's passion for a particular long-term goal or end state, coupled with a powerful motivation to achieve their respective objective. This perseverance of effort promotes the overcoming of obstacles or challenges that lie with-*

*in a gritty individual's path to accomplishment, and serves
as a driving force in achievement realization. Commonly
associated concepts within the field of psychology include
'perseverance', 'hardiness', 'resilience', 'ambition', 'need for
achievement' and 'conscientiousness'."* (50)

*"Resiliency is the ability to overcome challenges of all
kinds-trauma, tragedy, personal crises, plain 'ole' life prob-
lems-and bounce back stronger, wiser, and more personally
powerful."* (51)

A leader is one who keeps the end goal in mind. The
journey may be tough and rough, the obstacles may be too many,
discouragements may be all over the place, but a leader refuses
to give up. The ability to persevere sets the leader apart from
the rest of the group. Many people are willing to continue the
journey only if it is smooth and easy, but when they face difficulties, they quit. Grit means the journey continues even under
seemingly impossible conditions. Resilience helps the leader to
keep standing up even after several falls. A resilient leader keeps
bouncing back. Grit, resiliency, and perseverance turn failures
into victory.

One great story of perseverance, grit, and resiliency is that
of the president of Ghana, Nana Addo Dankwa Akufo-Addo.
This is a man who could have given up a long time ago. He was
a prominent politician for 40 years before he was finally able to
secure a victory to become Ghana's president. By the time he
secured the presidency, he was already 72 years old. This is what
was said about him:

*"Over forty solid years in the wilderness, amid insults,
public ridicule, outright insults of his personality and that
of his family, and his resilience to withstand all this political madness, finally bore fruits on Saturday, when he
held the national sword, and lifted it up after taking the*

oath office to signify his coronation as the new President of Ghana." (52)

Perseverance, grit, and resiliency made Nelson Mandela endure the harshest prison conditions for 27 years and took him to the highest office in South Africa. His resiliency made him leader over those who oppressed him for almost three decades. Today he has become an icon, one of the greatest human examples of perseverance. He is celebrated worldwide for not giving up, even when it seemed like the only possible option. His grit, which can be seen in his passion to see his ultimate, long-term goal of putting an end to the apartheid regime, was realized in his old age.

Perseverance helped Job endure extreme suffering and remain faithful to God. Even though he lost everything, his wealth, his children, and his health, he persevered. Even when the situation was almost humanly impossible to endure, and even when his wife challenged him to curse God, Job held on to his integrity and persevered through the most difficult trials any human can ever go through. Consider the exchange between Job and his wife:

> "*His wife said to him, 'Are you still maintaining your integrity? Curse God and die!' He replied, 'You are talking like a foolish woman. Shall we accept good from God, and not trouble?' In all this, Job did not sin in what he said.*"
> Job 2:9-10

Perseverance pays off. After Job persevered through the harshest trials any human can ever go through, God blessed him more than He did before. He gave him more children and made him richer than before.

When Jesus persevered through the trials of the crucifixion, God exalted Him to the highest level. Perseverance is not easy, but it is worth it for anyone who wants to be a leader, or simply anyone who wants to live a victorious life. It was not easy, even for Jesus, when He was in the flesh. He got to the point where the pain was too much. He prayed to His Father to provide an escape for Him so that He would not be crucified. But He asked that it be his Father's will and not his own will. Because of the end goal ahead of Him, He persevered through the trials and crucifixion. Here are two passages of Scriptures to show how difficult the suffering was and how exalted Jesus was as a result of His victory over the crucifixion:

> *"Going a little farther, he fell with his face to the ground and prayed, 'My Father, if it is possible, may this cup be taken from me. Yet not as I will, but as you will.'"* Matthew 26:39

> *"He humbled himself by becoming obedient to death, even death on a cross! Therefore God exalted him to the highest place and gave him the name that is above every name, that at the name of Jesus every knee should bow, in heaven and on earth and under the earth, and every tongue confess that Jesus Christ is Lord, to the glory of God the Father!"* Philippians 2:6-11

Jesus' perseverance resulted in His exaltation and in our salvation!

However, it is important to know that it is possible to persevere in the wrong way. It is good to persevere when we have a good goal, an unselfish one, to achieve. A leader should not persevere in power when everyone else is praying, wishing, and hoping he would leave. It is not positive resiliency when you are crushing and oppressing everyone else so you can maintain yourself in power by force. Good grit is when a leader is passionate enough to make a difference in the lives of others, to succeed not only for himself, but for others as well. Perseverance and resiliency are great when you are enduring difficulties with hope to make things better.

But the fact is that leadership is not easy, and it requires a high level of perseverance. You know someone is not a leader when any simple roadblock or any problem he faces makes him want to quit. Quitters are neither achievers nor leaders. Leaders persevere; they give their very best and have to get to the end before they can stop the journey.

Leaders do whatever right things it takes to succeed, even if they are difficult. If it means doing the same thing 20 times, they do it joyfully until they get to the finish line. For Naaman, the leper, it took seven times going under water for him to be healed of leprosy:

"So he went down and dipped himself in the Jordan seven times, as the man of God had told him, and his flesh was restored and became clean like that of a young boy." 2 Kings 5:14

I once worked with someone who mastered perseverance. Dave was truly resilient and tenacious. He was doing a night shift; his work begun when I was leaving. For a night shift worker, you would expect him to come dressed in jeans and runners, basically his work clothes. But he always wore a suit and dress shoes to work. One day, I asked him why he always wore fancy clothes and shoes to come work a night shift. Then he told me his story. He had a Master's degree in Business Administration, and he had been applying for jobs in his field for a long time. He told me how he had already applied to more than 100 jobs and went through so many interviews, some of which he came close to getting the job, but did not. You would think that after so many disappointments, many unsuccessful job interviews, he would quit and comfort himself for having tried many times. But he said that, instead of giving up, he used every interview in which he did not get the job as training or practice. He told me how he had become so good at interviews that he had heard almost all possible questions that they usually ask on interviews in his dream field.

He told me that he considered every day as a possible opportunity for his dream job, and so he dressed as if he was going for an interview. He said that he was always ready for the elevator speech which could land him his sought-after job.

> "*An elevator pitch, elevator speech or elevator statement is a short summary used to quickly and simply define a process, product, service, organization, or event and its value proposition.*" (53)

After about six months of working with him, he was called for an interview and he got his dream job, as area manager for the Province of Alberta in an American company. I learned from him that perseverance may be painful, but in the end, its dividends can be plenty.

Lord, help me persevere in difficult situations and make me gritty and resilient enough to reach the end of the journey successfully!

Application of Day 30

1. In your own words, what is perseverance? What is tenacity?

2. Why should leaders be people of perseverance?

3. Can you describe a situation where perseverance is the wrong thing to do?

4. Why is it important to be resilient?

5. Do you persevere or give up easily?

6. Are you resilient and tenacious?

7. How does perseverance, grit, resiliency, or tenacity for a leader inspire his followers?

DELEGATOR

To delegate is to share responsibilities!

Delegation is one of the top qualities of a successful leader. Delegate, and you will make your job easier and more effective; do it all by yourself and you will surely burn out and fail. The "I can do it alone" attitude does not work. To be a leader, you need people. If you choose the route of the one-man show, then you can be sure that your fall is not a matter of if but when, because it will surely happen sooner than later. Ask someone who has ever run the show by himself, and he will tell you how impossible it is for any human, any leader, to do it alone. Go to the Bible and ask Moses how it is to do it all alone. Ask him why his father-in-law, Jethro, was his wisest counselor! Let us look at Moses' problem and Jethro's answer to it"

> "Moses answered him, 'Because the people come to me to seek God's will. Whenever they have a dispute, it is brought to me, and I decide between the parties and inform them of God's decrees and instructions.' Moses' father-in-law replied, 'What you are doing is not good. You and these people who come to you will only wear yourselves out. The work is too heavy for you; you cannot handle it alone.

Listen now to me and I will give you some advice, and may God be with you. You must be the people's representative before God and bring their disputes to him. Teach them his decrees and instructions, and show them the way they are to live and how they are to behave. But select capable men from all the people—men who fear God, trustworthy men who hate dishonest gain—and appoint them as officials over thousands, hundreds, fifties and tens. Have them serve as judges for the people at all times, but have them bring every difficult case to you; the simple cases they can decide themselves. That will make your load lighter, because they will share it with you. If you do this and God so commands, you will be able to stand the strain, and all these people will go home satisfied.' Moses listened to his father-in-law and did everything he said. Exodus 18:15-24

The mistake that some leaders make is to think that when they delegate, they lose power or control. I wish they knew that when they delegate is when they gain power and control. What they could not do by themselves or what they could do very poorly because they are overstretched, is done by others who have more time to dedicate to the project. They would be more effective also because they are not overstretched like the leader.

It is important to note a great lesson from Jethro in the biblical text above; delegating responsibilities to others does not mean the leader sits around and does nothing. No. The leader must have the primary responsibility to lead the community, to be the representative of the people. He must set the direction for the community. He must teach and exemplify the values of the organization or community. Jethro made clear that he was not advising Moses to just sit on the couch and let others work. It is worth repeating:

"You must be the people's representative before God and bring their disputes to him. Teach them his decrees and instructions, and show them the way they are to live and how they are to behave. But select capable men from all the people—men who fear God, trustworthy men who hate dishonest gain—and appoint them as officials over thousands, hundreds, fifties and tens. Have them serve as judges for the people at all times, but have them bring every difficult case to you; the simple cases they can decide themselves."
Exodus 18:19b-22a

Moses was being advised to share his load with his team. Jethro asked him not to do it alone, as it would hurt both the people and himself. Instead, Moses had to value the team and ask them to help him. He still needed to keep his responsibility as the representative of the people to God. He still needed to be the lead teacher, in charge of instructing people on the ways of the Lord and how to live as God's people. He was still responsible for handling tougher cases, which would be too difficult for the judges he appointed to settle. So, it is clear that delegating is not abandoning the leadership altogether, but rather giving up on doing everything alone and letting others help the leader.

When a leader delegates, the success that comes out of it is still to the leader's credit. When Canada's economy did well, yes, people acknowledged the contributions of Paul Martin or Jim Flaherty, both finance ministers, but credits went to Prime Ministers Jean Chretien and Stephen Harper, respectively.

This is why delegating works to the advantage of the leader and his people. When delegation happens, everyone, the whole team, wins. The good thing about the leader having a team is that he can then delegate many responsibilities and tasks. The leader does not have to do it all by himself or herself. When you have a team, delegation contributes to the team success. You assign people tasks they are capable of executing. In sports such as basketball, you see coaches assigning specific players to defend certain players. Sometimes, if you are playing against a team that has one or two superstars, you really need to delegate responsibilities. You know your primary defender, but if the player he is defending is too hard for one person, coaches will assign a secondary defender to support the primary one. It is called double-teaming.

> "In basketball, a double team (also double-team, double teaming, or double-teaming) is a defensive alignment in which two defensive players are assigned to guard a single offensive player." (54)

Delegating requires trust. When you delegate responsibility to someone on your team, trust him to do the job. It is counter-productive when you delegate responsibility, and yet keep holding onto it. You appoint an ambassador to represent you in a foreign country, but for any deal to be signed, you have to fly and be the one to sign the deal, which could have been signed by your ambassador. When you do that as a leader, you are disempowering your own delegate. Yes, for some rare big missions or deals, your active participation is necessary, but showing up at every deal is disrespectful to yourself and to your ambassador.

One of the areas of leadership we must improve on as Africans is delegation. There is very little delegation in African leadership. The president and the prime minister want to go to every event and every mission, especially missions abroad. This is one of the areas in which we can learn from Western leaders. During the Obama and other US administrations, the president did not have to make many foreign trips; at least not as many as his Secretary of State. The Secretary of State and the ambassadors dealt with many foreign issues and diplomatic missions and the president only went to the ones deemed of high importance. As a president, you appoint people you trust. Once you have done so, then, let them operate without your interference.

President Dr. John Magufuli has done a great job of trusting his ambassadors and letting them do all that is required to represent Tanzania. President Magufuli was sworn in as president on November 5th, 2015. After a year in office, he had not visited any Western country, and even in Africa, he had visited less than five countries.

Delegation must also be fiscally responsible. Some leaders have used delegation as a means of filling up their inner circle's pockets. For a mission that could be done with two or three delegates, they will send 20 or 30 instead. Every delegate makes more during a one-week mission trip than they make in two months at home. When you are a leader of a nation, you need to be respectful of the tax-payers' money. They pay taxes for you to manage it well so that it can in turn benefit all the people. Again, President Magufuli has done well in this area, cutting foreign mission delegations in a big way, thereby saving money that they used to benefit many.

Delegation should be based on merits, skills, talents, experiences, and qualifications, not based on family ties or connections. It is harmful when we delegate people close to us just because we want them to benefit from our influence, even when we clearly know that there were others much more qualified than our chosen ones. There is nothing wrong with delegating those close to us if they are qualified. I know sometimes it does not look good; hence the need to avoid what may appear as conflict of interest. I remember one time, Prime Minister Jean Chrétien sent his nephew Raymond Chrétien on a mission in the D.R. Congo because he was the one most qualified to carry out that mission. But still, it did not stop people from considering his act as a conflict of interest or pure favouritism.

When there is a possibility of our actions being seen as a conflict of interest, we should avoid delegating our family members or friends. I remember when I was vice president at the Council for the Advancement of African Canadians (CAAC); we had an issue that concerned the Somali community.

The president of the CAAC board at the time was a Somalian. He was also at the same time the president of the Somali community. He was the one to decide on the issue as president, but due to the potential conflict of interest, he delegated me to make the decision, which was very smart on his part. I decided on the action to be taken and everything went well.

After the president's tenure ended, I replaced him and became the board president. But I was also the executive director of Christian Immigrant Support Services (CISS). Sometimes, I participated in meetings where both CISS and CAAC were present. On those occasions, I had to delegate responsibility to avoid the conflicts of interest.

My father had an opportunity years ago to get three teachers appointed as headmasters. My mother was a teacher at that time and was as qualified as anybody else. But he chose not to give her the job because it would not look good. As children, and people close to Mum, we did not like his act of appointing others and not giving Mum the opportunity. But it makes sense when you really want to avoid any misunderstandings. So, as a rule of thumb, when delegating, pick the most qualified and, at best, not a close relative; especially if it is not a personal or family business. The case of former Alberta Premier Alison Redford, while Alberta Minister of Justice, is a good example why it is necessary to avoid acting in any way that will put our ethics in question.

> *"Premier Alison Redford, while justice minister, personally chose her ex-husband's law firm for a government tobacco-litigation contract worth potentially tens of millions of dollars in contingency fees, a CBC News investigation has found. One of Canada's top experts in conflict of interest says Redford was in a clear conflict and should have not made that decision.*

> *"The minister of justice, as she then was, Alison Redford, in my view behaved unethically and possibly illegally by not*

recusing herself from making a decision in which she had a private interest, and was in a conflict of interest situation." (55)

Regardless of the abuse in delegation, as a principle, it is essential to effective leadership. The fact is that no one can do everything. Any human being is limited and prone to burning out. Delegating gets the job done without the leader losing his sanity. Sharing responsibilities, as opposed to doing it all alone, is the way to go, and is the most efficient way. Western countries have been developed based on, among other things, delegation.

We see that in Canada where there are town, municipal, provincial, and federal governments with city counselors, provincial members of legislatures, and Members of Parliaments, all doing each their part for the building of the country. Even though the Prime Minister still bears the biggest responsibility, his or her load is shared because he delegates many responsibilities to other members of government. We need to see more appropriate delegations happening in Africa.

As a leader, you just have to trust your teammates and let them share in the responsibilities. When you delegate responsibility and trust your team members to execute them, often you would have already empowered them so much that they usually do not disappoint.

We see that in the church. Those who often complain and criticize whatever is going on in the church are the ones without responsibilities. But once people get involved, they take on tasks and responsibilities. Suddenly the church ceases to be others' church, but their church. They start to own both the good and the blame too. They become ambassadors and advocates of their church.

Lord, help me be a delegator, knowing that alone, I cannot do much, but with the support and contributions from our team, we can accomplish much.

Application of Day 31

1. What is the value of delegation? Why delegate?

2. What can happen to leaders who do not delegate?

3. How did Jethro's advice prevent Moses from burning out?

4. Why are leaders so reluctant to delegate?

5. When faced with delegating a family member or someone else competent, why should a leader guard himself against a conflict of interest?

6. Do you delegate or do you try to do it all alone?

CONCLUSION

I hope that as you have read this book, you have been able to identify some of your areas of strength and your areas of weakness. My intention for you, dear reader, was to get you inspired by the principles in this book so that you can become the best leader God created you to be. Take time to read and to consider how you can apply these principles in your life and in your leadership.

A leader is one who is constantly working on getting better. The world is relying on you to get better so that you can make the world better. Please read this book daily so that the knowledge in it can sink in and be part of you enough to be put it into practice.

If we each do our part in applying the principles in this book, I have no doubt that we will experience personal growth that will translate into making ourselves, those around us, Africa, and the world better. Knowledge is power, we have heard it said. Let us equip ourselves with knowledge from this book so that we can help contribute to building a better world. Now that you have learned these principles, you will make the world better by applying them and teaching them to others.

This book is Christian-based, but I have written it with a wider audience in mind. It can help any leader and anyone aspiring to become a leader. It will be helpful for those already in leadership. It will be very helpful to students preparing themselves to become leaders. It can help leaders with knowledge of how to be exemplary good leaders to those who work under them.

Although I put much emphasis on African leadership, this knowledge is necessary to leaders from all over the world. The principles from this book apply to all leaders. For example, the first principle talks about being knowledgeable, starting with knowing God. Knowing God is foundational for any leadership that truly wants to be great.

Now that you have learned or been reminded of these principles, these truths, you need now to produce good fruits. A great leader makes sure his learning translates into actions, which also translate into victory. Just like professional athletes, we do not play just for fun; we play to win a championship for our team. Leaders too need to acquire knowledge and skills in order to provide above average leadership that makes a tangible, positive difference for their people or their team. Just like a woman labours for nine months in order to end up delivering a baby, leaders too must labour with perseverance to propel their people to community victory. The time has come when we need to gather all of our strength and be super motivated and totally determined to build the best Africa and the world ever seen. We can do it with God's help and working together as a team.

Africa and the world are waiting for the Moses, Joshua, and Aaron type of leaders whom God has chosen to lead His people to the Promised Land. The reason why you are a leader or becoming one is because you have an entire community or communities waiting patiently for you to help them build a better society. You may be a church leader or pastor; God has called you and employed you to participate actively in His mission of making disciples and to lead His people to a growing relationship with Him and with one another. You may be a Christian and community leader; God has called you to help lead people into making a difference in their communities. I believe the time has come when the Evangelical church must now go a step further to fully realize that the so-called 'social gospel' is actually true gospel, as 'faith without deeds is dead'.

You may not be a Christian leader or a Christian at all, (even though I pray and hope you would become one) but this book still applies very much to you as well. The principles discussed in this book are helpful to any leader, regardless of the status of their faith. For example, you do not have to be a Christian leader to apply delegation or being principled or being a hard worker. So, regardless of where you are in life, these principles will help you lead well.

Keep reading this book so that you can keep equipping yourself to be the best leader you can possibly be, the kind of special leader God designed you to be. Remember that your leadership is unique, because God made you to be an original. There are no other you on planet Earth, not even your twin brother or sister. So, use your unique God-given gifts and talents to be the kind of leader you are meant to be.

Now, as I conclude this book, I want to emphasize one thing that we must do. I want to emphasize the need to work together. Two are better than one, the Bible tells us, and we know and we see that to be true. Even when one can achieve something, two can achieve way more. John Maxwell is right when he says:

"One is too small a number to achieve greatness." (56)

Take, for example, Africa. Africa has its children all over the world. Many of them are experts in their fields and could contribute greatly to building a better Africa. But due to everyone working in isolation, their impact is often felt only in their immediate families. Imagine if we worked together in teams! Imagine if we worked together as African Diaspora wherever we are! Let us build unity! Let us find ways to team-up to achieve big things together. We are here on Earth to live a purposeful life and we will achieve that purpose better with unity among us. We have to build and enhance the 'we', and together we will succeed. We all have to make our contribution, giving of ourselves for the betterment of us all. Nick Vujicic says it better:

"The greatest rewards come when you give of yourself. It's about bettering the lives of others, being part of something bigger than yourself, and making a positive difference." (57)

May God help us to know these principles and to apply them to make ourselves, those around us, and those far away, better! Together, and especially with God, we will lead better and leave this world a much better place than we found it. Remember that knowledge that is not applied is of no value. May God bless you as you reflect on and apply these principles!

Now the ball is in your court. You can choose to play or to simply wish others will play. If you just wish change will happen because others will make it happen, you have chosen for that change not to happen. The change that will happen is the one you make happen.

Do not expect someone else to bring change. Change is not someone else's responsibility; it is each person's responsibility. Do your part; be that change that you want or wish to see happen. Nick Vujicic has another great statement regarding making change happen. He says:

"To wish for change will change nothing. To make the decision to take action right now will change everything!" (58)

For change to happen in our world, we all need to do our part. Each one of us must now bring his or her contribution to build a better world. I am in agreement with the late Dr. Myles Munroe, whose view is that every human being is a leader, because everyone has something unique that, if developed, can be his area of expertise and in which he can lead others.

This is why I believe that everyone can exercise his God-given gift, skill, or talent to bring about needed positive change. The problem the world is facing today, especially in Africa, is that there are too many spectators and too few players. Many wish to see change, but few want to practically contribute to bring about that change. It is like someone who really wants a certain candidate to win, but does not even go to vote for him or her. I can see God saying, "Who are you waiting for when you are the one I have chosen to bring about that change?" So, be the leader God designed you to be and take on the assignment. Like Gandhi said:

"Be the change you want to see in the world." (59)

I know something about preaching and hoping others will put your message into action. But I also know something about applying what you preach to yourself. I have tried both, and trust me, I know that the latter is much better and more effective. People are much smarter than you think. They can tell if you mean what you say or if you are not serious. The moment you first apply what you ask others to do, then it becomes easier for others to do it also.

When I was president of the board for the Council of the Advancement of African Canadians, I spoke quite a bit about the need for African Canadians to fully participate in Canadian affairs, including politics, because they had become as fully Canadians as anyone else. In 2012, I ran for the Progressive Conservative nomination for the Edmonton South West constituency. Even though I did not win the nomination, I am glad that it inspired other Africans to get involved; just as I was inspired by other Africans, such as Chinwe Okelu, who ran for political offices before me. I am encouraged to see that, from 2012 to 2017, a number of Africans ran for political offices; and it looks like this trend will likely continue.

I used to urge and encourage Africans in the Diaspora to go back to Africa and serve, even for a short period of time. But it was not until I packed up my whole family and we went to serve as Canadian missionaries in Burundi for 14 months that others could really listen to me. So, be that change; do something. Together, and with God, we will make the world a better place for all.

Can you imagine what the world would be like if we each took part in effecting positive change? If you are compassionate toward orphan children, you decide to adopt two or three orphans. As you share your story of adoption, others feel compelled to also adopt one or two orphans. Soon, there are more children adopted and to whom being hungry becomes history. Imagine what would happen when these children grow up to make their own difference in the world!

You see, the enemies of positive change are passivity, inactivity, fear, discouragement, apathy, laziness, pessimism, and selfishness. This list is not by any means exhaustive. A leader must avoid being caught up in any of these enemies of change. A leader must be active, determined, purposeful, passionate, loving, confident, a person of conviction, hardworking, optimistic, and selfless. A leader with such qualities will achieve what seems impossible.

In October 2017, we saw Jagmeet Singh become the first non-White to lead a federal party in Canada, at only 38 years old. When you hear his story, his background, you can see someone who was determined to effect change, to contribute to the elimination of racial or skin color discrimination:

"Growing up with brown skin, long hair and a funny sounding name meant I faced some challenges. I've been stopped by police multiple times for no other reason than the colour of my skin. It makes you feel like you don't belong, like there's something wrong with you for just being you. And that's why, as prime minister, I will make sure

that no one in Canada is stopped by police because of the
way they look, or the colour of their skin." (60)

Singh spoke about creating sustainable work, because he knows what it means to go from pay cheque to pay cheque. His compassion for the poor workers is not just from theory, but from personal experience. This is what he said:

"While I was in university, my father became very ill and my father was unable to work. We needed to pay the bills, so in my 20s I became the sole income earner in my family. We were lucky to find a way out of this precarious situation, but many people don't. Many people face far more difficult struggles. I caught just a little glimpse of the pressure they feel, the weight of living paycheque to paycheque knowing the consequences of falling short; letting your family down and losing the basics like shelter, food and education. That's why it's unacceptable for the government to tell people to just get used to unstable work." (61)

The change we want to see happen, we must work hard to make it happen. Let us not be like some Christian leaders who want to see a Christian leader in power, but at the same time forbid Christians to get involved in politics because, they say, it is evil. They just do not realize that it does not work to want something and its opposite at the same time because that is a total contradiction.

I therefore urge leaders, wherever they are, to work to effect change. We are living in difficult times, with so many challenges. There is extreme poverty that we must combat wholeheartedly. There is a rise in the gap between rich and poor that must be addressed. More countries acquire nuclear bomb capabilities with massive potential damage proportions that are threatening the entire planet; there again, leadership is needed. The rate of suicide is going up as people do not want to live anymore. We are living in a time when people are willing to be suicide bombers in order to kill innocent people. There are wars everywhere, especially in the Middle East and in Africa. Racism and discrimination that should have been history by now seem to be on the rise. There are just too many problems in our world today, so much that we cannot seem to catch a break. We desperately need the establishment and the rise of effective and wise leadership to address the many challenges our world is facing today.

ACTION PLAN

Jesus did not just preach change; He effected change. When the sick needed healing on a Sabbath day, He did not ask them to come back the next day; He healed them. It was more important for Him to do the right thing than to not offend the Pharisees. Even though Jews and Samaritans did not get along, at the well, Jesus took time to have a conversation, not only with a Samaritan but a Samaritan woman. And because of that conversation, not only did the Samaritan woman become saved, her community also became saved. The woman who was once renowned for her sinful nature became enrolled as Christ's ambassador, or Christ's agent of change, who shared the good news of Jesus Christ that changed the entire village.

Like Jesus, we too can be agents of change in our world. So, examine yourself; think of a cause that you can champion. Think of a situation that you must change, or can at least contribute to changing it. There are so many causes that are waiting for your contribution to bring about positive change. While you cannot champion all of them, you can ask God to show you which one/ones you need to be involved in.

Is it sharing the gospel of faith demonstrated with works?

Is it adopting an orphan?

Is it supporting orphans or starting an orphanage?

Is it paying for education for children from poor families?

Is it training single mothers and helping equip them to stand on their feet and be productive members of society?

Is it getting involved in politics?

Is it improving your employees' wages?

Is it being a better husband or parent?

Is it going as a missionary into a foreign country?

Is it starting a business and creating suitable employment for others? Is it teaching business principles to others?

Is it teaching farming to uneducated or untrained farmers?

Is it advocating for fair wages for the poorly paid, the mistreated, and the abandoned?

Is it caring for the elderly?

Is it creating a centre for physically challenged people?

Is it caring for street children and teaching them skills?

Is it mowing the lawn for the elderly or the physically challenged?

Is it fighting for human rights (e.g. for equality between men and women)?

Is it helping provide wells for communities without water?

Is it training leaders?

Is it fighting corruption and bribery?

Is it speaking to leaders and playing an advisory role?

Is it volunteering in various humanitarian projects?

Is it starting a school or serving in an established one?

Is it supporting financially the propagation of the gospel and various humanitarian causes?

Is it establishing micro-finance for women and girls?

Is it establishing a clinic?

Is it partnering with us to teach these principles?

Could it be mentoring or coaching an individual or a group of people?

Could it be starting a mentoring or coaching program?

As you can see, there is no shortage of causes one can be involved in. We just have to ask God what He wants us involved in, listen to our hearts, and do it. My prayer and hope for you is that you will realize that there is a specific purpose for you being here on Earth. There is a gap that only you are meant to fill. May you discover who you are meant to be and what you are meant to do in life! So, be that person you are meant to be and do that which you are meant to do, and you will contribute to making this world better.

In summary, here is an action plan based on all the principles we addressed in this book. I can assure you that you will be a great leader if you put in action these principles by being:

1. **Knowledgeable:** Being knowledgeable will set you apart. Remember that ignorance is deadly and keeps a person in bondage. Always start with knowing God and making Him known. Do whatever it takes to keep acquiring knowledge.

2. **Visionary:** You need vision to get to where you want to go and where you want to take those under your leadership. So, make sure you develop your vision. The clearer your vision is, the clearer your destination, because without the vision you are simply beating around the bush, going nowhere.

3. **Purposeful:** There is a purpose for everyone's existence. Find your purpose and follow it. This is a critical area of life and actually foundational to a meaningful living. Ask God, yourself, your family and your friends to help you know what you are meant to be and to do and be it and do it. Do not be passive about it. Be proactive in living in your purpose.

4. **Person of Integrity:** Sometimes we are tempted to compromise our integrity because we see ourselves failing while dishonest people prosper. But in the long run, integrity always wins. Always be a person of integrity, and sooner or later, it will pay off for you.

5. **Caring:** You can never go wrong when you care for others. Even though some may take advantage of you, keep caring for them anyway, as Mother Teresa would say. Being car-

ing speaks volumes more than words can. When people see you care, they receive your message with open arms. Keep caring, and keep finding more ways to care, and you will change people.

6. **Good Listener:** There is nothing fun about talking with a poor listener, as the conversation is often one-sided. Develop your listening skills, and it will help establish you as an effective leader. Make everyone you are talking to feel that you value them and that you are willing to give them your undivided attention.

7. **Humble:** Humility is priceless. Pride and arrogance are ugly. Humility makes you approachable, and you need that to lead people. A leader is a servant and servanthood goes hand in hand with humility.

8. **Joyful:** Being joyful has a lot of emotional, social, physical, and spiritual benefits. If you are a Christian leader, it is imperative that you be joyful. Joy is fun and good. Remain joyful, and you will be positively contagious.

9. **Thinker:** One of the top gifts God gave us is the brain, the ability to think and to be creative and innovative. A leader must be a thinker. To be a step ahead as a leader you must think more and deeper and ahead of the people under your leadership. Be a creative and innovative thinker.

10. **Team player:** To achieve much, you need a team. The good thing about a team is that even your weaknesses get overcome by the strengths of your teammates. You do not have to carry the heavy load alone; share it with the team and together you will succeed.

11. **Disciple:** Be a disciple of Jesus Christ and He will help you make other disciples and help you lead well. A disciple is a student. Keep learning and adopt the attitude that you will never know everything. If you are a disciple of Christ, help make other disciples.

12. **Courageous:** Life has so many discouragements and challenges. As a leader, you need courage to face those challenges, and to keep moving in the face of discouragements. Courage helps a leader not only in his personal challenges, but it also helps inspire others. It is the leader's responsibility to exemplify courage to those under his leadership.

13. **Advocate:** Advocacy is critically important for a leader. We are living in a world in which so many people are mistreated, abused, underpaid, discriminated, and oppressed. A leader is an advocate for justice, fairness, and equality. To see injustice and keep silent about it is to side with the perpetrator. Part of a leader's responsibility is to advocate for and defend those who cannot defend themselves. Do your part!

14. **Builder:** A leader builds up and encourages others. Are you an encourager? Do you build others up? When people come to see you, do they leave built-up and encouraged, or beaten-up and discouraged? To build a better world, we need to start building up and encouraging people.

15. **Accountable:** Everyone must be accountable. It does not matter how big you think you have become, you still must be accountable to someone else or to other people. It is a very good idea for all leaders to have accountability partners, people who can speak the truth to them even when such truth may hurt. Do not get an accountability partner who always tells just what you want to hear, for that is not true accountability. Find someone who can confront you with the truth in a caring manner.

16. **Grateful:** It is very important to be grateful, to be thankful. We deserve nothing. We must continually be grateful. Saying thank you does not cost anything and yet it can open doors for more blessings. In fact, gratitude is pleasing to God. So, do yourself a favor, and always say thank you.

17. **Developer:** What you know is not just for yourself; it should be used to develop others. It is the leaders' responsibility to

develop others so that at any time others can take over from him and do as well as he did or even better than him. Jesus developed his disciples so well that in his absence, they took over the responsibility and today there are more than a billion followers of Jesus because of that.

18. **Doer:** Some people just talk, but they do not do. A leader is a doer. A leader is a hard worker. If you want those under your leadership to be doers and hard workers, then be a doer, be a hard worker! Set an example! In Africa especially, leaders need to be hard workers. Leaders do not just order or command others to work hard, they exemplify hard work.

19. **Fair:** Being fair is a must-have quality for a leader. Fairness is needed everywhere. If you are a parent, you need to be fair to all your children. Showing favoritism or being unfair to some is damaging to both the favored ones and the unfavoured ones. It is important that a leader is fair to everyone. As an employer, it is important to pay fair wages and to generally treat all your employees fairly and justly.

20. **Principled:** A leader must be principled. Being principled is about doing the right thing even when everyone else is doing the wrong thing. For example, bribing is wrong, and yet there are places where everyone does it with their conscience at peace. Being principled in that case is saying no to giving or accepting bribes, even though it might cost you something. For the sake of building a better world, can you decide to be a principled person?

21. **Relational:** Good relationships make us better. Each one of us is incomplete in some areas and often needs the contributions of others in order to be complete. A leader must relate, be friendly to everyone, rich or poor, young or old, male or female, Asian or Indigenous/Aboriginal or Black or White. Every human being is worth relating to. Think of the people you have not related to, people that may be considered the outcasts of society, and make a point to befriend and relate

to them. Being relational is also about breaking the barriers. Jesus related to everyone; we too must do that. So, go ahead and make a point to relate to everyone, and a special point to relate to the marginalized or the misunderstood of society. You can invite them for coffee. You can invite them to your house for a meal. Just do something that you have not done before and keep improving in that area. When you relate to people you have never related to, you will be surprised at how ignorant you used to be. Do your best to graduate from stereotyping people, because it is false, more often than not. For example, get to know the indigenous people of Canada, and you will realize how intelligent they are; it will help free you from the prison of stereotyping. We have to be friendly to everyone.

22. **Optimistic:** Are you an optimist or a pessimist? A leader must be optimistic. Think today of a situation that requires you to be optimistic. It may be a difficult situation or a challenge. Are you a hope-full or a hope-less person? Think of a situation in your life right now that demands that you be hopeful. No matter how difficult the challenge or situation is, being hopeful gives you the hope to overcome it. Optimism is not just mere hoping for something good to happen. It is giving your best to whatever you want to achieve, and then hoping for the best. So, decide today to live an optimistic life, and you will not regret it.

23. **Person of Conviction:** Our convictions impact how we live our lives. If your convictions are that men and women are equal, that will influence how you as a man treat women, and how you as woman treat men. If your convictions are that one race is superior to another race or that all races are equal, that will influence how you treat people of a different race than you. What are your convictions? Think about your convictions, examine them, and see if they are good for building a better world or not. The good news is that

we can change our convictions. Will you choose today to have good convictions that contribute to making you a better person and a better leader?

24. **Intentional:** Intentionality goes beyond just wishing something good would happen or hoping someone will know you love them. Being intentional means making that good thing happen; it is about doing your part. If you love someone, then tell them you love them or show in tangible ways that you love them. If you would like to see people graduate from poverty, practically help them get out of it. If you wish all orphan children to have a family, be intentional and adopt two or three; that is a step toward achieving your goal. Think of the causes that require you to be intentional in doing something about them, and then do it.

25. **Finisher:** While starting is critical in any process, it is really finishing that validates the whole process. Your leadership success will be determined by how well you finish. There are many leaders who started well but whose end damaged everything. A leader must prepare to finish well. It is such a waste when we begin a good project and we abandon it without finishing. What is it that you started but you did not finish? Can you decide to finish it before it is too late? It would be better to not start than to start and never finish the project. Think of all that you need to finish and go back to complete whatever it is, as long as it is a good thing.

26. **Dependable:** Do you always honor your word? Do you always fulfill your promises? How reliable are you? Can people trust you? Those are very important questions for a leader. When people cannot truly trust you, you have at that very moment lost them. Think about yourself and ask yourself if you are worth being trusted or depended on. Work on establishing yourself as a dependable person, a trustworthy and reliable leader. The success of your leadership depends on it.

27. **Motivator:** One of the key responsibilities of a leader is motivation. A leader must motivate others. Much can be achieved when people are motivated. Are you motivating your team? What are you doing to motivate those under your leadership? You can motivate people by praising them when they do something good. You can motivate your employees by offering them a better pay or a pay-raise. You can motivate people by taking time to be with them and listen to them. As a leader, you must make motivating others a priority if you want to lead successfully and to be a healthy and thriving organization or community.

28. **Mentor:** Everyone needs a mentor. The effectiveness of mentoring can never be under-estimated. Are you mentoring someone or a group of people? Do you have a mentor? Who is cheering you on? Who are you cheering on? Who are you fire-lighting? Think of someone or a group of people that can use your mentorship and find a way to be their mentor. Also think of someone you would like to mentor you, and ask him or her to be your mentor. The world will be a better place if each person could have a mentor or mentee.

29. **Selfless:** Selflessness is the opposite of being selfish. Being selfless is about considering the needs of others and doing something about it. It is about giving to the community. It is about being generous. It is about thinking less of self and thinking more of others. The good thing about being selfless is that the more you think of or give to others, the more God blesses you. Selflessness is like an investment; the more you give to others, the more you receive back, even more than you gave. You do not give so that you receive, and yet, the more you give the more you receive. Think of people who need your help right now. How about a child needing school fees or school uniforms; can you be selfless and pay those fees or for uniforms for them? How about a hospital bill for someone who cannot afford it; can you pay

their bill? I have mentioned many causes in this section; ask yourself which one or ones you should be involved in? You might already been thinking of another cause; be selfless and do something about it. The more selfless you are, the more you are already making our world better.

30. **Perseverance:** Perseverance can be the difference maker between success and failure. There is a tendency today to try just a little bit, and when it does not seem to work, we give up easily. Perseverance is about holding on a bit longer. It is about not quitting easily. It is about giving it your best and holding on even more. In the end, perseverance, more often than not, takes a leader to victory or success. Are you in a situation where you feel like giving up? Holding on may be the best decision you have ever made. Remember, perseverance is only a bad thing if we hold on to what we should now let go. Sometimes, the best thing to do is calling it quit, rather than holding on to it. May God clearly show us what we must persevere in, and what we should now let go of.

31. **Delegator:** Delegating is a leader's best friend because a leader cannot do everything. We all need the help of others to do more. Delegating saved Moses' leadership, and it can save yours too. Trying to do everything yourself may cause you to achieve nothing. Delegating is about sharing the load with others. Are you a delegator, or a do-it-all-yourself kind of a leader? Take stock of your leadership responsibilities and ask yourself which responsibilities you must keep, and which ones you must delegate to others. Delegating some of your responsibilities to others will increase your effectiveness as a leader.

May God help us as we apply these principles! The world is counting on you and me to each do our part, which is to apply these principles. Together, and with our God, we will make our world better. Thank you!

Special message to the African Leaders

I could not finish this book without a special message to our African leaders. Everyone is looking at Africa and wondering why there is still so much poverty in a continent blessed beyond measure. Why are we still having, in many African countries, children without access to a primary school education? How can we justify having children living in the streets? Where did the African concept of 'it takes a village to raise a child' go?

Why have we not done all we can to eradicate rape and free our mothers and daughters from the biggest crimes against humanity? Why are we still paying our poor workers, in some countries, less than a dollar a day? Why are we spending more on a lunch with our families or friends than we pay our servant or employee to work for us for the whole month? Why have many African countries not established the minimum wage to ensure fair wages to all working Africans?

Are we competing with the colonial masters, the slave masters, and the apartheid masters on who can mistreat our people the most? Africans are becoming the worst masters to their fellow Africans; how tragic! Many African employers do not even take time to have a mere conversation with their servants or employees. Have you ever taken time to think about the servant-quarter housing where we accommodate our servants while we enjoy our own mansions?

When I was in Africa for my first book tour, I was shocked to see that in the year 2017, we still have people with physical challenges who have to walk with their hands and feet because they do not have a wheelchair. What is happening to caring for our own who are disabled?

Why are we still having wars and conflicts among ourselves? Who benefits from those wars and conflicts? Think of the damages that those wars and conflicts are inflicting on all of us and our economies. Think of how the money we spend on wars and conflicts could help us build our continent!

Why are many African countries still not giving dual citizenships to their native children of the Diaspora? Put yourselves in the shoes of the African Diaspora who have to pay a visa, just like any foreigner, to go home to their country!

Do you want to see Africa emerge as the superpower of the future? Do you believe, like me, that Africa has all it takes to be the most powerful continent on planet Earth?

We have no more excuses now. As of 2017, most African countries have been independent for more than 50 years. In March 2017, Ghana celebrated 60 years of independence. Everywhere you go in Africa now, there are many PhD holders and many highly educated people. We are our own leaders now, so what is holding us back from realizing the Lumumba, Nyerere, Kwame Nkrumah, and others' dream of a totally independent and prosperous Africa? Like Professor PLO Lumumba, I wonder how our Independence heroes would feel if they were to come back and see what Africa has become!

Let me propose some solutions. Before I do that, I want first to appreciate the efforts I am seeing from many of our former African leaders teaming up with current African leaders to work towards building a better Africa, the kind of Africa that we all want and desire. Their work and efforts are commendable and we need to build on that.

As a proud African and one who wants to see Africa emerge as a just, peaceful, and prosperous continent, I am proposing:

1. That African countries reinforce democracy and the rule of law. I think that democracy is good because it helps prevent leaders from overstaying in power. It gives people the power to choose their leaders. It provides for a proper system of leaders passing on the baton and letting others take Africa further forward. For those countries struggling with term limits, I am proposing a maximum of three terms. I think two terms is too short for countries trying to get established, and four terms is too long and tempting for a leader to want to keep going by trying to change the term limit. Three terms should be enough for a leader to accomplish his plan and then pass on the baton to his successor.

2. That all African countries that have not adhered to dual citizenship do so, to facilitate the full involvement of the African Diaspora. It is such a waste of resources not to allow the African Diaspora's full rights to citizenship and consequently to full involvement in the development of their countries and their continent. Just imagine what Africa can be in 10 years if only 10 percent of the African Diaspora went back home to contribute to the development of Africa!

3. That the African Union do everything possible to end immediately the slavery of Black Africans in Libya and anywhere else. It is horrible that in 2017, in the 21st century, Blacks are still being purchased as slaves and treated worse than objects. The Black race has suffered enough and for too long. It is worse enough that Blacks have continued to suffer all over the world; it is much worse that they are being made slaves in their own African land. The African Diaspora has done its part of denouncing, demonstrating in

massive numbers and advocating against the barbaric, in-human, slavery treatment of Black migrants. African leaders must act with a full sense of urgency to restore dignity to their people in captivity of slavery. I hope that these crimes against humanity committed to Blacks will be a wake-up call for Africans and friends of Africa to put an end to the mistreatment of Blacks all over the world. Blacks deserve full right to being human.

4. That the African Union does all it can to end wars and rape against women and girls in the Democratic Republic of Congo. The African Union should do the same in South Sudan and other African countries that are experiencing wars and conflicts. Consider this article on rape in the DRC, and realize why staying silent can no longer be an option:

Woman 'publicly raped and beheaded for serving fish in Congo' © Provided by Independent Print Limited

A woman has been raped in public and killed by a rebel militant group in the Democratic Republic of Congo, reportedly because she served the gunmen "forbidden food". France 24 said it had compiled footage and witness statements documenting the incident, rare evidence of the atrocities being committed on the front lines of a year-long conflict between the Congolese Army and a rebel movement known as the Kamuina Nsapu. Witnesses said the gunmen forced the woman's step-son, who was working with her when the food was served, to rape her in the main public square of Luebo, a town of 40,000 people that was briefly occupied by the Kamuina Nsapu earlier this year. Both were then killed by the armed rebels who, according to the report, then drank some of the victims' blood. The killing has been linked to protection rituals which are observed

by the Kamuina Nsapu during periods of fighting, includ-
ing the perceived need to avoid certain foods. The woman,
who owns a small restaurant, apparently served gunmen
fish - which is banned, along with meat, cassava leaves and
vines. She is reportedly seen in the footage being held by the
hair and told she "must die" for committing "high trea-
son". One resident of the town, who has asked to remain
anonymous, told France 24: "She was accused of serving
fish to rebels who were fighting on the frontlines in Kabao.
They said she gave them beans that contained pieces of a
small, local fish. "Convinced that she had broken their pro-
tection charms, the council of rebels led by a man named
Kabata sentenced both the woman and the son of her hus-
band's second wife [the young man was also working there
that day] to commit incest in public." The witness said
people were forced to watch the executions. "We had no
choice: to stand up to them would have meant death. We
were left to fend for ourselves against the armed militants.
The police fled a week earlier. "The two bodies - decapitated
and mutilated - stayed there, out in the open, for two days.
Eventually, they were buried on the spot. After the village
was liberated, the Red Cross moved in and helped move the
bodies to a cemetery." (62)

Where are the African leaders to put an end to the horrific torture of women? Where does the help for these innocent
mothers come from to free them from rape and horrific death?
This woman and her stepson are just two of the many that are
being raped, tortured, and dying daily. Can we please do all we
can to restore dignity and safety for the innocent women of the
Democratic Republic of Congo?

5. That African leaders put strong systems in place to ensure
   disabled Africans are taken care of. There should be no one
   walking on their hands and feet in Africa anymore. The
   blind should be supported, and so should all the people

whose disabilities make it difficult for them to earn an income.

6. That all African countries establish a minimum wage system to all working Africans. No one working full-time in this world should be making less than a dollar a day in the 21st century. Leaders should stand in the gap and defend the weak and the mistreated. Establishing the minimum wage is a strong way to defend the poorly paid workers. Zambia is a good example for establishing the minimum wage. Other African countries that do not have the minimum wage established can follow the example of Zambia and other countries that have it established.

"Zambia has a government-mandated minimum wage, and no worker in Zambia can be paid less then this mandatory minimum rate of pay. Employers in Zambia who fail to pay the Minimum Wage may be subject to punishment by Zambia's government. Zambia's Minimum Wage is the lowest amount a worker can be legally paid for his work. Zambia's yearly minimum wage is $917.00 in International Currency. International Currency is a measure of currency based on the value of the United States dollar in 2009." (63)

7. That equality between men and women be established. To balance the inequality in African education, which has more boys than girls educated, the government could introduce an incentive program to boost the education of girls so as to reach parity between boys and girls in education.

8. That free education up to grade 12 be offered to all Africans. Children's education should be made mandatory up to grade 9.

9. That African countries, through their leaders, combat corruption, bribery, and waste of resources forcefully.

10. That agriculture be developed enough to ensure no African dies of hunger. There is enough land that a small portion of land could be given to everyone to allow every African to grow food for their family.

11. That African countries invest in building quality schools to reduce the massive exodus of Africans going abroad for quality education.

12. That Africa builds adequate medical centres and hospitals so that no one, including African leaders, has to go overseas for medical treatment.

13. That Africa develops its own industry so that vehicles, machinery, and electronics can be manufactured in Africa. We must also ensure the basics, such as electricity and water, are fairly abundant to allow countries to increase their productivity. If electricity is in abundance, people can work during the day or the night.

14. That Africans support each other so that Africans can spend money in Africa, vacation in Africa, build in Africa, and invest in Africa. This is not a call to isolate Africa from the rest of the world, but rather a balanced approach that encourages Africans to first love and care for their continent before they do it for other continents. We have heard it said that 'Charity that is in best order begins at home.' We need to stop enriching everyone else but Africans. We must be the primary supporters of our fellow Africans.

15. That Africans should start supporting their own ventures and teams. Why should Africans know and support European soccer/football teams, but not their own African teams? Europeans do not spend their time watching African football; why should Africans always be glued to their televisions to watch European football? Africans must support, promote, and invest in African culture and businesses.

16. I think it would be beneficial if African leaders were to wear African clothes at African Union meetings. We can all follow President Thomas Sankara's example of African patriotism. We should promote African food, African clothing, African culture, African books, and African music. Again, this is not a call to abandon Western things because the West has good things too that we can also enjoy. There are many Africans who live in the West and have become citizens of different Western countries. Those must also live in the new countries as full citizens, and contribute fully to the building of their countries. The world has become such a small village that we need each other, and Africa cannot be in isolation. But there is an urgent need for Africa to boost its self-esteem and the pride of being African.

17. That African leaders must be the defenders of the poor and less privileged. Leaders must be the voice of the voiceless. We are to think of every raped mother as if she was our own mother and a raped girl as if she was our own daughter. We have the power to end such barbaric crimes from becoming a norm of our society. Think of any street boy or girl as your own. Think of your house-servant as an equal fellow human being, an equal fellow African, and treat him or her as such.

18. That we improve wages of army and police men, women, teachers, nurses and doctors, customs agents and all the hard working civil servants who are daily tempted to accept bribes to subsidize for their meager wages.

19. That Africans build adequate infrastructures. I was in South Africa and was impressed by how good their roads were. I was equally impressed by the Rwandan and Zambian roads. But I have been in some other African countries where it takes the whole day or more to travel 200 kilometres. We must do better.

20. That we must take care of our orphans. It is not right that almost all of our orphans have foreign sponsors. It does not speak well of us Africans that foreigners have to be the ones taking care of our children. Philanthropy should not only be for Westerners; it should also be for Africans.

21. That we must restore the African *Ubuntu*. We must be concerned for each other, especially the less fortunate of our society. With true *Ubuntu*, we will build a better and greater Africa that will be the envy of the world.

22. That a partnership between Africans in Africa, Africans in the Diaspora, and friends of Africa be established to help Africa join other continents in development. There are many non-African friends of Africa who love Africa just as we do. If included in the partnership with Africans in Africa and Africans in the Diaspora, that partnership can perform wonders. The African Diaspora, if utilized, could greatly impact Africa's development and economy. African leaders should find ways to strike a strong partnership with their African Diaspora, as such an alliance could perform wonders for Africa.

"'Teacher,' said John, 'we saw someone driving out demons in your name and we told him to stop, because he was not one of us.' 'Do not stop him,' Jesus said. For no one who does a miracle in my name can in the next moment say anything bad about me, for whoever is not against us is for us. Truly I tell you, anyone who gives you a cup of water in my name because you belong to the Messiah will certainly not lose their reward." Mark 9:38-41

For Africans, partnership should be done first with Africans. Partnership among Africans will build the kind of Africa we want and desire. Partnership among Africans should be done in a mutually beneficial relationship. It should also be truthful. A true partner tells you the truth. African leaders will help build a better Africa by speaking the truth to each other. In November 2017, Botswana President Ian Khama did just that. He advised President Robert Mugabe, who had stayed 37 years in power, to leave, arguing that African presidents are not monarch to stay that long in power. Mugabe listened and left power and that has led to one of the bloodless and peaceful transition of power.

> I don't think anyone should be President for that amount of time. We are Presidents, we are not monarchs. It's just common sense. (64)

For Africans, partnership should include everyone who loves and cares for Africa. Africa is now a multicultural society, where we find the majority Blacks, but also Whites, East Indians, Asians, and Arabs. Anyone who loves Africa and wants to contribute to the building of a better Africa should be welcomed.

The list above is not by any means exhaustive. It gives us a starting point. Let us look at ourselves, the many challenges that we are facing, and start addressing them seriously. Friends can help us, but as Africans, we must deal with our own problems. Waiting for help outside the continent is not the responsible way to address our African challenges. African leaders such as the ECOWAS proved that when united and determined, they can deal with serious African problems. Their efforts to force former President Yahya Jammeh from power following his election defeat remains one of the successful demonstrations of African leaders' power to act successfully for the benefit of the rule of law and democracy. We need more of that kind of leadership in Africa; African leaders working together for the benefit of all Africans.

I am optimistic that if we apply these 31 essential principles, we will make Africa the best place on Earth to live. Let us rid ourselves of the devastating focus on self and start to think and operate as 'we' and 'us', and we will contribute to building a better world for all.

I want to thank all the leaders who are already working hard to make their people and countries better. I want to thank leaders who are thinking as Pan-Africans, making it easy for Africans to move and operate in Africa. I want to thank African leaders who are making education affordable for all children. I want to thank countries that have established or are working on establishing the minimum wage system to combat exploitation of the poor by the rich. I want to thank leaders who are making healthcare affordable and/or subsidized so as to help even the poor to receive medical treatment.

There are some good things happening in Africa and I thank God, our African people, the friends of Africa and our exemplary African leaders for that. But looking at the level of poverty, injustice and suffering of the majority of Africans, much must still be done.

African leaders and all Africans must work on making Africa the best place to live in and to prosper. If we build the kind of Africa that is just, peaceful and prosperous for all there will be no need for Africans to be perishing in the Mediterranean or to risk being sold as slaves in search of a better life overseas. We can do much better. Let me urge every African leader and all Africans to reflect and act on these timely and powerful words from President Nana Akufo-Addo of Ghana during the visit of French President Emmanuel Macron to Ghana in November 2017:

> We can no longer continue to make policy for ourselves, in our country, in our region, in our continent on the basis of whatever support that the western world or France, or the European Union can give us. It will not work. It has not worked and it will not work. Our responsibility is to charter a path which is about how we can develop our nations ourselves. It is not right for a country like Ghana – 60 years after independence – to still have its health and education budgets being financed on the basis of the gen-

erosity of European tax-payers. By now we should be able to finance our basic needs ourselves. We have to get away from this mindset of dependency. This mindset about 'what can France do for us?' France will do whatever it wants to do for its own sake, and when those coincide with ours, 'tant mieux' [so much better] as the French people say... Our concern should be what do we need to do in this 21st century to move Africa away from being cap in hand and begging for aid, for charity, for handouts. The African continent when you look at its resources, should be giving monies to other places...We need to have a mindset that says we can do it...and once we have that mindset we'll see there's a liberating factor for ourselves. (65)

To build this kind of Africa President Nana Akufo-Addo talked about that will make Africa so good that its children will not need to go elsewhere for green pastures requires selfless and community focussed leaders. Africa and the world need leaders who think of and put their community needs above their own. Africa needs leaders with the right convictions, intentions, will and power to do good for their people.

To build this kind of Africa requires a strong partnership and real unity among Africans, especially the African leaders. We have to build Africa with the Pan-Africanism spirit. Together and with God, we can build a better Africa, the kind of Africa that is just, prosperous and peaceful for all. Together and with our God, we can build a better world for all.

May God help us apply these principles and contribute to building a better world for everyone! Thank you!

REFERENCES:

#	PAGE	REFERENCE

1:   p.6   Internet quote on Sojourner Truth.

2:   p.10   Why East Africa wants to ban second-hand clothes, article on internet on March 2, 2016.

3:   p.20   Haile Selassie, Internet quote.

4:   p.24   George W. Bush, Internet quote.

5:   p.26   Foundation for Cross-cultural Education, Internet quote.

6:   p.30   Rick Warren, Internet quote.

7:   p.31   Miles Munroe, Internet quote.

8:   p.33-34 Nelson Mandela, Internet quote.

9:   p.34   Oprah Winfrey, Internet quote

10: p.35   Wikipedia, Internet quote on Father Damien.

11: p.36   John Bevere, Internet quote.

12: p.46   Martinez Javier in movie Courageous, Internet quote.

13: p.48   Theodore Roosevelt, Internet quote.

14: p.52   Mother Teresa, Internet quote.

15: p.55-56 Internet quote on C.S. Lewis.

16: p.62   J. Kikwete, Internet quote.

17: p.71   Internet quote on José Mujica.

18: p.76   Internet quote on the value on joy in job performance.

19: p.77   John Maxwell, Internet quote.

20: p.76   David Lucatch, Internet quote.

21: p.81   Napoleon Hill, Internet quote.

22: p.91   Barack Obama, Internet quote.

23: p.91   Joseph Biden, Internet quote.

24: p.94   Patrice Lumumba, Internet quote.

25: p.112-113 Patrice Lumumba, Internet quote.

26: p.121-122 Matthew West, Internet quote.

27: p.122   Desmond Tutu, Internet quote

28: p.123   Internet article on William Wilberforce

29: p.141   Internet article on Pastor Cal Switzers.

30: p.146   Definition of gratitude, Internet quote.

31: p.159   Harvey Firestone, Internet quote.

32: p.167-168 Internet article on John Stephen Akhwari.

33: p.169   John Hardon, Internet quote.

34: p.172   Martin Luther King, Internet quote.

35: p.175   Golden rule, Internet quote.

36: p.178-9 Aaron Motsoaledi, Internet quote.

37: p.180   Article on Thomas Sankara, Internet quote.

38: p.181   John McCain, Internet quote.

39: p.186   Article on Obama, Internet quote.

40: p.186-187 Article on Magufuli, Internet quote.

41: p.189   Mahatma Gandhi, Internet quote.

42: p.209   Martin Luther King, Internet quote.

43: p.221   John Wooden, Internet quote.

44: p.222   Brian Tracy, Internet quote.

45: p.238   Myles Munroe, Internet quote.

46: p.239   Andy Karl Irambona,Internet quote.

47: p.242-243 John Osmers, Conversation with the author.

48: p.255   Kevin Durant, Internet quote.

49: p.258   Definition of perseverance, Internet quote.

50: p.258-259 Definition of grit, Internet quote.

51: p.259   Definition of resiliency, Internet quote.

52: p.259-260 Article on Nana Addo Dankwa Akufo-Addo, Internet quote.

53: p.263   Definition of elevator speech, Internet quote.

54: p.267   Definition of double-team in basketball, Internet quote.

55: p.269-270 Article on Alison Redford, Internet quote.

56: p.274 John Maxwell, Internet quote.

57: p.275 Nick Vujicic, Internet quote.

58: p.275 Nick Vujicic, Internet quote.

59: p.276 Mahatma Gandhi, Internet quote.

60: p.277-278 Jagmeet Singh, Internet quote.

61: p.278 Jagmeet Singh, Internet quote.

62: p.293-294 Article on crime against humanity, Internet quote.

63: p.295 Article on Zambia minimum wage, Internet quote.

64: p.299 President Ian Khama advises President Mugabe, Internet quote.

65: p.301 President Nana Akufo-Addo answering a question during President Macron's visit, Internet quote.

https://pagemasterpublishing.ca/by/charles-balenga/

To order more copies of this book, find books by
other Canadian authors, or make inquiries about
publishing your own book, contact PageMaster at:

PageMaster Publication Services Inc.
11340-120 Street, Edmonton, AB T5G 0W5
books@pagemaster.ca
780-425-9303

catalogue and e-commerce store
PageMasterPublishing.ca/

ABOUT THE AUTHOR

Charles Balenga is a husband and father of five children; a Canadian originally from the Democratic Republic of Congo. He has a Master of Intercultural Ministry from Ambrose University.

His experience includes being a Pastor of the Gospel Chapel of Youngstown, Alberta; Immigrants Settlement Counselor; Missionary Chaplain at Gitega International Academy in Burundi; Founder and Executive Director of Christian Immigrant Support Services and Board President of the Council for the Advancement of African Canadians.

As a public speaker, he has presented the message of 'Africa, It's Time!' in Canada and abroad.

He wrote *31 Essential Principles of Leadership* to help train leaders to lead more effectively. He is also the author of the well thought after book *Africa, It's Time!*

He is a passionate advocate of justice for all. His calling in life is to equip and to call leaders to build a just, prosperous and peaceful society.

If you are interested in inviting me to do a seminar, conference, or leadership training on *31 Essential Principles of Leadership* and/or on my first book, *Africa, It's Time!*, I can be reached at:

Charles Balenga

cbalenga@gmail.com

780-221-6263

www.balengaleadership.com

Facebook: cbalenga2000@yahoo.ca

Or 'Africa Its Time' Facebook page

Together, and with God, we can build a better world for everyone. I am a phone call or email away and I am excited and committed to do my part. Thank you. May God bless you!

www.ingramcontent.com/pod-product-compliance
Lightning Source LLC
Chambersburg PA
CBHW060003100426

42740CB00010B/1385